PSYCHOLOGY
FOR GCSE LEVEL

The
Manchester
College
be amazing

SEC

PSYCHOLOGY

FOR GCSE LEVEL

SECOND EDITION

DIANA DWYER & CRAIG ROBERTS

Psychology Press
Taylor & Francis Group

Published in 2009 by Psychology Press
27 Church Road, Hove, East Sussex, BN3 2FA

www.psypress.com

Psychology Press is part of the Taylor & Francis Group, an Informa business

Copyright © 2009 by Psychology Press

AQA examination questions are reproduced by permission of the Assessment and Qualifications Alliance.

OCR examination questions are reproduced by permisssion of Oxford Cambridge and RSA examinations.

British Library Cataloguing in Publication Data
A catalogue record for this book is available from the British Library

ISBN 978-1-84872-018-3

Cartoons by Sean Longcroft
Typeset by Newgen Imaging Systems (P) Ltd, Chennai, India
Printed and bound in the UK by
Ashford Colour Press Ltd, Gosport, Hampshire

Contents

Preface

Welcome to the fascinating world of psychology. Whenever we, as teachers, are asked what psychology is about, it doesn't matter which topic areas we describe, the invariable response is "That sounds interesting". It most certainly is. We believe that, as you go through the course, you will be intrigued by all the various facets of behaviour that will be discussed. You will begin to learn how the thinking of young children differs from that of adults, why people are prejudiced, why some people experience phobias, how your memory works (and why it sometimes doesn't!), how much we communicate non-verbally, to name but a few. We hope by the end of the course you will not only have gained a qualification but also have enjoyed being drawn into the absorbing world of psychology. Beware – some of you may never escape!

Di would like to thank her partner, Len Jackson, for his enormous support in preparing this manuscript. His enthusiastic willingness to read, discuss, and offer suggestions has been of great practical help; of even more importance has been his emotional support, which has been invaluable.

Craig would like to thank the following people for their endless support and love: Jav, Jayne, Julie, Elle and Bagpuss. He would also like to thank his family for just being ace.

This book is dedicated to all of the students we have ever taught and who made our jobs worthwhile and fulfilling. Keep us smiling, please!

How to use this book

This second edition of *Psychology for GCSE Level* has been revised and expanded to provide thorough coverage of the new OCR and AQA specifications for teaching from September 2009. It has been tailored to match each specification, and so can be used as the main textbook for either course.

Each chapter is clearly signposted at the beginning as being for either OCR or AQA. The "**What you need to know**" sections list the key points that students will need to know, based on the specification requirements. Within chapters, headings are clearly labelled to identify the text that applies to OCR, AQA, or both – for example:

AQA Defining aggression

OCR Common types of phobia

OCR AQA Sex and gender

These headings make it easy for students to focus on the content within the chapter that applies to their particular course. However, students may want to read the whole chapter as it will provide a useful background and aid understanding of the subject as a whole.

Chapter 1 provides an introduction, clearly separated into sections about the OCR course and sections about the AQA course. It also contains invaluable guidance for students on how to revise and how to cope in the exam.

Chapters 2–14 are on the specific topics covered by each of the specifications, representing five psychological approaches.

The final chapter (Chapter 15) covers research methods in psychology, and includes a separate section giving guidance on planning an investigation.

The book is divided into colour-coded sections for each part:

- Part 1: Social Psychology 1
- Part 2: Social Psychology 2
- Part 3: Biological Psychology
- Part 4: Developmental Psychology
- Part 5: Cognitive Psychology
- Part 6: Individual Differences
- Part 7: Research in Psychology

These are the chapters relevant for the OCR course
1. Preparing for the GCSE exam
2. Social influence
5. Non-verbal communication
6. Sex and gender
7. Criminal behaviour
8. Attachment
9. Cognitive development
10. Memory
11. Perception
12. Learning and atypical behaviour
14. The self
15. Research methods

These are the chapters relevant for the AQA course
1. Preparing for the GCSE exam
2. Social influence
3. Stereotyping, prejudice and discrimination
4. Aggression
5. Non-verbal communication
6. Sex and gender
10. Memory
12. Learning and atypical behaviour
13. Development of personality
15. Research methods

Each of the topic chapters is structured in the same way:

- They begin by outlining the specification requirements in the "**What you need to know**" section.
- Next, a **case study** introduces the chapter and puts the topic in an everyday-life context to help students see how psychology applies to the real world.
- The main body covers all of the necessary specification content, and includes (for OCR) all of the key concepts, core theories, core studies and applications, and (for AQA), the required definitions, descriptions and evaluations.
- Each study is highlighted in the text with a green line in the margin and is thoroughly evaluated, with positive ⊕ and negative ⊖ aspects identified where appropriate.
- Ample **classroom activities** are given throughout the text, to help students develop their understanding and to give teachers suggestions for preparing lessons.
- A clear **summary** is provided at the end of each chapter, to reinforce the content and help with revision.
- Lastly, **exam-style questions** are provided for each specification, written in the style of the GCSE Psychology examination for either OCR or AQA as appropriate. Sample answers to these questions are given in the online Teacher Resources.

The book also includes the following special features that have been designed to support the GCSE Psychology specification requirements:

Exam hints

These are positioned alongside sections of the text that students can find particularly challenging, or where common mistakes are made in the exam. The hints are designed to help students identify the main issues in the text, and provide focused guidance on how to use the information from the text in the exam.

Key terms

These provide useful definitions, in the margins of the text, of terms and concepts that will help students to understand the material.

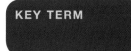

Aims and learning outcomes

Both the OCR and the AQA specifications list seven identical "Aims and Learning Outcomes" of the GCSE Psychology course, which are designed to inspire students in their studies and help them develop both an enthusiasm for the subject and an insight into how they could take psychology further. Students should be encouraged to:

- Engage in the process of psychological enquiry in order to develop as effective and independent learners, and as **critical and reflective thinkers** with enquiring minds.
- Develop an awareness of **why psychology matters**.

- Acquire knowledge and understanding of **how psychology works** and its essential role in society.
- Develop an understanding of the relationship between psychology and social, cultural, scientific and contemporary issues, and its impact on **everyday life**.
- Develop an understanding of **ethical issues** in psychology.
- Develop an understanding of the contribution of psychology to individual, social and cultural **diversity**.
- Develop a critical approach to scientific evidence and **methods**.

Everyday life

Throughout the book, boxes like the one shown here appear in the margins at points where the text relates to one of the above Aims and Learning Outcomes. They provide brief, interesting observations to enhance students' understanding of psychology and encourage them to think about how the topic relates to these wider themes. They can also be used to prompt lively classroom debate.

For more information on the GCSE in Psychology, please go to the OCR and AQA websites:

www.ocr.org.uk
www.aqa.org.uk

Preparing for the GCSE Exam

1

OCR AQA **About your GCSE course**

OCR **If you are studying OCR**

The OCR GCSE is made up of three units. Their official numbers are B541, B542 and B543. We will refer to them as Units 1, 2 and 3. The following is the content of each. You will notice that there are five main approaches (Biological, Cognitive, Developmental, Social, Individual Differences) that are repeated in Units 1 and 2 using different topic areas.

Unit 1: Studies and Applications in Psychology 1

- Biological Psychology: sex and gender
- Cognitive Psychology: memory
- Developmental Psychology: attachment
- Social Psychology: obedience
- Individual Differences: atypical behaviour

Unit 2: Studies and Applications in Psychology 2

- Biological Psychology: criminal behaviour
- Cognitive Psychology: perception
- Developmental Psychology: cognitive development
- Social Psychology: non-verbal communication
- Individual Differences: the self

Unit 3: Research in Psychology

- Planning research
- Doing research
- Analysing research
- Planning an investigation

A little more detail on the topic areas

Each topic area consists of key concepts, one core theory, one core study, and an application. Use the following tables as revision checklists.

Unit 1

Biological Psychology: sex and gender

- Key concepts: sex, gender, masculinity, femininity, androgyny
- Core theory: biological theory
- Core study: Diamond and Sigmundson (1997)
- Application of research into sex and gender: equal opportunities for the sexes

Cognitive Psychology: memory

- Key concepts: information processing, input, encoding, storage, retrieval, output, accessibility problems, availability problems
- Core theory: multistore model
- Core study: Terry (2005)
- Application of research into memory: memory aids

Developmental Psychology: attachment

- Key concepts: separation protest, stranger anxiety, secure attachment, insecure-avoidant attachment, insecure-ambivalent attachment
- Core theory: Bowlby's theory
- Core study: Hazan and Shaver (1987)
- Application of research into attachment: care of children

Social Psychology: obedience

- Key concepts: obedience, defiance, denial of responsibility
- Core theory: theory of situational factors
- Core study: Bickman (1974)
- Application of research into obedience: keeping order in institutions and situations

Individual Differences: atypical behaviour

- Key concepts: typical behaviour, atypical behaviour, fear, agoraphobia, social phobia, school phobia, acrophobia, arachnophobia
- Core theory: behaviourist theory
- Core study: Watson and Rayner (1920)
- Application of research into atypical behaviour: behaviour therapy for phobias

Unit 2

Biological Psychology: criminal behaviour

- Key concepts: crime, measures of crime, criminal personality
- Core theory: biological theory

- Core study: Mednick et al. (1984)
- Application of research into criminal behaviour: crime reduction

Cognitive Psychology: perception

- Key concepts: sensation, perception, depth cues, linear perspective, height in plane, relative size, superimposition, texture gradient
- Core theory: constructivist theory
- Core study: Haber and Levin (2001)
- Application of research into perception: advertising

Developmental Psychology: cognitive development

- Key concepts: invariant stages, universal stages, sensorimotor stage, pre-operational stage, concrete operational stage, formal operational stage
- Core theory: Piaget's theory
- Core study: Piaget (1952)
- Application of research into cognitive development: educating children

Social Psychology: non-verbal communication

- Key concepts: non-verbal communication, body language, facial expressions
- Core theory: social learning theory
- Core study: Yuki et al. (2007)
- Application of research into non-verbal communication: social skills training

Individual Differences: the self

- Key concepts: individuals as unique, free will
- Core theory: humanistic theory
- Core study: Van Houtte and Jarvis (1995)
- Application of research into the self: counselling

Unit 3

Research in Psychology

Planning research

- Hypothesis
- Variables
- Experimental designs
- Sampling techniques
- Ethical considerations

Doing research

- Experiments
- Questionnaires
- Interviews
- Observations
- Types of studies

Analysing research

- Types of data
- Descriptive data
- Tables
- Charts and graphs

Planning an investigation

- Investigation skills
- Design skills

OCR Structure and content of the OCR examinations

There are three examinations for OCR, corresponding to each of the units.

Paper 1 examines Unit 1 and is out of 80 marks (40% of the total GCSE marks). It is 1 hour 15 minutes long.

The question paper is in five sections (Sections A–E) corresponding to the approaches:

- Biological Psychology: sex and gender
- Cognitive Psychology: memory
- Developmental Psychology: attachment
- Social Psychology: obedience
- Individual Differences: atypical behaviour

The topic areas can be in any order. Four of the five sections are worth 15 marks each, and the fifth section is worth 20 marks.

The first three sections contain only short-answer questions, with questions worth between 1 and 4 marks each. The fourth section also consists of short-answer questions but the last one is out of 6 marks. The last section is out of 20 marks, with the last question being worth 10 marks.

Paper 2 examines Unit 2 and is identical in time and structure to Paper 1. In this case the sections ask questions on:

- Biological Psychology: criminal behaviour
- Cognitive Psychology: perception

- Developmental Psychology: cognitive development
- Social Psychology: non-verbal communication
- Individual Differences: the self

Paper 3 examines research methods. It is 1 hour long, worth 20% of the total GCSE marks. It is in two sections. See Chapter 15 for an example question.

Section A is worth 25 marks. You are given some source material (e.g. an account of a study) and asked a series of questions around it.

Section B is worth 15 marks and requires you to plan a study. You will be told what method to use (e.g. an observation, questionnaire, interview, experiment). See Chapter 15 for an example question.

AQA If you are studying AQA

The course consists of two units.

Unit 1: Making Sense of Other People
The content of this is:

- Memory
- Non-verbal communication
- Development of personality
- Stereotyping, prejudice, discrimination
- Research methods

Unit 2: Understanding Other People
The content of this is:

- Learning
- Social influence
- Sex and gender
- Aggression
- Research methods

AQA Structure and content of the AQA examinations

There are two examination papers, one for each unit.

Paper 1 and **Paper 2** are the same in length and structure: each is worth 50% of the GCSE marks, is 1 hour 30 minutes long and is out of 80 marks in total.

There are five questions and you must answer them all. There are five sections; the first four are the topic areas and the fifth section is Research methods.

So, on Paper 1 the sections are: Memory, Non-verbal communication, Development of personality, Stereotyping, prejudice and discrimination, Research methods.

On Paper 2 the sections are: Learning, Social influence, Sex and gender, Aggression, Research methods.

The sections on the topic areas are all out of 15 marks and the Research methods section is out of 20 marks.

OCR AQA Quality of written communication (QWC)

Regardless of the exam board specification you are following, you will be examined on the quality of your writing. This means that, in order to maximise your marks in an exam, you should:

- Make sure that your writing is legible (that it can be read) and that spelling, punctuation and grammar are accurate so that the meaning is clear.
- Organise the information clearly. Try to avoid bullet points where possible and write in full sentences, with appropriate use of capital letters and full stops. On the longer answers, paragraph your work.
- Use psychological terms wherever possible and appropriate.

Don't be defeatist about spelling, punctuation and grammar. Don't simply say "I'm no good at spelling". Well, perhaps you're not but it is something that you can learn (and you can easily test yourself or rope in mum/dad/friends to do it). In all walks of life, you need to be able to spell and punctuate properly, so it's best to learn it now. Psychology teachers are well aware that many of the names of psychologists are unusual and appear awkward to spell, but it is easy to learn the correct spelling as an incorrect one, so try to learn them accurately from the start. Perhaps you could suggest to your teacher that you have regular spelling quizzes with a prize for the highest score (using the psychological principle of positive reinforcement!).

For some of the longer questions on the exam paper you will be asked to write "in continuous prose". This is an indication that QWC will be assessed in the answer. Be particularly careful to avoid using note form or bullet points in these answers because this will reduce your QWC marks. (In the other answers you probably will not lose marks by using bullet points, but it's a good habit to try to avoid them so that you are not tempted to use them on the answers in which QWC is assessed.)

OCR AQA Revision

Organise yourself

1. Know exactly what you have to learn for each of your exams.
2. Make sure you have notes on everything. Whether you are studying AQA or OCR, there is no choice of questions in the exam, so be aware that you need to know everything.
3. Make a list of what you need to learn. You can tick things off as you go.
4. Look at past papers. Your teacher will probably be able to show you these. If not, you can order some from the examination board or get them online.

5. Sort out the times you will revise. Try to allow a reasonable length of time but give yourself frequent short breaks. Do about 30 minutes and then take a 5-minute break. Repeat this for three sessions and then take a good break (at least half an hour). Most of the time this will be sufficient in any one session but there may be times (such as study leave) when you can revise for longer than this. You just need to develop a routine.
6. Sort out a quiet, comfortable place to revise.

How to revise

There are many ways to revise – the key is to find a method that suits you.

Revise in a quiet spot and in an organised fashion

Suggested revision activities

Write revision notes. Revision notes are brief notes made from your class notes or a textbook. The key is that you reword them (don't just copy), as this means you have to understand what you are writing and this is crucial for remembering. When you write your notes, make them well organised (lots of numbered points) and visually memorable – use different colours and illustrations that might help you to remember, as in the box below.

> Cognitive Development Piaget
> 4 stages of cognitive development =
> 1. sensorimotor stage = **explores world using senses. Develops object permanence.**
> 2. pre-operational stage = **starts using symbols. Features = egocentric, inability to conserve.**
> 3. concrete operational stage = **can conserve, no longer egocentric, unable to think in abstract terms but can reverse concepts.**
> 4. formal operational stage = **can think in abstract way.**

Summarise the main studies. In an exam you may have to summarise a study in a few lines. In the textbook, some studies are briefly worded and may not need summarising. However, some of the longer, more complicated studies do need a summary. For example, Milgram's study in the chapter on social influence (Chapter 2), Sherif's summer camp study in Chapter 3. Pretend you are summarising it for an intelligent person who knows no psychology. This means you need to include all the important points of procedure (but can miss out a lot of the trivial details) and most of the findings. Do this as you go along – don't wait until it's time to revise.

Always learn core studies in terms of aim, method, findings, conclusion.

Draw pictures. Whenever possible, draw pictures to illustrate what you are trying to remember. It doesn't matter if you can't draw very well, no one except you is going to see them. For example, labelled storage jars for the multistore model of memory, each jar representing one store and surrounded by pictures that illustrate the characteristics of the store. Another example would be a picture of a car crash for the eye-witness testimony study of leading questions by Loftus et al.

Do mind maps. This is a different way of writing revision notes. Mind maps are useful for seeing an overview of a topic; they really do help to summarise the whole topic area and to see how concepts fit together. See the example on the opposite page.

Make revision cards. Write a question or concept on one side and the answer on the other, for example:

1. Define the term "prejudice".
2. Who proposed the theory of the authoritarian personality?
3. Name three characteristics of the authoritarian personality.
4. Outline the main points of social identity theory.

With respect to methods, you could do three cards for each method (observation, questionnaire and so on), one asking for the definition (see the example on the opposite page), one for an advantage, one for a disadvantage.

Writing these cards will be very helpful and then you will have a set to use whenever you have a spare few minutes. Make a set at the end of every topic – don't wait until it's time to revise.

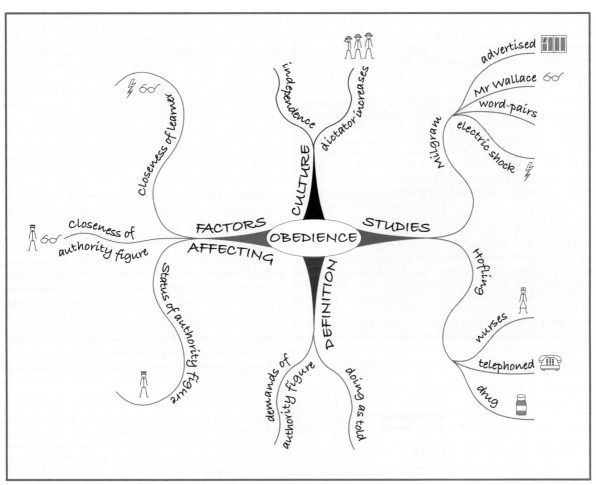

The beginnings of a mind map for obedience. Evaluations could be added. Note the small drawings as well as the words

Do more than just read. Repeat what you've read. Close your eyes and recite what you have just said. Then do it again. Reading your notes through is rarely enough to ensure you will remember them. If this is all you have time for though, try reading them out loud.

Use memory tricks – rhymes, silly associations, etc. The more ridiculous, unusual and distinctive, the better it will stick in your memory.

For example, if you have a list to learn, try to make up a mnemonic using the first letters (just like **R**ichard **O**f **Y**ork **G**ave **B**attle **I**n **V**ain for the colours of the rainbow). You could do this for the ethical guidelines: **D**eception, **C**onsent, **C**onfidentiality, **D**ebriefing, **W**ithdrawal, **P**rotection of participants, use of **C**hildren. Think of

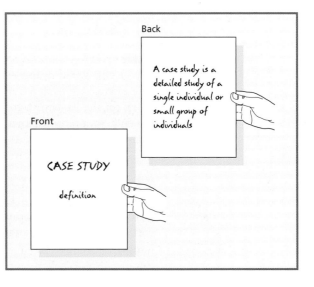

a silly sentence with the words starting with DCCDWPC, such as "Donkeys Can Clumsily Dance With Police Constables". The sillier the better, as long as it helps you remember. How about "So Piaget Can Fly" for Piaget's stages: Sensorimotor, Pre-operational, Concrete operational, Formal operational?

Alternatively, think in pictures. In the conformity section of the chapter on social influence (Chapter 2), the names of Sherif and Asch are mentioned. Think of a cowboy wearing a big sheriff's badge, smoking a large cigar with ash dropping off the end. The only thing to remember is that the spelling of the psychologists' names is different from the items in the pictures!

Practise exam questions in timed conditions. First of all, be very aware of how much time you have for each section of the exam and do NOT exceed this. The worst thing you can do in an exam is take too long on the early questions so you do not have enough time for the last questions. This can be especially damaging as the later questions carry more marks.

OCR AQA Time allocation in the exams

OCR

On Papers 1 and 2 (both 1 hour 15 minutes), you should aim to do each of the first four sections in about 13 minutes each, then use 18 minutes for the last section. This means that you will have about 5 minutes at the end to go over the paper. On Paper 3, which is 1 hour long, spend about 35 minutes on the first section and about 20 on the second one, leaving 5 minutes to go over it.

AQA

It is useful when doing AQA exams to think in terms of "a mark a minute". The exams are each 90 minutes long and worth 80 marks. Therefore, if you work on the basis of a mark a minute, you have 10 minutes checking time at the end. So, on both Paper 1 and Paper 2, spend 15 minutes on each of the first four sections (Sections A–D) and 20 minutes on the last one (Section E). This gives you 10 minutes for checking.

Whichever exam board – you will know what time the exam starts, so work out when you need to have finished each section. If you haven't finished, go onto the next section and return to the questions you've missed at the end. However, if you practise answering in the time allowed, this shouldn't happen.

OCR AQA In the exam

Read the questions very carefully

Make sure you know what you are being asked to do. Some important points to note are as follows:

1. Describing studies:

   - You are used to studies being in terms of aim, method, results, conclusion. In some questions, when asked to describe a study, you will have these side-headings but at other times you will not. Even when these are not provided, still use them as guidance. Sometimes instead of aim, you may be asked the reason. It's the same thing.
   - You may be asked for only one section (e.g. Outline the findings of...). Make sure that's all you write about. Some terms are interchangeable but the meaning is obvious. If the question asks for procedure, it means the method. If it asks for findings, it means results.
   - If asked to describe a study with the instruction to use continuous prose, make sure you do NOT use side-headings. Still approach the answer in terms of the sections, but write in sentences and paragraphs. You can start by saying "The aim of the study by... was to...". When it comes to the method, simply give an account of it (e.g. "Milgram placed an advertisement in the local paper and obtained a self-selected sample of 40 men..."). Do the same with the results ("They found that..."). It's probably best to cover the conclusion by making explicit reference to it (e.g. the researchers concluded that...). It is very important to use continuous prose when you are required to, otherwise you lose a considerable number of marks.

2. If asked to evaluate, do not describe.
3. If asked to describe and evaluate (either a theory or a study) be especially careful not to spend all the time you have on describing and do no evaluation. There are only a certain number of marks allocated to this part of the answer, so you can't get more than that however much you write. You may get maximum marks for that part of the answer but no marks at all for evaluation, so you will have wasted marks.
4. If the question gives you an article (a short paragraph on a topic area) or a piece of conversation and asks questions on it, make sure you refer to the article or conversation throughout.
5. When answering true/false questions, read the statements very carefully. Many students have thrown away marks by careless reading: for example, by saying "false" to a statement that says prejudice is treating someone differently.
6. Questions that start "from your study of psychology" require you to write about studies or theories you have learnt about. For example:
   Question: From your study of psychology outline two reasons why people obey authority. (4)
   Answer: Do NOT make up "common sense" reasons from your everyday experience. Use your psychology! So a suitable answer would be as

follows: "From his research Milgram identified a number of reasons why people obeyed. One reason was the power of the situation. There is a very strong social expectation that participants will do what the experimenter (authority figure) asks them to do in an experiment, especially as the participants have volunteered and been paid to take part in the study."

"Another reason that participants obeyed in this situation was that they did not feel responsible for what they were doing. They feel that it is the person in authority who is responsible for the action."

7. Some questions require you to fill in missing words, or draw lines between boxes, etc. Read the instructions carefully and make sure you do what is asked. If you do happen to make a mistake, cross out what you have done very clearly, so the examiner is certain of your final answer.

Look at the mark allocation for each question

This gives you a really strong clue as to how much you should write. If a question is only worth one mark you should be very brief. If it is worth four marks you obviously need to write more. Think about your answer from the examiner's point of view – have you given enough detail for them to award you all the available marks? If you have not, try to expand your answer, perhaps by giving an example to illustrate what you mean.

Pace yourself

This was referred to above and is extremely important. You MUST make sure you don't spend too much time on any one section/question and run out of time. Take the advice offered earlier about how much time to spend on each section.

What not to do in the exam

1. Do not write in the margin. If you run out of space, go to the back of the answer booklet and indicate this to the examiner so they know where to look.
2. Do not spend ages thinking about an answer you are not sure about. Go on to the next question and come back to it later.
3. Do not forget to read through your answers at the end of the exam if you have time.
4. Do not decorate the exam paper.
5. Do not write notes to the examiner – especially rude or offensive notes.
6. Do not leave questions unanswered because you're not sure of the answer. You get no marks for blank spaces. Write something!

Part 1

Social psychology (1)

Social psychologists are interested in the ways people affect each other. Social psychology is the study of the thoughts, feelings and behaviour of individuals and groups as influenced by other people.

For example, you may have noticed that you can run faster when competing with a friend than when alone – this means that your performance has been affected by the presence of another person. You may have laughed at a joke because your friends did, even though you didn't understand it. So others can influence your behaviour, even though no one asked you to behave differently.

Chapter 2 • Social influence

We will look at why we obey an authority figure, and why we often conform and behave in a similar way to others.

Chapter 3 • Stereotyping, prejudice and discrimination

We will look at why we use stereotypes, explain why people become prejudiced, and investigate ways in which we could reduce prejudice.

What you need to know OCR

The specification lists the following things that you will need to be able to do for the examination:

- Distinguish between obedience and defiance
- Explain what is meant by the term denial of responsibility
- Explain the effect of environment on obedience (setting, culture)
- Explain the effect of authority and the power to punish on obedience
- Explain the criticisms of situational factors as an explanation of obedience
- Consider dispositional factors as an alternative theory, with specific reference to the role of the authoritarian personality in obedience
- Describe and outline limitations of the Bickman (1974) study
- Outline an application of research into obedience, e.g. keeping order in institutions

What you need to know AQA

The specification lists the following things that you will need to be able to do for the examination:

- Describe definitions of conformity, obedience, social loafing and deindividuation
- Describe and evaluate studies into conformity, obedience, social loafing and deindividuation
- Explain factors affecting conformity, obedience, social loafing and deindividuation
- Explain factors affecting bystander intervention
- Describe and evaluate studies into bystander intervention, including Latané and Darley (1968), Batson et al. (1983), Piliavin, Rodin and Piliavin (1969) and Schroeder et al. (1995)
- Consider contemporary practical implications of studies and research into social influence and their benefits and drawbacks, e.g. keeping order in institutions

Social influence

2

The Russian pilot involved in a mid-air crash last week that killed 71 people was given conflicting orders by Swiss air traffic control and his automatic warning system, German investigators said yesterday.

Ground staff told the pilot to dive to avoid an oncoming cargo plane, but the TCAS on-board crash-avoidance device ordered the plane to climb. The pilot of the Tupolev 154 airliner, Alexander Gross, obeyed the second command from controllers to descend and 30 seconds later crashed into a Boeing 757 freight jet.

Voice recorders recovered from fragments of the two planes scattered across the Swiss–German border showed that the on-board system on the Boeing had told its pilot to climb. The systems are designed to communicate so that aircraft are sent in opposite directions to avoid a collision.

If the Russian pilot had obeyed the machine rather than the air traffic controller, the disaster might have been avoided.

OCR AQA
Obedience and defiance

What is obedience?

Obedience is when people behave in a certain way because they go along with the demands of an **authority figure**.

Who do you think are good authority figures? Who do you think are not so good authority figures? You may wish to generalise first to certain occupations.

What is defiance?

Defiance is when people want to resist the demands of authority and *not* do as they are told.

Why do you think some people defy authority figures? What makes someone want to defy an authority figure? Is it ever a good thing to defy authority?

OCR AQA
Studies into obedience and the effect of authority and power to punish on obedience

STUDY ONE: MILGRAM (1963)

Aim: Milgram had an interest in why during the Second World War hundreds of people obeyed the orders of others in authority. Millions of innocent people were killed on command. He wanted to test out this potential **destructive obedience** in a laboratory.

Method: Milgram advertised for **participants** (see the figure below). Forty participants were then used in the study. Each participant met a "Mr Wallace" (a confederate) thinking that he was also a participant in the study. The participant was told that one of them would be the teacher, while the other was the learner. The study was introduced as an investigation into whether punishment affects learning. However, it was always "fixed" that the participant was the teacher while Mr Wallace was the learner (both slips of paper that the participant had to choose from had the word "Teacher" on them, plus Mr Wallace always chose first and said he was the learner).

After this, Mr Wallace was seen being strapped into an "electric chair" device in the next room. Electrodes were attached to Mr Wallace's wrist. The participant was then made aware that the shocks would be extremely painful but they would not cause any tissue damage to Mr Wallace.

The participant then left to sit in front of the "shock generator" in the next room. He was told that he would read out a series of word pairs (e.g. blue box). After reading out the pairs, he was instructed to read just one word (e.g. blue) and then a choice of four words (e.g. sky ink box lamp). It was then the job of Mr Wallace to choose the correct one (in this case – box).

Public Announcement

WE WILL PAY YOU $4.00 FOR
ONE HOUR OF YOUR TIME

Persons Needed for a Study of Memory

*We will pay five hundred New Haven men to help us complete a scientific study of memory and learning. The study is being done at Yale University.

*Each person who participates will be paid $4.00 (plus 50c carfare) for approximately 1 hour's time. We need you for only one hour: there are no further obligations. You may choose the time you would like to come (evenings, weekdays, or weekends).

*No special training, education, or experience is needed. We want:

Factory workers	Businessmen	Construction workers
City employees	Clerks	Salespeople
Laborers	Professional people	White-collar workers
Barbers	Telephone workers	Others

All persons must be between the age of 20 and 50. High school and college students cannot be used.

*If you meet these qualifications, fill out the coupon below and mail it now to Professor Stanley Milgram, Department of Psychology, Yale University, New Haven. You will be notified later of the specific time and place of the study. We reserve the right to decline any application.

*You will be paid $4.00 (plus 50c carfare) as soon as you arrive at the laboratory.

TO:
PROF. STANLEY MILGRAM, DEPARTMENT OF PSYCHOLOGY, YALE UNIVERSITY, NEW HAVEN, CONN. I want to take part in this study of memory and learning. I am between the ages of 20 and 50. I will be paid $4.00 (plus 50c carfare) if I participate.

NAME (Please Print)..
ADDRESS ....
TELEPHONE NO... Best time to call you..............................
AGE .... OCCUPATION .... SEX ....
CAN YOU COME:
WEEKDAYS.............................. EVENINGS........................... WEEKENDS...........................

The announcement placed in a local newspaper to recruit participants for Milgram's study

The participant was instructed that if Mr Wallace got one of them wrong they were to give him an electric shock via the "shock generator". The generator had a series of 30 buttons to press. Each button was labelled with a number that corresponded to a certain voltage level. The first button was for 15 volts and then every button increased the shock by 15 volts. So, the second button was 30 volts, the next 45 volts and so on. The maximum they could give was 450 volts!

Also, across the top of the buttons were words ranging from Slight Shock above the early buttons to Danger: Severe Shock over the higher-voltage buttons. The last two buttons simply had XXX over them.

So, for every incorrect answer the participant had to go to the next button up. The first incorrect answer would therefore get 15 volts. When the next error came they had to give 30 volts. This continued until the participant reached 450 volts.

The photographs show the electric shock machine used in Milgram's classic experiment

The experimenter was in the same room as the participant. If the participant said that they did not want to continue then the experimenter had to "prod" them in the following ways:

- Prod 1 – say "Please continue" or "Please go on."
- Prod 2 – say "The experiment requires that you continue."
- Prod 3 – say "It is absolutely essential that you continue."
- Prod 4 – say "You have no other choice, you must go on."

Have you asked yourself yet why the experiment always had Mr Wallace as the learner? Well, it was to keep everything the same for all participants (called a control). Another thing that was kept the same was Mr Wallace's responses to the "shocks" given. Yes, you may have guessed it but Mr Wallace was never ever really shocked! It was all set up. Mr Wallace would always get the same answers wrong for every participant. Also, his responses to the "shocks" were always the same, as they were tape-recorded and played to the participant every time they pressed a specific voltage on the "shock generator".

An interesting thing to note is when the participant gave Mr Wallace the 300-volt shock, the response was that Mr Wallace hit the wall repeatedly so that the participant could hear it. From that point on, Mr Wallace did not answer another word-pair task.

Ethical issues

There are several ethical issues here, particularly deception and stress. Nevertheless, some ethical issues were addressed by a full debrief and follow-up of participants to discuss any problems arising from their experience.

An illustration of the control panel of the apparatus used in Milgram's study

75 volts	Ugh!
90 volts	Ugh!
105 volts	Ugh! (*louder*)
120 volts	Ugh! Hey this really hurts.
135 volts	Ugh!!
150 volts	Ugh!!! Experimenter! That's all. Get me out of here. My heart's bothering me. Let me out of here! You have no right to keep me here! Let me out! Let me out of here! Let me out! Let me out of here! My heart's bothering me. Let me out! Let me out!
210 volts	Ugh!! Experimenter! Get me out of here. I've had enough. I won't be in the experiment any more.
225 volts	Ugh!
240 volts	Ugh!
255 volts	Ugh! Get me out of here.
270 volts	(*Agonised scream*) Let me out of here. Let me out of here. Let me out of here. Let me out. Do you hear? Let me out of here.
285 volts	(*Agonised scream*)
300 volts	(*Agonised scream*) I absolutely refuse to answer any more. Get me out of here. You can't hold me here. Get me out. Get me out of here.
315 volts	(*Intensely agonised scream*) I told you I refuse to answer. I'm no longer part of this experiment.
330 volts	(*Intense and prolonged agonised scream*) Let me out of here. Let me out of here. My heart's bothering me. Let me out, I tell you. (*Hysterically*) Let me out of here. Let me out of here. You have no right to hold me here. Let me out! Let me out! Let me out of here! Let me out!

Adapted from Milgram, 1974

Part of the script used by Milgram

Results: All of the participants gave a minimum 300 volts to Mr Wallace, and 65% of the participants gave 450 volts despite the caption XXX above the button. Some continued to give 450 volts repeatedly, as Mr Wallace's silence meant a wrong answer!

Conclusion: The study clearly demonstrated that people do show high levels of obedience to an authority figure when placed in a situation where they had to give an electric shock to a complete stranger.

ACTIVITY 2.1

You have been asked to write a much briefer version of the Milgram study described in depth here. You need to pick out what you feel are the "crucial" bits of the study so that your non-psychology friends can understand it. Write up to two sentences for the aim, up to six for the method, up to two for the results, and a one-sentence conclusion. They must all be in your own words and not copied straight from this book!

KEY TERMS

Laboratory experiment: an experiment carried out in very tightly controlled surroundings (but not necessarily a laboratory), often with special equipment.

Ecological validity: the degree to which the behaviour observed and recorded in a study reflects behaviour that actually occurs in natural settings.

Ethics: a standardised set of guidelines for researchers in psychology. Key ethical considerations include informed consent, right to withdraw, confidentiality (anonymity), debriefing, and protection of participants against stress and harm.

Informed consent: always applies to research participants, and refers to written or verbal consent to take part after they are given information about what they will be asked to do.

How psychology works

This research has important applications in many walks of life, as it indicates that most people are willing to obey an authority figure even if it causes harm to others. Before this research, that was not the view of the general public or even of psychiatrists.

Critical thinking

Migram had an interest in why, during the Second World War, millions of innocent people were killed on command. What application can Milgram's findings be used for?

EXAM HINT

If you choose to evaluate Milgram on ethics, make sure you use two ethical guidelines to assess him on (e.g. right to withdraw and deception). However, you can take this further if you want to. Argue that ethical guidelines had not been formalised at the time Milgram conducted his study, so assessing him on today's ethical guidelines might be unfair.

EVALUATION

➕ The study was well controlled because it was a **laboratory experiment**. So, Milgram could control many variables and be confident that the situation the participants were placed in directly affected the shocks given by the participants.

➖ However, many psychologists would say that because it was a laboratory experiment Milgram's study lacks **ecological validity**. That is, the task may not represent whether we would be obedient in a real-life situation. Also, the task is not one that we usually come across in everyday life.

➖ Many psychologists criticise Milgram on **ethics**. They believe that he did not get **informed consent** (nowhere on the advertisement does it state the true aim), was deceitful, did not allow people the right to withdraw and placed all of the participants under high levels of psychological stress. This is now in breach of ethical guidelines (however, there were no such guidelines in the early 1960s when Milgram was conducting his study).

➕ However, Milgram did follow up the participants to make sure that they were all fine months after participating. Virtually all of the participants were pleased to have taken part in the experiment as they believed they had learnt a lot about themselves during the experiment.

STUDY TWO: HOFLING ET AL. (1966)

Aim: Hofling and his colleagues wanted to examine obedience in more of a real-life setting. They wanted to see whether nurses were obedient to a potentially life-threatening order given to them by a doctor.

Method: Hofling and his team decided to make up an incident that would cause conflict in the mind of the nurses who were unknowing participants:

- the nurse would be asked to give an excessive dosage of a drug
- the order would be via telephone (this is not allowed in hospitals)
- the drug would not be on the ward stock-list
- the order would be given by someone the nurse did not know.

A total of 22 nurses took part in the experiment. Each of the nurses was telephoned by a doctor (given a name that was not known to the nurse, e.g. Dr Hanford in one case) and told to give a patient 20 milligrams (mg) of the drug "Astroten". The nurses were not aware that the pink pills inside the Astroten box were simply glucose tablets! On the box of Astroten it clearly stated that the usual does was 5 mg and the maximum daily dose was 10 mg. So the nurses were being asked to give twice the maximum dosage. The telephone conversation with the doctor was recorded. Also, the behaviour of the nurse was observed after the telephone call had been completed.

Within 48 hours of the study, each of the nurses was interviewed and reassured that no harm had been done. They were also told that they would remain **anonymous** and absolutely no action would be taken against them.

Results: Of the 22 nurses in the study, 21 simply completed the telephone call and gave the patient 20 mg of Astroten. The average length of telephone call was around 2 minutes. This indicates that the nurses offered no resistance and simply followed the orders of an authority figure.

Conclusions: Hofling had shown that people are obedient in real-life situations (and in life-threatening situations).

It should be noted that a group of 21 student nurses were given the scenario on paper and asked what they would do. All 21 stated that they would never have given the patient Astroten.

KEY TERM

Anonymous: having no known name, source, or identifying features. Used to maintain participants' confidentiality in psychological research.

Ethical issues

There is the ethical issue of deception here; however, with a lot of social psychological studies, telling participants the purpose ruins the study and so researchers have to decide whether the deception is justified.

EXAM HINT

When asked to *describe* a study (e.g. Hofling et al.) make sure you do the following: Identify the study (by stating Hofling), write out the aim, then a few sentences on the procedure, then a few more sentences on the results, then a conclusion. You should not begin to evaluate (e.g. "it has high ecological validity because"). This will gain you no marks because you are not answering the question!

ACTIVITY 2.2

What do the findings of the Hofling follow-up study tell us about questionnaires as a measure of real-life behaviour?

EVALUATION

➕ As the study took place in a real hospital using real nurses, the study has some level of ecological validity. That is, as the situation was "real" Hofling could believe that his findings do relate to real-life nurse behaviour.

KEY TERM

Extraneous variables: any factor or variable, other than the variable being studied, that causes an effect (or potential effects).

As the main experiment was in a real-life setting there could have been many **extraneous variables** that could have affected the nurses' responses (remember that in a laboratory you can control for these variables). So it may not always have been the doctor's instructions causing the nurses to obey.

Hofling has been criticised because of ethics. Many psychologists believe that he placed the nurses under psychological stress and did not get any informed consent from the nurses.

Everyday life

This study has enormous implications for nurse training (and that of similar professions). Nurses need to be reassured that they do not have to give unquestioning obedience.

ACTIVITY 2.3

Look at the negatives for the Hofling study. What extraneous variables do you think could have affected the nurses? Also, why couldn't Hofling really get informed consent?

It should also be noted that Rank and Jacobson (1977) attempted to replicate Hofling's study to see if nurses would still obey in such a way. There had been other criticisms of Hofling's study after it had been published in terms of the *task*. The nurses were being asked to administer an unknown drug and did not communicate with their fellow nurses before administering it. This rarely happens in real life. In the Rank and Jacobson study, a doctor telephoned 18 different nurses and asked them to administer a non-lethal dose of Valium to a patient (they were asked to give a dosage three times larger than recommended). All 18 nurses accepted the telephone request with little resistance. However, only 12 went and got the amount of drug asked for, and only *two* broke open the drug and were prepared to give it to the patient. Rank and Jacobson believed that there were three main reasons why so many "refused" to give the drug: (1) an increased willingness to challenge doctors' orders, (2) self-esteem increasing within the profession, and (3) the fear of possible lawsuits for incorrectly administering a drug.

ACTIVITY 2.4

Can you think of any other reasons why the nurses failed to be obedient in the Rank and Jacobson study?

OCR AQA # Factors that can affect levels of obedience

We will look at factors that can affect obedience by looking at variations on the study conducted by Milgram (1963).

Closeness of the "learner"

In a series of experiments highlighted in Milgram (1974), the closeness of the learner (Mr Wallace) was varied to see if it made a difference to obedience levels.

Remember the set-up for the original experiment – you may wish to draw it in your notes.

In one of Milgram's experiments the participant had to push "Mr Wallace's" hand onto the "shock plate"

The three experiments that looked at the closeness of the learner were:

- *Voice feedback*. In this study Milgram got Mr Wallace to shout out the responses to the shocks. His voice could easily be heard through the wall so the participant knew that Mr Wallace was just behind it (remember that in the original, the responses were pre-recorded).
- *Proximity*. In this study Milgram got Mr Wallace to be in the same room as the participant. He was seated just a few metres away so the participant could see *and* hear Mr Wallace's reactions.
- *Touch-proximity*. In this study Milgram got Mr Wallace to place his hand on a "shock plate". This was really just a piece of metal that Mr Wallace placed his hand on. So the participant thought that Mr Wallace was receiving a direct shock from the metallic "shock plate". However, once a participant had reached 150 volts, Mr Wallace would refuse to place his hand on the "shock plate". Therefore, the participant had to push Mr Wallace's hand onto the "shock plate" for him, so the participant had to physically touch Mr Wallace.

Below is a table showing the percentage of participants who gave the maximum 450 volts. The table also highlights the percentage of participants who gave 300 volts (remember that in the original experiment 100% of participants gave this). Finally, it tells you the mean voltage given by the participants in the series of experiments. The results can be compared to the "original" experiment (also featured in the table).

Condition	% of participants who gave 450 volts	% of participants who gave 300 volts	Mean voltage given by the participants
Original	65.0	100.0	405 V
Voice feedback	62.5	75.0	360 V
Proximity	40.0	62.5	300 V
Touch-proximity	30.0	40.0	255 V

> **ACTIVITY 2.5**
>
> What conclusions can you draw from the data in the table? Take one of the columns and plot a bar chart of the results. This may help you to remember the findings.

Closeness of the authority figure

Milgram also decided to look at whether having the experimenter in the same room as the participant had an effect. So he conducted another experiment where the authority figure was absent from the room. To do this, Milgram got the authority figure to meet the participant but then leave the room and give the orders via a telephone.

Below is a table similar to the one used in the *Closeness of the learner* section on the previous page, comparing the original experiment with this variation.

Condition	% of participants who gave 450 volts	% of participants who gave 300 volts	Mean voltage given by the participants
Original	65.0	100.0	405 V
Order given over the telephone	20.5	42.5	270 V

> **ACTIVITY 2.6**
>
> Remember the Hofling experiment with the nurses? That study also had instructions given over the telephone. Try to recall how many nurses were "obedient" in that study and compare it to this study by Milgram. Think of reasons why the results appear to be very different.

OCR AQA Culture and obedience

Kagitcibasi (1996) conducted a wide-scale study on parental attitudes to their child's behaviours and what is expected of them. This review examined these ideas across a wide range of nationalities. In certain countries, such as Turkey and Indonesia it was expected that children were obedient to their parents with little room for independence. However, other countries like USA and Korea were the opposite: independence was encouraged and obedience discouraged.

Munroe and Munroe (1972) also noted that many African cultures are rated as the highest for obedience in their people. Unsurprisingly, Triandis (1994) reported that in countries where there is a dictator, obedience levels rise to very high levels (think about Nazi Germany in the Second World War, or the regime of Milosevic in Serbia), meaning that it may not be the culture itself that affects obedience, but the situation people find themselves in that affects it more.

Kilham and Mann (1974) part-replicated Milgram's study in Australia and found obedience rates in one sample to be as high as 68%. Other replications have shown similar patterns, including Italy where it was 80% (Ancona & Pareyson, 1968) and Austria where it was 85% (Schurz, 1985).

Finally, some psychologists will use the individualistic–collectivist argument for obedience – cultures that are **individualistic** are theoretically less likely to be obedient compared to **collectivist** ones.

OCR The effect of environment on obedience

In this section on obedience, we will examine the status of the authority figure. Milgram was interested in whether the white coat worn by the experimenter giving the orders had an effect on obedience.

He was also interested in whether the status of the setting affected results. The original experiment took place at Yale University. This is a prestigious university in America that is well respected. He thought that people may have been in awe because the study was at Yale and therefore were more obedient in his experiment.

Milgram's experiments that looked at the status of the authority figure included:

- *Ordinary man*: In this study Milgram chose to have an ordinary man as the person giving the orders (authority figure). He was dressed in normal clothes (so no white laboratory coat!).
- *Run-down building*: In this study Milgram changed the setting. He chose to run the experiment in a run-down commercial building in a shopping area.

Below is a table similar to the one used in both the *Closeness of the learner* and *Closeness of the authority figure* sections, comparing the original experiment with this variation.

Diversity

This research, in considering the extent to which culture affects levels of conformity and obedience, provides an indication of how much Western research (like that of Asch and Milgram) can be generalised to other cultures.

Condition	% of participants who gave 450 volts	% of participants who gave 300 volts	Mean voltage given by the participants
Original	65.0	100.0	405 V
Ordinary man	20.5	30.0	240 V
Run-down building*	47.5	62.5	300 V

*It should be noted that here two participants refused to give even the lowest shock of 15 volts. This is the only variation on Milgram's experiment where some participants gave no shock whatsoever.

KEY TERM

Confederates: people who pretend to be participants in psychological research, but are in fact aware of the research aim and have been told how to respond by the researchers.

ACTIVITY 2.7

Read over all of the variations again. Which scenario had the highest level of obedience and which one had the lowest level of obedience?

OCR **The effect of consensus on obedience**

One way we can look at this is by examining another variation of the Milgram study. In this variation, four apparent participants turn up to take part in the study, but three of them are **confederates**. As with the original, one of the confederates is always the learner, and the participant is always given the role of "Teacher Number 3". As in the original experiment, the participant sees the learner being strapped into the chair. The roles for each teacher are then clearly defined. Teacher Number 1 (confederate) is given the job of reading the word pairs. Teacher Number 2 (confederate) is given the job of telling the learner if they got it right or wrong. Teacher Number 3 (real participant) is given the job of administering the shocks.

To measure the effect consensus has on obedience the following happens:

1. At 150 volts, Teacher Number 1 refuses to go any further with the experiment. The authority figure (the experimenter) insists they continue but this teacher sits in another part of the room. The real participant is then given the job of reading out the word pairs as well as giving out the electric shocks.
2. At 210 volts, Teacher Number 2 now refuses to go any further. The authority figure yet again insists they continue but the teacher sits elsewhere in the room, stating "I'm willing to answer any of your questions, but I'm not willing to shock that man against his will. I'll have no part of it."

Therefore, after 210 volts the participant is left doing all three jobs (as in the original study).

The results do show a large effect of consensus on whether we become obedient. Four participants (10%) refused to go further at the 150 volt mark. A further 21 refused to go further than 210 volts – meaning that 62.5% of the sample refused to break the consensus view of *not* going to the very end. Only four participants continued to 450 volts. This study clearly shows that as more people have a consensus to *not* be obedient, more and more people join them.

OCR **Criticisms of situational factors as an explanation of obedience**

One of the main criticisms of research that has assessed the role of situational (environmental) factors is that they are not real situations being tested out. For example with Milgram, the task asked of the participants in the various settings is not what could happen in those settings in real life. Also, if we use case studies of *real* obedience being shown in a variety of settings, there is no control over other variables that could be affecting the obedience levels. One such variable could be the dispositional (e.g. personality) factors of that person. As can be clearly seen in the next section, these factors can play a large role in whether we are obedient or not. However, this is evidence to suggest that the situation people find themselves in can affect obedience (see the earlier section on culture and obedience for examples).

OCR Dispositional factors and obedience

Dispositional factors refer to personal factors that might affect the obedience levels in individuals. One such idea is that of the **authoritarian personality**. According to Adorno, a person with this type of personality is intolerant of others with differing views, is dominating, is attracted to groups where there are strong leaders and respects higher authority figures. Adorno stated that an authoritarian personality is formed by having parents who are strict, cold and expect obedience in their child. As a result the child knows nothing different and takes on these traits as part of their own personality. Therefore when the child grows up they begin to be dominant, cannot tolerate people of lower authority and are strict with others. They are much more likely to be obedient to an authority figure as this relates back to their upbringing. One way in which people can be assessed for this type of personality is to complete the F-Scale that was created by Adorno. The person reads a range of statements and has to state how much they agree with each one. Statements can include "Obedience and respect for authority are the most important virtues children should learn" and "People can be divided into two distinct classes: the weak and the strong."

OCR A study into the effects of uniform

OCR CORE STUDY: BICKMAN (1974)

Aim: To investigate the social power of a uniform.

Method: Bickman ran a series of experiments that tested out whether people were more obedient to certain types of uniform. We will focus on his first experiment here.

Participants were the 153 pedestrians who happened to be around when Bickman was running his study. The setting was a street in New York. A pedestrian was chosen as a participant if he or she was the first person to come along who had not seen the previous interaction. All pedestrians were always alone. Forty-three per cent were male, with 57% females, 86% were white, 11% black and the race of the remainder could not be determined.

The type of authority figure was varied:

1. The authority figure wore a sports jacket and tie.
2. The authority figure wore a milkman's outfit.
3. The authority figure wore a uniform that appeared to be that of a policeman.

> **KEY TERM**
>
> **Authoritarian personality**: according to Adorno, a person with this type of personality is intolerant of others with differing views, is dominating, is attracted to groups where there are strong leaders, and respects higher authority figures.

> **EXAM HINT**
>
> The work and theory of Adorno et al. are discussed in more detail in Chapter 3, on stereotyping, prejudice and discrimination. It would be useful to read that section.

Obedience can be related to the amount of perceived authority.

Also, the type of situation was varied:

1. *Picking up a bag scenario*: The experimenter stopped the pedestrian and pointed to a small paper bag on the floor and said '*… pick up this bag for me!*' (p. 50). The pedestrian was noted as obeying if they picked it up.
2. *Dime and meter scenario*: The experimenter pointed to a confederate (someone in on the experiment) beside a parked car at a parking meter and said "*… this fellow is over-parked but doesn't have any change. Give me a dime!*" (p. 50). The pedestrian was noted as obeying if they gave a dime or made a sincere effort to find one in their purse or wallet.
3. *Bus stop "no standing" scenario*: The experimenter chose a participant if they were standing alone at a bus stop. The experimenter said "*… don't you know you have to stand on the other side of the pole? The sign says no standing*" (p. 50). If the pedestrian did not then comply the experimenter added "*… the bus won't stop here, it's a new law*" (p. 50). If the pedestrian moved this was taken as obeying.

Results: As can be seen, for all of the situations, the pedestrians were more likely to obey the guard, then the milkman, then the civilian (the sports jacket and tie).

Conclusion: Bickman could conclude that a uniform has the power to make people obey simple demands like picking up a bag, lending a dime to a stranger, or moving at a bus stop.

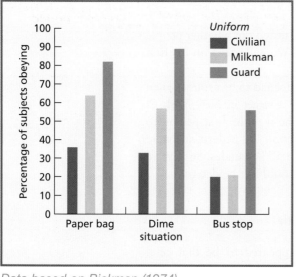

Data based on Bickman (1974)

Limitations: The small sample sizes in each of the conditions could be criticised as not being large enough to make generalisations to other pedestrians. Also, as the study was a field experiment, there are many variables that Bickman could not have controlled for that could be affecting the dependent variable of obeying. For example, some of the participants may have been late for an important meeting and therefore did not help. However, in a normal situation they would obey. The sample was predominantly white so it may be difficult to generalise to other races, especially as all of the experimenters were white. As we will see in the Piliavin et al. (1969) study on page 42, the race of a person can affect the level of helping behaviour. Also, Bickman did not report whether a certain race obeyed more often than not.

ACTIVITY 2.8

What other variables might have been affecting the dependent variable other than the "late for a meeting" one noted above? See if you can think of three others that could not have been controlled for by Bickman.

AQA Conformity

Conformity is when people behave in a certain way because of the pressure exerted on them by other group members.

Types of conformity

• *Informational*: the desire to be right
• *Normative*: the desire to be liked.

AQA Studies into conformity

STUDY ONE: ASCH (1955)

Aim: Asch wanted to see how the judgements of others in a group affect the decisions of an individual on a simple task.

Method: In the initial study a group of seven to nine college students (all male) were assembled in a classroom. They were told it was a "psychological experiment" about visual judgements. Not known to the participant the other people were confederates (in on the experiment). In all, there were 123 participants. The experimenter held up two cards and asked the group which line on the right-hand card was the same length as line X. Each person answered in turn individually, with the confederates answering first. The true participant answered last or next to last. On the first two trials the confederates stated the correct answer. However, on the third trial the confederates stated the wrong answer. The study

Even the most independent of individuals can feel the need to conform under social pressure from peers.

Cards like those used in Asch's (1955) experiment

Critical thinking

There are important ethical issues here, including protection of participants. The participants probably felt really awkward and embarrassed. Can you think of a way in which Asch could have done the studies so that this was avoided? See if you can find out about the work of Richard Crutchfield to give you a clue.

EXAM HINT

This is a laboratory study, so it has enough controls to show cause and effect but may lack ecological validity.

lasted for 18 trials. On 12 of them the confederates stated the wrong answer.

Results: In the trials where the confederates gave the correct answer, the true participants got it correct over 99% of the time. In the trials where the confederates gave the wrong answer, the true participants also got it wrong on 36.8% of them. Also, 25% of participants *never once* conformed to a wrong answer that the confederates gave.

EVALUATION

➕ The research method used was a laboratory experiment that allowed Asch to control many variables. This means that he could confidently conclude that the set-up was directly affecting the conformity rates.

➖ However, many psychologists would say that because it was an experiment his study lacks ecological validity. That is, the task may not represent whether we would conform in a real-life situation. Also, the task is not one that people usually come across in everyday life.

➖ Some psychologists would say that this study is not ethical. This is because the participants were put under psychological stress by having to choose an incorrect answer.

➕ The task was not ambiguous. That is, there was a definite answer and the task was easy to measure. Compare this to the task used by Sherif, described next.

STUDY TWO: SHERIF (1935)

Aim: Sherif was interested in how people may change their individual view once placed in a group situation.

KEY TERM

Autokinetic effect: perceiving a stationary point of light in the dark as moving. This is caused by constant eye movement that keeps your retina active and working.

Method: Sherif tested conformity via an illusion called the **autokinetic effect**. The effect is simple. Participants entered a darkened room where they could see a dot of light. They were asked to estimate how far it moved. However, the light never moved at all but the majority of participants stated that it did! Why? Well, this is where the autokinetic effect comes in. Your eyes are constantly moving to keep your retina active and working. So, with nothing to focus on in the dark, the constant shifting of your eyes gives the illusion of movement.

Once the participants had given their estimations of movement (they did this a few times) they were placed in groups. During their time in a group they were asked to discuss just how far the light had moved. However, Sherif had selected people who had reported a large movement, a medium movement and a small movement.

After the discussion Sherif asked the participants to re-estimate how much the light had moved.

Sherif's study used a darkened room with one dot of light

Results: Individuals were very consistent in their estimations before being put in a group to discuss it. However, estimations did change after the discussion. A *group norm effect* tended to be seen. That is, people changed their estimations towards the average for the group. So, for example, the person who had a large estimation of movement reduced it after discussion. Those who stated there was little movement increased their estimations after discussion.

EVALUATION

➕ The study was well controlled because it was a laboratory experiment. So, Sherif could control many variables and be confident that the group discussion directly affected the final responses of the participants.

➖ However, many psychologists would say that because it was a laboratory experiment his study lacks ecological validity. That is, the task may not represent whether we would conform in a real-life situation. Also, the task is not one that people usually come across in everyday life.

➖ The task itself was ambiguous. By this we mean that there was no real answer as the dot never moved. Some psychologists believe this to be a weakness of Sherif's study as it could have affected the outcome of the study. Participants were not being tested with something straightforward, like in the Asch study on page 29.

AQA Factors that can affect levels of conformity

Size of the group of people

In the Asch study there were between seven and nine people in the room at one time. Asch was then interested in whether the size of the group affected conformity levels. The table below shows the conformity rates for different sized groups.

Conformity rates shown in Asch's study		
Description of group	Group size	% of trials where P gave the incorrect answer
The participant + **one** confederate	2	0
The participant + **two** confederates	3	13.6
The participant + **three** confederates	4	31.8
The participant + **four** confederates	5*	33

*Any subsequent increase in size of group did not increase rates of conformity.
P = true participant.

Status of the group members

Imagine you were in the Asch study and everyone else in the room was described to you as a doctor. What would happen to your chances of conformity? Of course they would increase and you'd be more likely to conform to the incorrect answer. As status increases so do conformity rates.

ACTIVITY 2.9

Make a list of the types of people you would conform to in the Asch study. Also, think about the people you would not conform to.

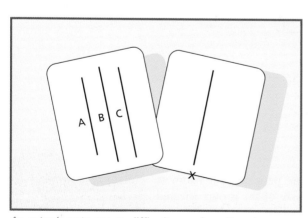

As a task gets more difficult, conformity rates increase

Task difficulty

When Asch made the task more difficult by having Lines A, B and C of very similar length (making the task much more difficult), conformity increased a great deal.

Culture and conformity

Psychologists have been interested in whether certain cultures are more likely to conform to the majority. For this, cultures can be classified into two main groups: individualistic and collectivist. Individualistic cultures tend to promote independence in their children, including being self-reliant and "thinking for themselves". People in these cultures may have personal goals that rarely overlap with other people in their culture. However, collectivist cultures tend to promote working as a team (or a complete family unit) and place less emphasis on doing things individually and independently of groups. If people do have individual ideas and goals these are sacrificed if a collective goal is more important (Moscovici, 1980).

ACTIVITY 2.10

Research using books and the internet, and find information about cultures that are seen as being individualistic or collectivist. What are the common features of the individualistic cultures, and what are the common features of the collectivist cultures?

There has been some research examining whether culture affects the rate of conformity on the Asch task (do you remember the Lines on the Card task?). Moghaddam (1998) reported on a range of studies that had assessed this. Nationalities such as Brazil and China all showed similar levels of conformity but these *differed* from the American sample used in the original Asch study by showing *higher* levels. Other nationalities such as Zimbabwe (Whitaker & Meade, 1967) and Fiji also showed much *higher* levels of conformity compared to the American sample. Frager (1970) reported that participants from Germany and Japan were *less* conformist compared to the Americans. Subsequent studies then showed that other samples in Brazil, China and Lebanon showed similar levels of conformity to the Americans.

In a more recent thorough review of this area of psychology, Smith and Bond (1996) found some solid evidence for the idea that individualistic cultures conform less than collectivist cultures. People from Zimbabwe, Fiji, Japan, Ghana and Brazil (seen as collectivist) showed higher error rates on Asch-type tasks. People from the UK, the USA, France, Belgium and Portugal (seen as individualistic) made fewer errors in total.

Critical thinking

Conformity is a very complex issue. Teenagers tend to view themselves as non-conformist because this is the age at which they often begin to rebel against authority figures. However, others might argue that this is the age when people are most conforming. Have a discussion about the pressures you are under to conform to certain standards but not to conform to others. Think about the reasons why conformity rates may be different in different cultures. Does it depend on the tasks people are asked to perform? Could there be circumstances in which a collectivist culture was less conforming than an individualistic one?

AQA Social loafing

Social loafing refers to situations when a person is likely to put in *less* effort in a group task. As a group is working towards some form of common goal, the individual members of that group put in less effort compared to what they would do if they were individually responsible for that task.

ACTIVITY 2.11

Think about some real-life examples of social loafing with people in your class. Make a list and see if there are any similarities.

KEY TERM

Social loafing: situations where a person is likely to put in *less* effort in a group task.

AQA Studies into social loafing

STUDY ONE: LATANÉ, WILLIAMS AND HARKINS (1979)

Aim: To assess the role of social loafing in cheering and clapping behaviour.

Method: Male students were asked to clap or cheer as loudly as they could. They did this either alone, in a pair, or in groups of four or six people.

Results: The amount of noise produced by the students decreased sharply as the number of students in the group increased. Therefore, there was a negative correlation between noise made and group size.

Conclusion: These findings support the idea of social loafing. This is because the group was putting less effort into cheering when there were more people around.

EVALUATION

➕ The task given to the students was quite artificial. As a result the study may lack ecological validity, and these results may not happen in a real-life situation when spectators can clap and cheer (e.g. at a football match).

➕ As the study was well controlled, Latané et al. could be confident that it was the group size that affected the amount of social loafing that happened. That is, they could be more confident that it was the independent variable affecting the dependent variable.

STUDY TWO: ARTERBERRY, CAIN AND CHOPKO (2007)

Aim: To investigate whether social loafing exists when children are asked to solve problems.

Method: Participants were 192 5-year-old children in America. The children were randomly assigned to either working alone or in pairs. None of the children assigned to the pairs condition knew each other. The children were then given either an easy or a hard puzzle, so there were four conditions:

1. alone with easy puzzle
2. alone with hard puzzle
3. in a pair with easy puzzle
4. in a pair with hard puzzle.

For each of the four conditions, half of the children were told that their work would be evaluated after completing the task, while the other half were not told this.

The hard puzzle was a 60-piece jigsaw of a bear outside a shop, where the outer border had already been completed. The easy puzzle was another jigsaw that was simply columns of different colours.

The experimenter recorded how many pieces of the puzzle were in the correct place after 5 minutes.

Results: The table below shows the mean number of correct pieces in place after 5 minutes.

Mean number of pieces placed correctly within the first 5 minutes as a function of task difficulty (easy or hard puzzle), evaluation, and working context (alone or with partner)				
	Alone		Paired	
	Evaluation	No evaluation	Evaluation	No evaluation
Hard puzzle	8.25	10.56	9.56	14.31
Easy puzzle	17.63	19.38	25.06	14.88

As can be clearly seen, for the hard puzzle the paired condition, on average, did much better than the alone condition. Therefore, the researchers concluded that the children were helping each other out (psychologists refer to this as social facilitation). However, for the easy puzzle, when the children were not evaluated the paired condition performed much worse, which is evidence for social loafing happening.

Conclusion: Social loafing only happened when the children were not going to be evaluated with the easy puzzle. This is because the mean for this condition is much lower than that of the alone condition (14.88 compared to 19.38). This shows they were putting less effort into the task. However, this was reversed for all of the other conditions, which showed social facilitation (children helping each other out).

EVALUATION

➕ As the study was well controlled, Arterberry et al. were able to confidently conclude that it was the independent variable affecting the dependent variable. That is, they could confidently conclude it was the type of puzzle and group size that were affecting the amount of social loafing and social facilitation.

The sample consisted of children from America, therefore the results may only be applicable to American children in terms of the level of social loafing seen. There is no way of knowing whether the same would be seen in other cultures where group work is encouraged more or less. Therefore, this study needs to be replicated in other countries to see if similar results happen.

AQA Factors that can affect social loafing

Size of project or task

It has been shown that the larger the project given to a group of people, the more social loafing will take place. That is, if the task takes a long time because it has many parts to complete, then there is more time for someone to socially loaf. Therefore, if tasks are broken down into smaller parts, with each part having to be completed before moving onto the next part, there is less chance for social loafing to happen.

Group size

It has also been shown that the larger the group, the more social loafing happens. This is because you are less likely to be spotted doing some social loafing as there are more people to "carry you through" the task. Read the Latané et al. study on page 34 for an example of this.

Peer or teacher evaluations

The "threat" of having your work evaluated by your peers or by a teacher reduces the chances of you socially loafing. This is because if your work is being assessed then there is more chance that your loafing will be spotted by someone and you will be found out!

ACTIVITY 2.12

Read the Arterberry, Cain and Chopko (2007) study on page 34 about children completing jigsaw puzzles. Did evaluating their work make them more or less likely to socially loaf?

KEY TERM

Deindividuation: refers to situations when a person, in a group, loses their sense of individuality or personal identity and personal responsibility for their actions.

AQA Deindividuation

Deindividuation refers to situations when a person, in a group, loses their sense of individuality or personal identity and personal responsibility for their actions. This is because of decreased awareness of one's actions when part of a large body of people. Therefore you just "go along with the crowd".

ACTIVITY 2.13

Can you think of any real-life examples where deindividuation occurs? You may wish to think about football fans, gangs, etc.

AQA Studies into deindividuation

STUDY ONE: JOHNSON AND DOWNING (1979)

Aim: Johnson and Downing wanted to investigate the effects of deindividuation on antisocial behaviour.

Method: The participants were 60 female students from a university in America. Participants were either dressed in robes with hoods (antisocial as they looked like those worn by the Ku Klux Klan or executioners) or in a nurse's uniform (prosocial as this uniform is associated with helping and caring). In addition the participants were either identified with a name tag (individuation) or they did not have a name tag (deindividuation). Therefore the conditions were:

1. robes and hood with name tag
2. robes and hood without name tag
3. nurse with name tag
4. nurse without name tag.

There were 15 participants per condition.

Photographs were taken of the participants and used in the actual study as an example of who else was administering electric shocks.

The participants were asked to decide the level of electric shock another person should get for failing to perform a task. To do this the participants were given a choice from +3 to −3, where +3 was to increase the shock to a high level, and −3 was to decrease the shock to a much lower level. Before choosing, the participants saw the responses of a further three participants (they in fact did not exist, and Johnson and Downing made sure that the three responses averaged 0 each time; however participants did see photographs of them in similar clothing to themselves). The participants were finally told that the experimenters were not recording individual responses but would be looking at the group average.

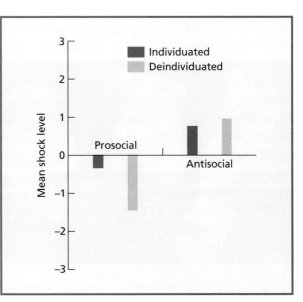

Data based on Johnson and Downing (1979)

Results: As can be clearly seen, when the participant was deindividuated (no name tag), the level of shock increased the most, particularly when the clothing was associated with antisocial behaviour (i.e. the robes and hood).

Conclusion: When a participant was deindividuated (e.g. no name tag present on the photograph) they began to follow the "norm" of that group. So, for example, when the participant was wearing antisocial clothing they acted more antisocially (giving high level shocks) and when they were wearing prosocial clothing they acted more prosocially (gave much lower level shocks).

EVALUATION

⊖ Johnson and Downing only used female, American students as their sample. This may make it difficult to generalise to male behaviour or the behaviour of females outside of America. Therefore, the findings may be unique to that sample of participants and deindividuation may not happen with other types of people.

⊕ As the study was well controlled, Johnson and Downing could be confident that it was the independent variable affecting the dependent variable. That is, they could be confident that it was the level of deindividuation affecting the level of antisocial behaviour.

⊖ There are ethical issues raised by the study. Participants may have been placed under psychological stress as they believed they were giving shocks to a stranger. As no shocks were delivered they were also deceived.

Participants in Zimbardo's deindividuation experiment

STUDY TWO: ZIMBARDO (1970)

Aim: Zimbardo wanted to test whether deindividuation makes people show more antisocial behaviour.

Method: He used groups of four female college students. They were asked to deliver electric shocks to another woman (they were fake though!). There were two conditions:

1. Each participant in the group dressed in a laboratory coat and hood immediately on arriving for the study. The room was dimly

lit and no names were ever used. This was the deindividuation condition.

2. No hoods or coats were worn, the laboratory was brightly lit and all the participants wore clear name tags.

Results: As Zimbardo expected, the participants in the deindividuation condition gave out electric shocks for much longer compared to the other group.

Conclusion: The study shows that deindividuation does make people show more antisocial behaviour.

EVALUATION

⊖ Zimbardo only used female, American students as his sample. This may make it difficult to generalise to male behaviour or the behaviour of females outside of America. Therefore, the findings may be unique to that sample of participants and deindividuation may not happen with other types of people.

⊕ As the study was well controlled, Zimbardo could be confident that it was the independent variable affecting the dependent variable. That is, he could be confident that it was the level of deindividuation affecting the level of antisocial behaviour.

⊖ There are ethical issues raised by the study. Participants may have been placed under psychological stress as they believed they were giving shocks to a stranger. As no shocks were delivered they were also deceived.

AQA Factors that can affect deindividuation

Group size

Like with social loafing, the larger the group, the more deindividuation can happen. This is because you are much less likely to be spotted engaging in some sort of group behaviour you would not normally do as there are so many other people doing the same! Think about being at a football match with everyone wearing their team's colours. People are more likely to engage in antisocial behaviour in this situation as it would be difficult to identify people who all dress the same.

Physical anonymity

If you are made to be anonymous then you are more likely to deindividuate. This is because, as with group size, you are less likely to be singled out or spotted as being the one who engaged in a certain type of behaviour.

KEY TERM

Denial (or diffusion) of responsibility: the feeling that one is less answerable for one's behaviour because there are other people around. Any "responsibility" is shared so no individual feels responsible.

ACTIVITY 2.14

Read the Johnson and Downing (1979) and Zimbardo (1970) studies on pages 37 and 38 respectively. Identify which parts of the studies show physical anonymity and then work out whether this increased or decreased deindividuation. Also consider what effect it had on the participants' behaviours.

OCR AQA ## Denial of responsibility and factors affecting bystander intervention

Denial (or diffusion) of responsibility refers to when people feel less answerable for their behaviour because there are other people around. Any "responsibility" is shared, so no individual feels responsible.

A good example of this came via the murder of Kitty Genovese as detailed in the box below.

Case Study: *The Kitty Genovese Murder* (as misleadingly reported by the *New York Times*)

At approximately 3.20 in the morning on March 13, 1964, 28-year-old Kitty Genovese was returning to her home in a middle-class area of Queens, New York, from her job as a bar manager. She parked her car and started to walk to her second-floor apartment some 30 meters away. She got as far as a streetlight, when a man who was later identified as Winston Mosely grabbed her. She screamed. Lights went on in the nearby apartment building. Kitty yelled, "Oh my God, he stabbed me! Please help me!" A window opened in the apartment building and a man's voice shouted, "Let that girl alone!" Mosely looked up, shrugged, and walked off down the street. As Kitty Genovese struggled to get to her feet, the lights went off in the apartments. The attacker came back some minutes later and renewed the assault by stabbing her again. She again cried out, "I'm dying! I'm dying!" Once again the lights came on and windows opened in many of the nearby apartments. The assailant again left, got into his car and drove away. Kitty staggered to her feet as a city bus drove by. It was now 3.35 a.m. Mosely returned and found his victim in a doorway at the foot of the stairs. He then raped her and stabbed her for a third time – this time fatally. It was 3.50 when the police received the first call. They responded quickly and were at the scene within 2 minutes, but Kitty Genovese was already dead.

The only person to call the police, a neighbor of Ms. Genovese, revealed that he had phoned only after much thought and after making a call to a friend to ask advice. He said, "I didn't want to get involved." Later it emerged that there were 38 other witnesses to the events over the half-hour period. Many of Kitty's neighbors heard her screams and watched from the windows, but no one came to her aid. The story shocked America and made front-page news across the country. The question people asked was why no one had offered any help, or even called the police earlier when it might have helped. Urban and moral decay, apathy, and indifference were some of the many explanations offered. Two social psychologists, Bibb Latané and John Darley, were unsatisfied with these explanations and began a series of research studies to identify the situational factors that influence whether or not people come to the aid of others. They concluded that an individual is less likely to provide assistance the greater the number of other bystanders present.

ACTIVITY 2.15

Read around the case of Kitty Genovese. What have subsequent reports found out about the original newspaper article?

AQA Studies into bystander intervention

STUDY ONE: LATANÉ AND DARLEY (1968)

Aim: Latané and Darley wanted to investigate whether being in a group affected reporting of an incident.

Method: All participants were male students living on campus at Columbia University. A situation was created to test out **bystander intervention**. The participants were seated in a small waiting room and then asked to complete a questionnaire. They were being observed through a one-way mirror as they did this. As soon as a participant had completed two pages of the questionnaire, the experimenter began to introduce smoke through a small vent in the wall. The time taken to report the smoke to the experimenter was noted. However, if after 6 minutes the participant had not moved, the experiment was ended. There were three groups who participated:

1. *The alone condition.* The participant was alone in the room ($n = 24$).
2. *The passives condition.* The participant was in the room with two confederates who did not react to the smoke ($n = 10$).
3. The group of three people in the room were all real participants ($n = 24$; 8 groups of 3).

> **KEY TERM**
>
> **Bystander intervention:** is when people help others who are in need. For example, if someone tripped up in the street and their shopping went everywhere and you helped, this would be bystander intervention.

Results: Participants were much less likely to report the smoke in the passives condition (10%) or when there were three real participants (38%). However, in the alone condition 75% of participants reported the smoke. Also, in the passives condition many of the participants tried to continue completing the questionnaire while waving the smoke away from their eyes!

Conclusion: Being in a group affected the reporting of the incident. When other people were around, participants were *less* likely to report the smoke incident. This could be because of a denial of responsibility (see page 40).

EVALUATION

⊖ Latané and Darley only used male, American students as their sample. This may make it difficult to generalise to female behaviour or the behaviour of males outside of America. Therefore, the findings may be unique to that sample of participants and bystander intervention may or may not happen with other types of people.

⊕ As the study was well controlled, Latané and Darley could be confident that it was the group size that affected the amount of bystander intervention that happened. That is, they could be more confident that it was the independent variable affecting the dependent variable.

⊖ The study could be seen as being unethical. Participants may have been placed under unnecessary psychological stress during the procedure. These people may now question themselves in similar situations, which may affect their behaviour.

STUDY TWO: PILIAVIN, RODIN AND PILIAVIN (1969)

Aim: Piliavin et al. wanted to investigate helping behaviour in a real-life setting.

Method: The method was quite complex. The field experiment had a setting of an express train in a New York Subway. Piliavin et al. described it as a laboratory on wheels. Four teams of students made up the research team. One played the victim, a second was a model and the other two were observers.

Around 4450 people on the train were the unknowing participants in the study over a period of 3 months. The train route selected meant there was a period of 7.5 minutes when there were no stops. Seventy seconds into

Methodology

This is a good example of a field experiment. The independent variable was manipulated in a natural setting. In this study there were several independent variables:
1. Black or white
2. Appearing drunk or appearing disabled
3. The model helps or does not help.

the journey, the victim staggered forward and collapsed. Below is a layout of the train carriage:

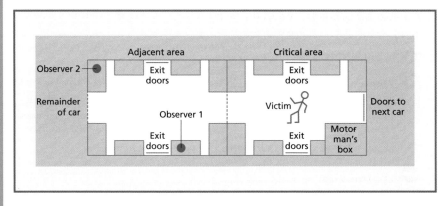

Layout of subway carriage showing the critical area and position of the victim

The situation was varied in the following ways:

1. The race of the victim was either black (1 student) or white (3 students).
2. The type of victim was either drunk or ill (the latter carried a black cane).
3. The model helping out (helped between 70 and 150 seconds after the collapse, especially if no one had helped already).

For each trial the observers noted the race, sex and location of every person in the train carriage. The total number of people who came to assist the victim was also recorded, as was the time taken to help.

Results: The observers reported that there was more immediate help if the victim had a cane compared to when the victim was drunk (many more helped the cane victim within 70 seconds of the collapse).

The percentage of conditions where help was given was analysed by race of helper and race of victim. Results are shown in the bar chart.

The table below shows the percentage of trials where helping behaviour occurred, by type of victim.

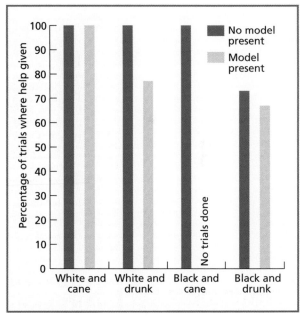

Percentage of trials where help was given, by race and condition of victim

	White victim – cane	White victim – drunk	Black victim – cane	Black victim – drunk
White helper	63%	91%	37%	9%
Black helper	75%	25%	25%	75%

Conclusion: There were two main conclusions that Piliavin et al. reported based on the data. The first is that an apparently ill person is more likely to receive help compared to someone who is drunk. Second, the race of the victim has little effect on the race of the helper, except where the victim is drunk.

EVALUATION

➕ The setting was in a natural environment for the participants, therefore it could be said that the study has ecological validity. That is, it was measuring the real-life bystander intervention of participants, showing what people will do in a real-life scenario involving someone requiring help.

➖ The study can be seen as being unethical. Participants could not give consent to take part in the study, and they were deceived because they would have believed the collapse was real. Finally, there is no way of assessing the psychological stress a participant was placed under during the collapse scenario or after (there would have been no way of following up the after-effects for each participant).

➖ As the study was conducted in a natural setting, there is no way that all variables could be controlled. There may have been other factors that affected the likelihood that someone helped out that had nothing to do with the race or type of victim. For example, a person may not have helped because a previous similar situation had not been favourable to them, or a participant may have been preoccupied with something happening in their lives. This means that Piliavin et al. would be less confident it was the type or race of victim affecting the amount of helping behaviour.

➕ The sample size was very large, which means that there was a much higher chance that the sample had a wide range of people in it. This makes generalisation stronger. That is, the sample's behaviours may reflect what people would do in a similar, *real*, situation.

STUDY THREE: BATSON, O'QUIN, FULTZ, VANDERPLAS AND ISEN (1983)

Aim: In a series of three experiments, Batson et al. were interested in what motivates people to help others. In study 1, which we will look at, they aimed to see whether making it difficult or easy to escape from an unpleasant situation would have an effect on helping.

Method: We will only look at study 1. A total of 40 students from an introductory psychology course were the participants. There were 20 males and 20 females. They were randomly assigned to either the *easy* or *difficult* escape conditions (as highlighted below).

The participants were always placed in the role of the observer. They watched closed-circuit TV footage (it was in fact a videotape) of a same-sex participant (who was in fact a confederate, called Elaine or Charlie) in the role of a worker. The participant watched the worker attempting to recall numbers, and while recalling, the worker received mild electric shocks at random intervals. After completing the observation, the participants were asked to report their impressions of the worker.

In the *easy* escape condition, just before observing the worker, the real participant was given the following information: "... *although the worker will be completing between two and ten trials, it will be necessary for you to observe* **only the first two** ..." (p. 710). In the *difficult* escape condition, the participant was given differing information: "... *the worker will be completing between two and ten trials,* **all of which you will observe** ..." (p. 710).

Unknown to the real participants, the worker would elect to do all 10 trials. However, after trial 2, the real participant had a chance to take the place of the worker.

Therefore, just after viewing the second trial, an experimenter appeared on screen, asking the worker if they were all right. The worker hesitantly said yes and revealed that they had had a traumatic experience with an electric shock in childhood. Hearing this, the experimenter came up with the idea that the real participants could "trade places" with Elaine or Charlie. Twenty seconds later, the experimenter appeared to ask the real participant if they would replace the worker for the remaining trials. Prior to this the real participants had completed a questionnaire measuring their emotional response towards the worker's distress.

One final point to note: participants were split into emotional response groups based on the questionnaire. They were classified as either *distress* or *empathy*. The *distress* participants were more likely to choose adjectives like upset, worried and alarmed as their emotional response towards the worker. The *empathy* participants were more likely to choose sympathetic, moved and compassionate. Batson et al. wanted to see which of these groups was more likely to take the place of the worker.

Results: As can be clearly seen, in the *easy* condition, the empathy group were much more likely to help and take part in more trials than the distress group. However, in the *difficult* condition, the distress group were more likely to help and take part in more trials than the empathy group.

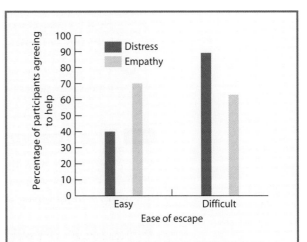

Conclusion: People's motivation to help differs depending on the scenario. If people are feeling compassionate or sympathetic, they are more

Proportion of subjects agreeing to help Elaine (Charlie) in each condition. Data based on Batson et al. (1983)

likely to help out if the situation is perceived as being "an easy way to help". However, if the situation is seen as being difficult, then people who feel distressed and upset are more likely to help.

ACTIVITY 2.16

There have been many studies in this chapter that have been evaluated for you. Your job is to evaluate this Batson et al. study. Think about things like sample size, the research method used, whether the study is ecologically valid, and if there are any ethical issues. Come on, you know you can do it!

EVALUATION

➕ The Batson et al. study cleverly took account of two variables (ease of escape and motivation to help) and their effect on helping behaviour. It could therefore look at the *interaction* of two variables.

➕ The study used both males and females as participants, so the findings can be generalised to both sexes. It randomly assigned people to the two conditions so there should not be any participant variables (individual differences) between the two groups to confound the results.

➖ The study uses rather an artificial situation in which people are seen on video in unusual circumstances, rather than in real life. It therefore lacks ecological validity and does not necessarily reflect how people would react to a real-life incident.

➖ There are ethical concerns with his study regarding protection of participants. The participants did experience distress when watching someone in pain.

➖ The sample consisted only of students, so the results do not necessarily generalise to other populations of people.

AQA The research of Schroeder et al. (1995)

Schroeder, Penner, Dovidio and Piliavin (1995) published a book reviewing the field of helping behaviour (including bystander apathy) up until 1995. The following were the main conclusions as to why people choose to help.

When will people help?

- People will help if they decide that something is wrong and that their help is needed. They will then go on to help if they can provide the necessary assistance. If not, then they do not help.

- People will conduct a cost–benefit analysis. If the costs (including money, amount of danger) outweigh the benefits then no help is given. However, if the benefit to the person requiring help is seen as not costing much and the benefits are high then people will help. This means, for example, that a young woman may not help a bleeding drunk (he may be sick on her, he may be aggressive, she may not be able to help him effectively, so the costs are high). People would, however, rescue a child from a river that was not deep enough for them to drown in but in which the child could drown, because the costs are low and the benefits are very high.

What motivates people to offer help?

- People are more likely to help if they have had direct or indirect experiences of similar events.
- If we feel "connected" to the person in need then we are more likely to help them.

ACTIVITY 2.17

Review the other studies into bystander intervention. Do any of them assess this issue of feeling "connected" to the person in need? What do you think Schroeder et al. mean by being "connected"?

Are some people more helpful than others?

- In many cases of bystander intervention, men and women react differently. People tend to help in ways that are consistent with what is expected as a male or female. For example, males help more when strength is required and females more so when emotional support is needed.
- People who show high self-efficacy tend to help more – that is, people who believe that their attempts to help will be successful will help out more often.

AQA Factors affecting bystander intervention

Bystander intervention involves helping others who are in need. For example, if someone tripped up in the street and their shopping went everywhere and you helped, this would be bystander intervention. However, there has been a lot of research that has tried to look at why people *do not* help others.

ACTIVITY 2.18

Before reading on, work in pairs and write down situations in which you would help out someone else in a crowd who needed assistance. Then repeat this for situations in which you would not help. You must justify your two lists!

Group size

The larger the group, the more people are likely to deny responsibility. As there are more people around who *could* help out, it appears sensible that people may *feel* less likely to want to help, believing someone else will do it instead.

ACTIVITY 2.19

Read the Latané and Darley (1968) study on page 41. Did group size affect intervention in that study?

The characteristics of the victim

This appears to be a crucial factor that can affect bystander intervention. How the victim is perceived by the people in the crowd or group can dictate whether anyone will help out.

ACTIVITY 2.20

Read the Piliavin, Rodin and Piliavin (1969) study on page 42. How did the characteristics of the victim affect helping behaviour? Under which conditions did bystander intervention happen?

Knowledge shared by the group

The knowledge about the victim or victims can also affect the likelihood that someone will help out. However, the "knowledge" may be faulty, as highlighted by Levine (1999). He analysed the testimonies of 38 bystanders linked to the murder of James Bulger (a 2-year-old who was murdered by two 10-year-olds). The bystanders in this event had all been given the knowledge that the three boys were brothers and there was nothing to worry about as a result. As you know, James was murdered.

OCR AQA Psychological theory behind keeping order in institutions (contemporary practical implications)

This chapter has covered a lot of ideas about why people are obedient and/or conform to social norms. These can be applied to keeping order in institutions, and there are other ideas and theories that can also be applied as highlighted next. We will relate the ideas to prisons.

Conformity

The idea of normative conformity can be applied to prisons. Inmates may conform to the prison system because of a desire to be liked. If a prisoner is "liked" and seen as being a follower of prison rules and regulations, then of course the prisoner may be considered for early release as a result. Therefore the prisoner is *more likely* to conform to rules to benefit themselves.

Adapting to institutional life (Goffman 1961)

With this idea, Goffman proposed that prisoners may do one of three things in a prison. These help to keep order in the prison. In the *colonisation* phase, prisoners make themselves fully at home in the prison and do not want to leave. As a result, prisoners will go along with the demands of the prison for this to happen. In the *conversion* phase, the prisoner imitates the actions of staff and is used by them on various tasks. Therefore, when a prisoner is in this phase they will follow the rules of the prison without question. Finally, in the *playing it cool* phase, the prisoner may not be fully cooperative with rules and regulations, but will follow them sufficiently to survive their stay in prison. If prison staff can identify which phase each prisoner is in they can use it to their advantage to help keep order in the prison.

Agency and obedience

Milgram's proposed agency theory can be linked to keeping order in prisons. In order for prisoners to be "happy" they need to stick to rules laid out by the prison. Obeying these rules may mean that at some point the prisoners have to give up their free will (the idea that we make our own decisions and think for ourselves). Milgram proposed that for a prisoner to do this they must have two social states:

1. *An autonomous state*: This is when we are free to act as we wish.
2. *An agentic state*: This is when we give up our free will in order to serve the interests of a wider group. In the case of prisons, this means going along with the orders of the prison guards to keep peace within the group of prisoners. So the prisoners are "agents" of those in authority and will do as they are told to ensure that the prison environment is a decent place to live in. They may not *agree* with the rules but that does not make any difference to their behaviour.

Therefore, if prison guards and the institution rules are used in a way to benefit the entire prison, then more prisoners will follow an agentic state and order will be kept.

ACTIVITY 2.21

Re-read the Bickman study on page 27. How could this study be used to try to keep order in a prison?

Chapter summary

- Obedience is when people behave in a certain way because they go along with the demands of an authority figure. However, defiance is when people want to resist the demands of authority and *not* do as they are told.
- Milgram's study using fake electric shocks clearly showed that when put under pressure from an authority figure, participants were willing to kill someone for getting a word pair wrong.
- Hofling's study using nurses showed that they were willing to administer a large amount of drug because a doctor (an authority figure) telephoned them and asked them to do it.
- There are also many factors that affect obedience, including the closeness of the learner, the closeness of the authority figure, and the status of the authority figure.
- Also, Milgram found that the environment in which obedience is asked for can have an effect (e.g. a run-down building versus a university). He also reported that consensus affects our obedience levels.
- Adorno mentioned that dispositional factors can affect obedience. People with authoritarian personalities tend to be more obedient.
- Bickman noted in his study that the uniform a person wears affects obedience levels. He concluded that a uniform has the power to make people obey simple demands like picking up a bag, lending a dime to a stranger or moving at a bus stop.
- Conformity is when people behave in a certain way because of the pressure exerted on them by other group members.
- Asch's study using the Lines on a Card procedure demonstrated that participants will conform to an answer that is clearly wrong because of the pressure from other group members who have also got it wrong.
- Sherif's study using the autokinetic effect showed that when people discuss their answers they move towards a group norm.
- There are many factors that can affect conformity, including the size of the group, the status of group members, and the difficulty of the task.
- Social loafing refers to situations when a person is likely to put in *less* effort in a group task. As a group is working towards some form of common goal, the individual members of that group put in less effort compared to what they would do if they were individually responsible for that task.
- Studies by Latané et al. and by Arterberry et al. show that people will socially loaf in different situations they find themselves in.
- There are many factors that affect social loafing, including the size of project, group size, and peer or teacher evaluations.
- Deindividuation refers to situations when a person, in a group, loses their sense of individuality or personal identity and personal responsibility for their actions. This is because of decreased awareness of one's actions when part of a large body of people. Therefore you just "go along with the crowd".

- Studies by Johnson and Downing and by Zimbardo show that people will easily deinividuate and quickly change their behaviours.
- Factors that affect deindividuation include group size and physical anonymity.
- Denial (or diffusion) of responsibility refers to when people feel less answerable for their behaviour because there are other people around. Any "responsibility" is shared, so no individual feels responsible.
- Studies by Latané and Darley, by Piliavin et al., and by Batson et al. all show that there are many factors that affect whether someone will help in times of need. Schroeder et al., reviewed the field in 1995 and reported different reasons why people will or will not help.
- Factors that affect bystander intervention include group size, the characteristics of the victim, and knowledge shared by the group.

`OCR` Exam-style questions for OCR

1. Using an example, what is the difference between obedience and defiance? (3 marks)

2. Using research evidence, describe **one** way in which the environment can affect obedience levels. (4 marks)

3. Describe what is meant by the authoritarian personality. (3 marks)

4. Describe **two** results from the Bickman (1974) study. (4 marks)

5. Outline **one** limitation of the Bickman (1974) study. (2 marks)

6. You will have studied one application of research into obedience (e.g. keeping order in an institution). Write a brief report recommending ways in which you *could* make some follow the rules of an institution. (6 marks)

`AQA` Exam-style questions for AQA

1. Using an example, define social loafing. (2 marks)

2. Using an example, define deindividuation. (2 marks)

3. Describe **one** study into conformity. Make sure you mention the aim, procedure, findings and conclusion. (6 marks)

4. Outline **two** factors that affect levels of obedience. (4 marks)

5. Outline **two** factors that affect bystander intervention. (4 marks)

6. Describe the findings of (a) the Batson et al. study and (b) the Schroeder et al. studies into bystander intervention. (4 marks)

7. Evaluate the Piliavin, Rodin and Piliavin study into bystander intervention in terms of **one** strength and **one** weakness. (4 marks)

What you need to know AQA

The specification lists the following things that you will need to be able to do for the examination:

■ Define stereotyping, prejudice and discrimination

■ Describe and evaluate studies of prejudice and of discrimination, including the work of Adorno (authoritarian personality), Tajfel (in-groups and out-groups), and Sherif (Robbers' Cave)

■ Explain prejudice and discrimination

■ Describe ways of reducing prejudice and discrimination

■ Evaluate ways of reducing prejudice

■ Describe contemporary implications of research into stereotyping, prejudice and discrimination and their benefits and drawbacks

Stereotyping, prejudice and discrimination

As someone who is heavily overweight, Sonya is used to what she describes as "fatism" from the general public. What she hadn't expected her obesity to affect were her career prospects. "I knew the moment I turned up to my last job interview that my chances were low," she says. "Everyone had a certain look – thin, young and pretty. When I met my two interviewers, I knew I'd lost immediately because of the way they looked at me. The thing that was most upsetting was the fact that the telephone conversation I'd had with one of them beforehand suggested I had all the skills and experience necessary and the interview was just a formality."

"Lookism" is the latest discrimination to hit the workplace, according to the law firm, Eversheds. Victims of the trend are judged by employers on aspects of their appearance ranging from weight to clothing and from hairstyle to body piercing, and while some, like Sonya, are turned down for jobs, others miss out on promotion.

Stephen Hirschfeld, CEO [Chief Executive Officer] of the ELA [Employment Law Alliance], says discrimination claims involving alleged lookism are surging in the US. "On the surface, this may look like another symptom of a litigious society. But it goes much deeper than that as employers and employees struggle over the authority of management to ensure customer service satisfaction versus an employee's right to, for instance, sport a nose ring and a tongue stud." . . .

Lucy has a rare condition called agromegaly, which caused some of her bones to grow abnormally, particularly on the head, hands and feet, as well as causing puffiness around her face. She feels certain she was turned down for a number of jobs because of what she looked like before she was diagnosed and subsequently treated. "I did look odd," she admits. "But it didn't affect my ability to work, yet no employer seemed to want me anywhere near their customers. Eventually, I didn't want to go out at all."

Meanwhile, Sonya's interviewers came back to her the next day and said they'd "reconsidered the skills set required for the job". "There was nothing I felt I could do about it," she says. What's more, it's not only recruitment and promotion that is affected by lookism. A report last year by the University of Helsinki showed that overweight women earned up to 30% less than their more slender colleagues.

Some names have been changed.

> Adapted from the *Guardian*, Monday 16 May 2005

AQA Defining stereotyping, prejudice and discrimination

This article provides examples of stereotyping, prejudice and discrimination. We're now going to consider in a little more detail what these concepts involve.

ACTIVITY 3.1

Pretend you are an employer in a small business that needs a receptionist to deal with prospective customers. Write a paragraph defending the company policy that the person in this post should not wear a nose ring, tongue studs, or eyebrow studs because of fears that it might give the wrong impression to customers (there are no safety issues).

Pretend you are a young person who would like such a job but you feel that, since there are no safety issues, you should have the choice over whether to wear a nose ring, tongue studs, or eyebrow studs.

What is prejudice?

We live in a society that consists of many different social groups – blacks, whites, Asians, men, women, Jews, Muslims, Catholics, southerners, northerners, teenagers, members of a particular school, to name only a few. As we grow up, we develop attitudes towards some of these groups, often with very little if any knowledge of what they are really like. Sometimes we haven't even met people from these groups, but we still develop attitudes towards them.

An overall attitude to a social group is termed **prejudice** because it causes us to *prejudge* people on the basis of the group to which they belong. Prejudice can be positive or negative, although it is usually associated with negative feelings.

A definition of prejudice

Prejudice can be defined as "an attitude that predisposes us to think, feel, perceive, and act in favourable or unfavourable ways towards a group or its individual members".

KEY TERM

Prejudice: an attitude that predisposes us to think, feel, perceive, and act in favourable or unfavourable ways towards a group or its individual members.

Stereotyping

Stereotyping involves holding beliefs about the characteristics of groups of individuals and assuming that each individual member of that group has those characteristics. Common **stereotypes** are those based on race, religion, social class, sex, sexuality and attractiveness.

Examples of stereotypes are that fat people are jolly, French women are elegant, the Welsh are good singers, university professors are forgetful.

In principle, there is nothing wrong with stereotyping, in fact, it is an essential part of everyday life. For example, it is not unreasonable to assume that most 15-year-old boys will not be interested in knitting, or that most 75-year-old women will not play football on a regular basis. Most of us have stereotypes about many important social groups but that does not necessarily mean we are prejudiced. Stereotypes are simply beliefs about a group; prejudice, on the other hand,

Not everyone conforms to stereotypes

involves *emotion*. None of the stereotypes mentioned above brings with it great emotional feelings – they are just beliefs about groups of people. Nevertheless, if stereotypes involve negative or positive evaluations, they can form the basis of prejudiced attitudes and **discrimination**. For example, if an employer held the stereotyped belief that old people cannot learn new skills ("you can't teach an old dog new tricks"), then they would be unlikely to employ older people for jobs that require new training. Similarly, if an employer believes all young people are lazy and unreliable, they are unlikely to offer them a job or even interview them.

ACTIVITY 3.2

There are stereotypes based on all sorts of characteristics. Individually, give a very brief description of what characteristics you think people from the following countries have, then compare your answers in a group to see how similar they are: the French, the Spanish, the Italians, the Germans, the Swedes, the Danes, the Swiss, the Poles, the Norwegians.

Do the same for a group of car drivers – as a group, agree the types of cars beforehand. Then similarly for forenames, or indeed any other groups you can think of.

Discrimination

Discrimination involves the unequal treatment of individuals or groups based on arbitrary characteristics such as race, sex, ethnicity, and cultural background. Some stereotypes can lead to discrimination: in the example

KEY TERMS

Stereotype: an automatically activated "fixed" set of beliefs about the characteristics of a group of individuals that is then applied to individual members of that group. Stereotypes are based on limited information and are often incorrect.

Stereotyping: holding beliefs about the characteristics of groups of individuals, and assuming each individual member has those characteristics.

Discrimination: the practice of unequal treatment of individuals or groups based on arbitrary characteristics such as race, sex, ethnicity, and cultural background.

above, the employers would be discriminating again older people and young people by not employing them.

> **ACTIVITY 3.3**
>
> Discrimination has been a feature of societies for many years. See if you can think of (or can find) one or two examples of discrimination along the following lines:
>
> • Women in Britain up to the early 20th century
> • Homosexual men in Britain up to 1967
> • Blacks in South Africa during the apartheid regime
> • Blacks in the USA until the 1950s
> • Women in any other culture at the present time

The three components of a prejudiced attitude: ABC

We'll now take a more detailed look at prejudice and the relationship between this, stereotyping and discrimination.

As we have already said, prejudice is an attitude. Attitudes of all types have three parts or components, which we can refer to as ABC: an **affective component**, a **behavioural component**, and a **cognitive component**. Let's use an example to explain these three components. Suppose you have the attitude "I love horror films". The three components of this attitude are:

• The affective component – how you *feel*. In this case you love the films.
• The behavioural component – how you *act* or *behave* because of the affective and cognitive components. You watch these films at every available opportunity.
• The cognitive component – your *assumptions* and *beliefs*. Horror films are interesting and exciting.

Now we'll consider how these components apply to prejudiced attitudes.

The cognitive component is the assumptions we make about the object of our prejudice. With prejudiced attitudes this may well involve a negative (or positive) stereotype – a belief about the characteristics of a group of individuals.

The affective component of a prejudiced attitude consists of the feelings aroused in us by the object of prejudice. This is often a negative feeling, such as fear of all football supporters because you think they may be violent (even though most of them are not), or irritation and impatience towards old people. Common feelings associated with prejudiced attitudes are likes and dislikes, anger, fear, disgust, and, in the extreme, hatred.

The behavioural component of a prejudiced attitude is the way we behave towards the object of our prejudice. This could include discrimination, and may take the form of avoiding certain groups of people, verbal or physical

KEY TERMS

Affective component: the emotional part of an attitude.

Behavioural component: the action part of an attitude.

Cognitive component: the thinking part of an attitude.

attacks on them, not offering them employment, even large-scale persecution of them.

Types of prejudice

There are many types of prejudiced attitudes. Four important ones are the following:

- **Sexism** is a prejudice towards people based on their sex. It often (but not always) refers to contempt shown by men for women and may include discrimination against women.
- **Ethnocentrism** is the belief that one's own ethnic group, nation, or religion is superior to all others.
- **Racism** is a prejudice towards people based on their race or ethnic group. It may involve hatred, rivalry, or bad feeling between races. It is often related to ethnocentrism because it frequently includes the attitude that one's own racial group is superior to all others.
- **Ageism** is a prejudice based on age. It usually involves discrimination against the elderly.

ACTIVITY 3.4

Below are examples of the three components of the attitude of sexism as it might apply in the workplace. Think of examples of two statements for each of the three components (cognitive, affective and behavioural) for ageism and racism. Use a situation other than the workplace.

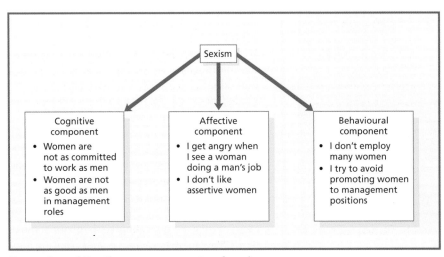

Examples of the three components of sexism

AQA Studies of prejudice and discrimination

STUDY ONE: THE "ROBBERS' CAVE" BY SHERIF ET AL. (1961)

Over several years in the 1950s, Sherif and his colleagues carried out a series of studies on boys attending a summer camp. We will look at the last one of these.

Aim: To look at the effects of group competition on prejudice and to investigate ways of reducing the prejudice by the use of common goals.

Method: Sherif selected 22 boys aged 11 to 12 years to go on a summer camp to a remote place near to a famous hideaway of Jesse James (an outlaw) called Robbers' Cave. The boys were all white and socially well adjusted, and came from stable lower-middle-class homes. None of them knew each other before the study started. They had no idea they were taking part in a study, since the researchers acted as regular camp staff.

The boys were there for 3 weeks and the study can be divided into stages, each corresponding to approximately a week.

- During week 1 the boys were separated into two groups broadly similar in terms of their physical ability, intelligence and how well they got along with others. At the camp each group occupied their own cabin and did not even realise the other group existed. Towards the end of the first week the researchers arranged that the boys would begin to be aware of each other by hearing the others' voices and seeing items left behind.
- During week 2 a series of competitions were organised between the groups, with valued individual prizes (of a medal and a multi-bladed pocket knife) for each member of the winning team and a team trophy.
- During the third week the researchers at Robbers' Cave deliberately set up a few "emergencies" that could only be sorted out with cooperation between the two groups. The intention was to provide the opportunity to work towards a common goal. (Such a goal, which is one that both groups must work together to achieve and that brings rewards for both groups, is known as a **superordinate goal**.)

This photograph shows the two groups of boys who participated in Sherif's study competing in a tug of war

Results:

- *Week 1:* The boys formed their own group identity, cooperated in such activities as pitching tents, preparing meals and playing sport, and developed their own hierarchy. They spontaneously gave themselves names, one group choosing to be called the "Eagles" while the other dubbed themselves the "Rattlers" and they stencilled these names onto their shirts and flags.

  Once the boys became aware of the presence of the other group, they responded by becoming quite territorial and there was a definite division into "us" and "them", in other words, into **in-groups** and **out-groups**.

- *Week 2:* Once the competition had been announced, the team identity increased while the unpleasantness between the two groups quickly got worse, with a lot of name-calling and singing of derogatory songs (songs that were rude about the other group). This became much worse once the competition started, so much so that the camp officials had to intervene several times to break up fights and prevent serious injury. The Eagles won the prizes of camping knives and trophies, and the Rattlers responded by raiding their cabin, stealing the knives, and telling their enemies they'd have "to crawl on their bellies to get them back".

- *Week 3:* One of the "emergencies" arranged by the researchers was that there was no water because of a leak in a mile-long pipe. The boys organised themselves into teams to inspect the pipe. Once the leak was found and repaired, the boys rejoiced together. Then a truck carrying food supplies got stuck in mud and it required all the boys to pull it clear. Having to work together cooperatively rather than in competition reduced the conflict, and by the end of the study the boys were playing together and cross-group friendships were formed. On the last day the majority of the boys thought it would be a good idea to travel back on the same coach and, when seating themselves, mixed with members of the other group.

> **KEY TERMS**
>
> **In-group:** the group to which a particular individual perceives him- or herself as belonging.
>
> **Out-group:** the group to which a particular individual perceives him- or herself as not belonging.
>
> **Field study:** any research that is conducted in an environment natural to the participants.

EVALUATION

➕ This type of study is known as a **field study**, a study done in a natural environment (though not necessarily a field!). Because it reflects everyday behaviour, this type of study has *high ecological validity*. This means that it tells us something about how people act in their ordinary lives.

➕ Sherif et al.'s research has important *implications*. It demonstrates the conditions under which prejudice can occur and the conditions needed to reduce this prejudice. This may be of use in trying to break down prejudice and stop discrimination in ordinary life.

➖ The research only involved a small number of people, all of whom were similar in terms of age, sex, and cultural and social background. It therefore does not necessarily tell us much about how other groups such as adults, younger children, girls or people from other cultural and social backgrounds would respond in such a situation.

There are ethical problems with such research. The boys had never consented to take part in this study. More importantly, they were placed in quite unpleasant conditions with a lot of hostility and bad feeling between them, at least in the first 2 weeks. It could also be argued that it is wrong to induce prejudice in people, especially in impressionable youngsters.

Exam advice for the Robbers' Cave study

In an exam you will not have time to write the study in as much detail as the account given in the text. In fact, it is easier to think of it as being two studies rather than one, as follows:

1. A study showing how prejudice is formed; this covers the first 2 weeks and answers such an exam question as: "Describe a study that shows how prejudice might be explained (or caused)."
2. A study showing how prejudice can be broken down; this covers the third week and answers any question asking for a study showing how prejudice can be reduced.

Study 1

Aim: To look at the effects of group competition on prejudice.

Method: The participants were 22 white, lower-middle-class boys aged 11–12 years who were attending a summer camp. They did not know each other before the study. They were first separated into two similar groups of 11 and spent the first few days in cabins in their own groups. They were then moved to one area and a series of competitions were organised between the two groups, with valuable prizes for the winners.

Results: In the first few days, while the groups were separate, they formed their own group identity and gave themselves names (the Eagles and the Rattlers). Once they were placed together they were very rude and unpleasant to each other, with taunting and name-calling. When the competition started, the situation got worse: they became aggressive with fights breaking out between the two groups. When the Eagles won, the Rattlers invaded their cabins and stole their trophies.

Conclusion: Competition between groups for valued resources (in this case, the prizes) can result in prejudice and discrimination.

Study 2

Aim: To investigate whether working on common goals is a means of reducing prejudice.

Method: The participants were 22 white, lower-middle-class boys aged 11 to 12 years who were attending a summer camp. During the early part of the study they had formed into two groups who had become very hostile and aggressive towards each other. The organisers set up a series of "emergencies" that required the groups to work together in order to solve them. One required the boys to inspect a length of water pipe in order to find a blockage or leak so that the water supply could be restored.

Results: The boys worked cooperatively on all the tasks and a lot of the hostility disappeared. They cheered together when the problems were solved. On the last day the majority of boys chose to travel back on the same coach and they seated themselves so that the groups were mixed.

Conclusion: When groups work together successfully on superordinate (common) goals, prejudice and discrimination are reduced.

ACTIVITY 3.5

Draw a story board of the Robbers' Cave study. Do this in a series of three sets of illustrations, one for each week of the study.

STUDY TWO: TAJFEL ET AL. (1971)

Aims: Tajfel et al. investigated the effects of splitting people into in-groups and out-groups.

Method: Schoolboys aged 14–15 from a comprehensive school took part in the study. The boys came into the laboratory in groups; each group was from the same class and knew each other well. They were told that the researchers were interested in how people make judgements about numbers, and that when people are asked to look very quickly at a picture containing a very large number of objects and guess how many are there, they tend to be either "underestimators" or "overestimators".

The boys were asked, one at a time and alone, to guess how many circles were in a picture that was flashed on a screen in front of them for a very short time. They were then told whether they were an overestimator or an underestimator.

The trick was that the researchers took no notice at all of the boys' guesses and had assigned them to the two groups on a random basis. What the researchers were really interested in was the effect that being split into groups on the basis of a characteristic that was totally unimportant would have on them.

Now comes the important part of the study. The boys were asked to perform a second task in which, on their own and completely confidentially, they were asked to give real money rewards or penalties to other boys with whom they had come to the study. This is the way it worked. They were given a grid similar to the one below:

Reward for no. of overestimators (your group)	4	7	8	8	10	11	12	13	14	15	16	17	18	19
Reward for no. of underestimators (the other group)	2	1	3	5	7	9	11	13	15	17	19	21	23	25

Sample grid used in Tajfel et al. (1971). Participants were asked to allocate points (representing money) to another member of their own and another group.

They then had to choose one pair, one from the top row and one in the same position on the bottom row. So, in the example above, they could give 7 to the overestimator and 1 to the underestimator, or 8 to the overestimator and 3 to the underestimator, and so on. No boy could give rewards to himself, as the grids were arranged so their own number only appeared on other grids. They could not identify who they were giving the money to, since only the researchers knew who the numbers referred to. However, the boys did know whether they were a member of their own group or of the other group.

Results: The boys consistently rewarded their own group members more than those of the other group, despite the fact that they personally did not gain from it. Even on the grids (like the one above) in which the overall amount of money that could be gained was more if they had been more generous to the out-group, they still tended to favour their own. It appeared that, on the whole, the boys preferred to allocate points in such a way that there was the maximum difference between the two groups, with their own group having more.

When the boys emerged from their rooms after making their decisions, they were asked by the others "Which were you?" and the answers received a mix of cheers or boos.

Conclusions: Once people are split into groups, no matter how random or trivial the criterion on which the groups are formed, they tend to like their group more, to treat other groups less well, and to behave competitively towards the other group even when no one benefits from it.

EVALUATION

➕ Realistic group conflict theory is supported by research such as that done at Robbers' Cave. There are also many instances in ordinary everyday life when prejudice appears to be rooted in groups competing for valued resources.

➖ Although conflict may account for how prejudice arises in certain situations, it cannot account for it all. The research by Tajfel et al. demonstrates that prejudice may arise even in the absence of conflict – all you need to do sometimes is to split people into groups.

Social identity theory

The Robbers' Cave studies showed how conflict and competition can lead to prejudice. The studies of Tajfel et al. show something rather different – that even when groups are formed on a random basis, such as by tossing a coin, there can still be prejudice between these two groups, with the in-group favouring their own group over the out-group.

To explain why people favour their own group, Tajfel (1982) put forward **social identity theory**. According to this theory, a person's identity or self-image has two parts, *personal identity* and *social identity*. Our personal identity derives from the knowledge we have of our self as an individual (I am a student; I'm hard working; I'm useless at sport). Our social identity derives from the groups with whom we identify (our family, our school, our friendship group). People's self-esteem is affected by both of these identities (self-esteem is how much you value yourself). We all have a need to boost our self-esteem and one way in which this can be done is by identifying ourselves with successful groups. This is especially important to people who have low self-esteem from their own personal identity, perhaps because they were not greatly valued in their family or were made to feel a failure. According to social identity theory, one way to gain a good social identity and boost your self-esteem is to belittle the out-groups. Unfortunately, this can often lead to negative stereotyping and prejudice.

In sum then, Tajfel's social identity theory argues that prejudice results from people's motivation to boost their self-esteem through a positive social identity.

ACTIVITY 3.10

Write down 10 words or expressions that are your personal identity (such as whether you are a boy or girl – that one doesn't count towards your total!) and four groups that you belong to that make up part of your social identity (the word "group" is used quite loosely – it could be a member of a fan club, not necessarily part of a group that meet each other on a regular basis or even at all). Is there any rivalry between these groups?

KEY TERM

Social identity theory: the view that prejudice against minority groups arises when people of low self-esteem identify with certain in-groups and bolster their self-esteem by belittling out-groups.

EXAM HINT
One way of evaluating a theory is to see whether it accounts for all instances of behaviour. For prejudice, it is very unlikely that any one theory can account for all prejudice, so this is a fair evaluation point for any of the explanations. To make your answer complete, make sure you (briefly) mention the alternative explanations, as is done here.

In order to have a positive social identity, people criticise or denigrate (put down) other groups. Can you think how that applies to football crowds or to different school groups? It is those people with low self-esteem who identify most strongly with certain groups and are particularly prone to prejudiced attitudes.

EVALUATION

⊕ Many studies, including those by Tajfel et al., have supported social identity theory. For example, one such study showed that people of low self-esteem are especially likely to denigrate out-groups, and that when people are given an opportunity to belittle a member of an out-group, their self-esteem rises (Fein & Spencer, 1993).

⊖ Social identity theory cannot account for cultural variations in prejudice, which are probably the result of differences in social norms between cultures (some cultures are far more tolerant of bigotry and discrimination than others).

⊖ Like most theories of prejudice, it is unlikely that social identity theory can explain *all* causes of prejudice. There are lots of other factors that may lead to prejudiced attitudes, such as upbringing (socialisation) and social norms (the attitudes that are acceptable within a community).

The authoritarian personality

When discussing the research done by Adorno et al., we mentioned that they argue that certain individuals have a personality type, called an authoritarian personality, that predisposes them towards prejudiced attitudes. Rather than seeing prejudice as being the result of group conflict or a certain social identity, Adorno et al. see it as being rooted in a certain type of personality.

The characteristics of an individual with an authoritarian personality can be summed up as:

- a rigid adherence to very traditional, conventional values;
- the belief in harsh punishment for violation of traditional norms;
- an extreme need to submit to those in higher authority together with enormous admiration for "strong" leaders;
- a belief that those they perceive as lower in the social hierarchy should submit unquestioningly to those above them;
- a lot of hostility and anger in general but particularly directed towards minority groups.

Adorno and his colleagues used Freud's theory (see Chapter 4) to explain how these childhood experiences are translated into a personality syndrome. The way these individuals have been treated as children causes considerable resentment and hostility, which cannot be openly expressed towards such harsh and aggressive parents and is therefore *repressed* into the unconscious mind. Now, although we don't realise what's in our unconscious mind, it still influences us and we need an outlet for this aggression. One way of doing this is to *displace* hostile feelings onto minority groups who cannot fight back. It is rather like thumping the door when you cannot get hold of the person who has made you angry, or snapping at your mum when your friend has upset you and gone off in a huff. However, there is a big difference – when feelings are in the unconscious you don't know the real cause of your anger or anxiety. People who are authoritarian have no idea that they are really angry at their parents. They believe that they have a right to be angry at minority groups and to disapprove of anyone who disagrees with their point of view – there is absolutely no "live and let live".

EXAM HINT

Summarise the authoritarian personality. Do this in three parts:

1. List two or three of the main personality characteristics.
2. Give a very brief account of the upbringing style of the parents.
3. Explain why this leads to prejudice against minority groups.

EVALUATION

➕ The personality pattern described by Adorno et al. (rigidity of thought, traditional attitudes, intolerance, aggression) is characteristic of highly prejudiced individuals. There is also a large body of evidence to indicate that people who are very rigid, conservative, and prejudiced have been brought up in the way Adorno described, with a great deal of corporal punishment and little chance to express their own opinions.

➖ Earlier, we criticised the questionnaires used by Adorno et al. Since these are used to support the theory, the theory can be criticised for using evidence gained in such a way.

➖ Like most theories of prejudice, it is unlikely that the authoritarian personality can explain *all* causes of prejudice. There are lots of other factors that may lead to prejudiced attitudes, such as social norms (the attitudes that are acceptable within a community).

ACTIVITY 3.11

Complete the table below – this will then provide you with a very good revision aid for evaluating the three theories we have covered. The first entry is done for you. Remember what we said before when evaluating realistic conflict theory – you can use the fact that no theory of prejudice can account for all instances of prejudice.

Theory of prejudice	What it can account for	What it cannot account for
Realistic group conflict theory	Why prejudice increases in times of economic hardship	
Social identity theory		
The authoritarian personality		

The boys in Sherif's study cooperate to solve a problem with the water tank

AQA Reducing prejudice

Establishing superordinate (common) goals

Earlier we looked at the Robbers' Cave studies carried out by Sherif. You will recall that in the third week the researchers attempted to reduce prejudice and discrimination by inventing tasks that the boys could only achieve if they worked together, in other words these tasks involved attempts to achieve *superordinate goals*. On the whole these were successful and, if you remember, the boys worked well together and became quite friendly with one another despite the groups of which they were a member.

One way of reducing prejudice, then, *is for both in-groups and out-groups to work in a non-competitive way to achieve a superordinate goal.*

How psychology works

Explanations of the causes of prejudice can suggest ways in which it can be reduced (or even prevented), although there may be many practical problems that psychologists have recognised and about which they have provided advice.

EVALUATION

⊕ Research studies like Sherif's have shown that cooperation between people who are of equal status and trying to achieve a common goal does break down stereotypes, increase liking, and reduce prejudice.

⊖ The superordinate goal strategy will only work if the people involved are successful in completing the task. If they fail, they simply blame each other and this can make matters worse. In real-life situations, it is not always possible to ensure success, so the strategy might simply increase the prejudice. (You can probably imagine what would happen if two groups who didn't like each other failed on a task they were trying to achieve – each would blame the other for their failure and negative stereotypes would be reinforced.)

The jigsaw approach

A variation on the idea of superordinate goals is to get people working together on a common task in such a way that they can all make a valuable contribution towards achieving the end goal. Aronson et al. (1978) devised a system specifically for school children in order to reduce ethnic conflict among white, Hispanic, and black children in primary schools in the USA. Classes were allocated to either a control or an experimental condition. Children in control classes were taught in a traditional way. Those in the experimental condition were divided into groups of six children of mixed ethnicity (so all groups had some black, white, and Hispanic children in them) and every group worked on a shared task that was broken up like a jigsaw, so that every piece was vital to a successful completion. Each individual was given a specific task and had to research information and teach it to the rest of the group. This meant that each child became an expert in turn. The jigsaw groups met for 45 minutes a day, 3 days a week, for 6 weeks, and followed the same curriculum as the control classes.

The results were encouraging. Compared to children following traditional methods in which every child worked alone and competition was encouraged, children in the jigsaw scheme showed significant improvements in self-esteem, achieved higher grades, and liked their classmates more.

What's more, as well as reducing prejudice this method improved learning. Some people have criticised systems that are not competitive as being academically inferior because children are not "pushed". Nothing could be further from the truth. Slavin (1983), in a review of 46 studies of schemes like the jigsaw one, found that 63% of these children did better academically in the cooperative classrooms, while in only 4% did the traditional classrooms prove to be superior. In the remainder, there was no difference.

ACTIVITY 3.12

Think of the reasons why the jigsaw technique might improve the self-esteem of ethnic minority children. Why might they have low self-esteem to start with?

EVALUATION

➕ This system appears to be successful in improving self-esteem, increasing a liking for school, and improving academic performance.

➕ This scheme uses young children. This is good because positive attitudes towards other ethnic groups fostered in the young are liable to stay with them for a lifetime.

➖ On the other hand, the method is limited as a means of reducing prejudice because it is only possible to use it on school children.

Demonstrating the effects of discrimination

In 1968, Jane Elliot, a school teacher in the small town of Riceville, Iowa, used a direct method to teach her class of all-white 8–9-year-olds the meaning of discrimination. She was inspired to do this by the assassination of Martin Luther King and TV interviews in which white reporters constantly talked in terms of "your people" when referring to King's supporters.

On the first day of the exercise, she divided the class according to eye colour into "brown-eyes" and "blue-eyes" and put collars on the brown-eyes. (Those

Critical thinking

Think about the reasons why this may have occurred and the wider implications of children feeling inferior to their classmates (even if this feeling has not been deliberately induced in them). Does it seriously affect their opportunities for academic success?

with neither blue nor brown eyes were put in a bystander group.) She then pointed out that blue-eyed people are better than brown-eyed people, they are smarter than brown-eyed people and more likely to succeed. To reinforce the point, she "picked on" brown-eyed children, pointing out how, for example, one brown-eyed child was sitting slightly slouched while a blue-eyed child was sitting nicely. She reinforced the division by giving the blue-eyed group extra privileges like a longer break, and removing from the brown-eyed group certain rights they had had before, such as drinking from the water fountain.

In no time at all the children's behaviour was transformed. From being a well-adjusted happy cooperative group of classmates, they became an unhappy, cruel, divided group. The blue-eyed children became bossy and arrogant and took delight in taunting the brown-eyed children. They, in turn, became cowed, extremely miserable and defensive. They reported feeling that Mrs Elliot was taking their best friends away from them. One child punched another at recess for calling him "brown-eyed".

The following day the tables were turned and Jane Elliot explained to the children that she had got it wrong the previous day and the brown-eyed children were actually superior. They took their revenge and the situation was equally unhappy and divisive.

Interestingly, on both days the superior children achieved academically much better than the inferior ones. Even very bright children appeared to be handicapped by being in an inferior group.

The final part of the exercise was to remove all collars and discuss with the children their experiences over the last 2 days. They were absolutely delighted to be one equal group again and felt that they did have a greater understanding of discrimination. As Elliot comments:

After you do this exercise, when the debriefing starts, when the pain is over and they're all back together, you find out how society could be if we really believed all this stuff that we preach, if we really acted that way, you could feel as good about one another as those kids feel about one another after this exercise is over. You create instant cousins. The kids said over and over, "We're kind of like a family now." They found out how to hurt one another and they found out how it feels to be hurt in that way and they refuse to hurt one another in that way again.

EVALUATION

➕ The effects of this exercise on the children were long lasting. Some 30 years later they were interviewed and still look back on the experience as being really worth while. They reported being much more aware of prejudice and tried hard to be non-prejudiced themselves.

➕ This exercise has been used with numerous groups of people, including many adult groups. It has been shown to increase awareness of the effects of discrimination and therefore reduce it.

There are ethical problems associated with this method, especially if used on children. In the original study the children were caused a great deal of distress and this resulted in antisocial behaviour. Jane Elliot herself advises that it should not be done unless the individual leading the group is extremely well trained. As she says, you could easily damage a child by this exercise.

Ethical issues

With all ethical issues, it is necessary to weigh up the costs and benefits. Think about whether you think this exercise was worthwhile if done well; in other words, did the children get any long-term benefit that outweighed their short-term distress. You may wish to have a class debate about whether you would let your son or daughter take part in such an exercise.

Optimal intergroup contact

Early investigators of prejudice reduction suggested that simply increasing the amount of contact between in-groups and out-groups might reduce prejudice between the two groups. It soon became apparent that contact alone was not sufficient to change attitudes, and that, in some circumstances, it may make it worse. You can probably imagine such situations – two groups of football fans at a "needle" match in which one team wins because of a dubious referee decision, or workers and managers coming together to negotiate pay unsuccessfully. It was generally agreed that prejudice would not decrease unless there *was* contact but in addition to this other conditions had to be met. Various extra conditions were suggested, including the fact that the groups had to be of equal status, that individuals should share common goals, and that contact should have the support of the authorities. When such conditions are met, this is known as optimal intergroup contact.

Everyday life

Many football clubs have had serious issues with racism of "fans" and have used practical means to reduce this. (The word "fans" is in inverted commas because although some racists may be fans, there is a strong suspicion that some groups use football grounds as places to promote racist views.) This has been an important application of psychology to everyday life.

In the context of looking at increased contact between groups, Harwood et al. (2005) investigated the reduction of prejudice between different age groups, mainly prejudice of young people towards older ones. This is interesting because most research has involved prejudice between different ethnic groups or sexes, while this looks at prejudice that might exist within families. Not only is it interesting, it is important because when we meet other people we are as likely to make assumptions about them based on their age as we are on other important characteristics such as race or gender. Young children easily recognise different age categories and often have negative stereotypes about older people. Young adults also hold negative attitudes towards older adults. It is important to study these ageist attitudes because they affect us all: most of us will be old one day and will probably have to tolerate these attitudes. We may understandably resent being patronised, a common complaint of older people.

Harwood et al. (2005) asked a group of university students to fill in a questionnaire about all four of their biological grandparents and another about their attitudes to older adults (those over 65) other than these grandparents. They were also asked questions to see how aware they were of the age difference between them and their grandparents, how much they thought about it and whether they thought their grandparents were typical of other older people. Finally, they were asked to say how well they got along with their grandparents on a scale ranging from "very poorly" to "very well". The researchers found that ageist attitudes were only affected by contact with the grandparent who the students saw most often and that the most important factor that resulted in them not having negative ageist attitudes was the extent to which they had a positive relationship with that grandparent *and* saw them as representative of the older age group. This means that having a positive relationship with a grandparent is not enough on its own to ensure that young people have a positive attitude to all older people – indeed the co-author's children had a wonderful relationship with her father but never perceived him as typical of other older people (as, indeed, he wasn't!) so this did not significantly affect their stereotype of older people. On the other hand, if the grandparent was seen as typical of the older group (the out-group), then the grandchildren's perception of older people in general was likely to reflect how they got along with their grandparent, be it well or poorly.

AQA Contemporary practical implications of research into stereotyping, prejudice and discrimination: Paracontact hypothesis

ACTIVITY 3.13

Think of a current TV show that involves a friendship or romance between a black and a white character and write down the name of the show and the characters. Do the same for a gay–straight relationship and a young–old interaction. Do you think that these TV shows have any impact on reducing prejudice about these groups? Have a class discussion about the issues raised by popular TV shows with respect to prejudice. Are there any shows that you think might increase such prejudice? If so, why?

Earlier we mentioned the increased contact hypothesis: the idea that prejudice could be reduced by increasing the contact between groups who held negative attitudes about each other. We also said that increased contact was not sufficient alone and that certain conditions must be met before attitudes were likely to change in a positive direction. These conditions include the fact that the individuals involved should be of equal status, share common goals and work together in a cooperative fashion to achieve such goals.

However, contact that meets these conditions can be difficult to achieve. If groups are hostile to each other, then individuals from one group may be reluctant to mix with individuals from the other group, especially if they are anxious about attempting to have a relationship with them. In addition, it is possible that when they encounter a likeable person who belongs to the out-group, they may see them as the exception rather than typical of their group, and therefore not change their attitudes.

If direct contact is difficult to achieve, could indirect contact, such as contact via the media, help to reduce negative attitudes? Some recent research tends to support this view.

Schiappa et al. (2005) has conducted experimental investigations into the effect of TV shows on prejudice reduction.

In one study, 150 students watched 10 early episodes of *Six Feet Under*, a programme in which the plot development during the first series involved a character called David Fisher coming to terms with his homosexuality and coming out to his family, friends and church. None of the students had ever seen the programmes before. Their level of prejudice was measured before and after watching the programmes, and there was a significant reduction in their reported prejudice towards gay men.

In the second study, 160 students were randomly assigned to two groups. One group watched three episodes of a programme called *Queer Eye for the Straight Guy*, a programme in which a number of openly gay men endeavour to "sort out" the life of a straight male in order for him to be fanciable to his girlfriend or a girl he wants to attract. The other 80, the control group, watched a stand-up comedy special. The researchers found that students who watched *Queer Eye* showed a significant reduction in prejudice compared to how they felt before watching the programmes, whereas the comedy programme had no such effect.

The presenters of Queer Eye for the Straight Guy. *Researchers found that students who watched this show showed a significant reduction in prejudice.*

The researchers believe that this was because the more they learned about gay men as a group, the more their attitudes became tolerant towards them. The amount of change in attitudes was greatest among those who previously had had very little direct contact with gay men.

Schiappa et al. (2006) have also done a correlational study of the effects of TV on prejudice against gays. This study showed that the more people watched the programme *Will & Grace* (a sitcom featuring a straight–gay friendship), the less prejudiced they reported towards gay men. Schiappa comments that "There is no question in my mind that *Will & Grace* has played an important role in changing attitudes about gay men."

Why should prejudice be reduced by these programmes? Schiappa believes that through the medium of television, viewers actually develop a relationship with characters and that this relationship (which he calls a *parasocial relationship)* leads to lessened prejudice. He has advanced the paracontact hypothesis, which suggests that positive experiences with minority characters can reduce prejudice in a way similar to direct contact with people. Schiappa believes that viewers treat TV characters as real, so watching them becomes very like direct contact with them, but with the important difference that there is much less anxiety involved concerning contact with this group.

Schiappa points out that this research is of importance because it is virtually the only research that has shown that TV can have a positive influence on prejudice. Almost all other research has focused on how TV can increase prejudice.

> **Why psychology matters**
>
> As the vast majority of people spend several hours a day watching TV, it is important to try to use it as a prosocial influence and to monitor any effects it might have.

ACTIVITY 3.14

Schiappa et al. measured prejudice by using the Attitudes Towards Lesbians and Gay Men Scale, developed by Professor Gregory Herek. See if you can obtain a copy of this in order to see how such an attitude scale is developed.

Chapter summary

- Prejudice can be defined as "an attitude that predisposes us to think, feel, perceive, and act in favourable or unfavourable ways towards a group or its individual members".
- Stereotyping involves holding beliefs about the characteristics of groups of individuals and assuming that each individual member of that group has those characteristics. Common stereotypes are those based on race, religion, social class, sex, sexuality and attractiveness.
- Discrimination involves the unequal treatment of individuals or groups based on arbitrary characteristics such as race, sex, ethnicity, and cultural background.
- The components of a prejudiced attitude are ABC: affective (how you feel), behavioural (how you behave), cognitive (what you assume and believe).
- Three important studies of prejudice and discrimination are:
  - Sherif et al.'s (1961) Robbers' Cave studies, in which prejudice was first induced then reduced in boys in a summer camp.
  - Tajfel et al. (1971), who divided schoolboys into two groups based on an arbitrary, unimportant characteristic and observed discrimination between them.
  - Adorno et al., who used questionnaires, including the F-Scale, and found that prejudice appeared to be a personality characteristic since people who were prejudiced against one group tended to be prejudiced against all minority groups.
- Explanations for prejudice based on this research include:
  - Realistic group conflict theory, which proposes that prejudiced attitudes are the result of competition for scarce resources, such as jobs and housing. This is based on research such as the Robbers' Cave studies.
  - Social identity theory, which suggests that when we categorise ourselves and others into social groups, we think in terms of "in-groups" and "out-groups". People with low self-esteem denigrate the out-group and feel their own group is better than others. This is based on Tajfel's research.
  - The authoritarian personality theory of prejudice, which holds that people with a certain personality type tend to be highly prejudiced. The characteristics of such an individual are that they are

unquestioningly respectful to traditional authority and very hostile to anyone who questions it. They have experienced a very harsh upbringing, resulting in repressed aggression towards their parents that is displaced onto minority groups. This is based on the research of Adorno et al.

- Several ways in which prejudice can be reduced were considered.
  - The establishment of superordinate goals. This involves two antagonistic groups working together successfully to achieve and bring rewards to both groups, as was done at Robbers' Cave when the boys worked together to get a trunk carrying food supplies out of a ditch.
  - The jigsaw approach, in which a group of children from different ethnic backgrounds work cooperatively on a common project. They each research a certain part and then fit the bits together like a jigsaw.
  - Demonstrating the effects of discrimination as was done by Jane Elliot, who discriminated against school children on the basis of eye colour. She has repeated this with adults and has found that making people aware of what it feels like to be discriminated against reduces the likelihood of discrimination against others.
  - Optimal group contact (Harwood et al., 2005), which looked at everyday life circumstances of a grandparent–grandchild relationship and found that if people had a positive, close and regular relationship with a member of a minority group who they considered to be typical of that group, then they showed less prejudice than people without such a relationship.
- Contemporary research has shown that certain TV programmes can reduce prejudice. Schiappa et al. have carried out experiments and correlational research demonstrating that positive images of minority groups (in this case, homosexuals) reduced prejudiced attitudes. Schiappa has explained this in terms of the para contact hypothesis, which suggests that positive experiences with minority characters can reduce prejudice in a way similar to direct contact with people.

AQA Exam-style questions for AQA

1. Define the following terms:

   (a) Prejudice. (2 marks)

   (b) Discrimination. (2 marks)

2. Using an everyday example, explain what is meant by a stereotype. (3 marks)

3. Read the following statements about the work of Adorno et al. on prejudice and discrimination and decide whether they are **true** or **false**.

   (a) Adorno used questionnaires and interviews to investigate prejudice. True/False

   (b) Adorno et al.'s research led them to believe that prejudice is the result of competition for resources. True/False

   (c) Adorno's research has been criticised because the questionnaires were not well constructed. True/False (3 marks)

4. Describe and evaluate **one** way in which prejudice could be reduced. (6 marks)

Social psychology (2)

In the second section on social psychology, we continue to look at how people influence one another.

Chapter 4 • Aggression

First we will consider what it means to be aggressive, and then consider both biological and psychological influences on aggression, including how we may learn aggression from observing and imitating the behaviour of others. We will also consider what different theories of aggression have to say about ways in which aggression can be reduced.

Chapter 5 • Non-verbal communication

We will consider the fascinating topic area of non-verbal communication – the ways in which we interact with one another by means of facial expression, body language and gestures, to name but a few. This chapter is divided into two parts depending on the specification you are studying, but all of it will provide interesting reading.

What you need to know AQA

The specification lists the following things that you need to be able to do for the examination:

- Explain aggression in terms of the following:
  - Biological explanations, including the role of hormones, brain disease and chromosomal abnormality
  - Psychodynamic explanations, including the frustration–aggression hypothesis
  - Social learning explanations, including modelling, punishment and monitoring
- Describe and evaluate studies of the development of aggressive behaviour
- Discuss ways of reducing aggression, based on these explanations
- Evaluate these ways of reducing aggression

Aggression

4

■ ■ ■ ■ ■ ■ ■ ■ ■

"I was 11 years of age, I was brought up in South London, I was in primary school. I got smashed in the nose in the classroom, I was only 11. I went home crying to my father. He said to me 'What you cryin' for?' I said 'a geezer punched me in the nose dad'. He said 'Oh did 'e, and you come crying to my front door', I went 'yea'. He said 'you see that milk bottle down by the door there, you pick it up, you go back to school and you rap it on 'is 'ead or you don't never come back to my door again.' And I was frightened (nervous laugh) and I thought that's what I 'ad to do. And I was frightened on my way back to school knowing I 'ad to go in the classroom and smash a geezer across the head with a bottle or I wouldn't be allowed back in my own 'ouse. It was unacceptable. My father was a very violent man so I went to the classroom, walked up to the geezer and put the bottle across his 'ead. And I found it solved the problem and I think I've used that since in life you know, you get into a problem, you get a fight and you just go out of your way to 'urt them, you know, quickly and as destructive as possible."

Quotation from a violent adult, *Horizon* "What You Lookin' At?" 1993

"A 30-year-old teacher with no criminal record killed a 7-year-old girl selling cookies door-to-door. Infuriated when she couldn't change a $20 dollar bill, he forced her into his basement where he beat her to death. Described by his mother as a 'good, gentle son,' in psychiatric interviews he displayed a range of psychological problems, including high anxiety and depression (Revitch & Schlesinger, 1978)."

From Forsythe, D. (1987). *Social Psychology*. (Brooks/Cole, p. 390)

KEY TERM

Aggression: any behavioural act designed to harm a living creature, such as hitting, shoving or throwing things, kicking, fighting, or biting; or any verbal act that is intended to hurt someone by non-physical communication, such as shouting, swearing, name calling, or saying nasty things about someone.

ACTIVITY 4.1

Before we define aggression, let's get your opinion of what is aggressive and what is not. Look at the list of actions below and decide whether or not you consider them aggressive. Put them into one of the following columns: "aggressive", "non-aggressive", "not sure". (Try not to put too many items in the last column!) When you've finished, compare your answers with others in the class and discuss any differences.

- A man tries to kick his dog but misses
- A driver hurls an insult at another driver who, in their opinion, has "cut them up" at a roundabout
- A young man fights a bull in a bull-fighting show
- A footballer kicks an opponent in order to prevent him getting further up the field with the ball
- A tennis player throws her tennis racket down on the ground when the match isn't going her way
- A boxer thumps his opponent
- A nurse gives an injection to a screaming child
- A bank robber is shot in the back while trying to escape
- A man thinks about a murder he might commit
- A woman, believing that a man is trying to open her car door in order to attack her, slams the door on his hand, badly hurting it
- Two wolves fight for leadership of the pack

AQA Defining aggression

The exercise above will probably cause considerable arguments because, although the word "**aggression**" is used very frequently, there is a lot of disagreement about what we mean by it. Some of the items, however, are easy to agree on. Most people would accept that the first action (trying to kick an animal) is aggressive, whereas the nurse giving the injection is not. Nevertheless, the man caused no pain, whereas the nurse did. The big difference, of course, is the *intention* behind the action. The man intended to hurt the dog with no motive other than causing pain, whereas the nurse caused pain as a by-product of protecting the child from disease. So any definition of aggression must take account of the motives behind the action.

With this in mind, we can define aggression as "The intention to inflict some form of harm on others" (after Baron & Byrne, 1997).

AQA Explanations of aggression

Biological explanations

Some researchers point to evidence that aggression could be caused by biological factors, such as hormones, genetics, brain disease or abnormal chromosomes. We will consider each of these explanations in turn.

Hormones

The hormone **testosterone** is thought be to be associated with aggression and may explain why males are often more aggressive than females. Adult males have much higher levels of the hormone testosterone than do adult females. This hormone is responsible for the sex drive but also plays an important role in aggression. Experiments on male animals show that aggressive behaviour increases dramatically if extra testosterone is injected into them. Further evidence that testosterone may be responsible for aggressive behaviour comes from several studies that indicate that the testosterone levels of violent male criminals may be higher than those of the ordinary population (e.g. Kalat, 1998). However, the situation may not be as clear-cut as it appears at first glance. Just because there is a **correlation** between testosterone levels and aggression, it does not tell us what is cause and what is effect (see the section on correlation in Chapter 15). Is it possible that rather than the testosterone causing the aggression, being a violent criminal actually increases the testosterone level? A study by Klinesmith et al. (2006) recounted in more detail later in this chapter implies that this may well be the case. It's possible that testosterone prepares the body to respond to competition or challenges from other males but that not all individuals would respond to this by being aggressive.

> **KEY TERMS**
>
> **Testosterone**: the male sex hormone required for sperm production and the development of male reproductive organs.
>
> **Correlation**: a statistical indicator representing the strength of a relationship between two variables. Correlations do not show cause and effect, only that a relationship exists.

Genetics

Genetics may also play a part in aggression. In one study the most aggressive mice from a group were bred and the most aggressive of their offspring were then interbred. This was carried on for 25 generations, by which time the mice were so aggressive that they would immediately attack any mouse put into their cage (Cairns et al., 1990).

> **EXAM HINT**
>
> If using this evidence in an exam, evaluate it with reference to the positive points and limitations of using animals in psychological research. The mice could be bred for many generations and this takes relatively little time and provides valuable information on the genetics of aggressive behaviour. However, we cannot necessarily generalise this to humans in whom social factors (including socialisation) have considerable influence.

Brain injury

In some cases, aggression appears to be caused by injury to the brain. This may occur through an accident, a stroke, a tumour or some conditions such as forms of epilepsy. Often people who show sudden outbursts of aggression, but who are not usually aggressive, are suffering some form of brain disorder. For example, Charles Whitman, a student at the University of Texas with no previous record of excessive violence, suddenly started engaging in fights, attacked his wife, and even sought psychiatric help because he had begun

> **ACTIVITY 4.2**
>
> The case of Charles Whitman is very famous and some psychologists have suggested other factors as well as a brain tumour that might have increased the likelihood of him becoming aggressive. See if you can find any of these alternative suggestions.

experiencing extremely violent urges. Shortly after this he murdered his wife and mother, then took a high-powered rifle to the top of a tower block at the university and for 2 hours fired at everyone he could, until he was shot dead by police. A post-mortem examination showed that he had a large tumour in the part of the brain called the amygdala, an area associated with aggression.

In 1848 a railway worker called Phineas Gage suffered serious brain damage when an explosion caused an iron bar to go through his skull, leaving

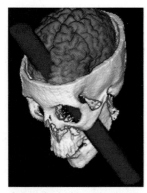

An artist's impression of Phineas Gage's skull with the metal rod that was fired through his head

a large hole in the front part of his brain. Although he survived, he changed from being a hard-working courteous individual into being impulsive, rude and, at times, rather aggressive.

In Chapter 13 we look at the work of Raine, who suggests that damage or abnormality of a part of the brain called the prefrontal cortex may result in a condition called antisocial personality disorder. One of the characteristics of this disorder is that people can be excessively aggressive.

ACTIVITY 4.3

The cases of Charles Whitman and Phineas Gage are case studies. A case study is a detailed investigation of one individual. See if you can find another example of a case study of a person who became aggressive as a result of brain injury.

Chromosomal abnormalities

As mentioned in Chapter 6, females have a pair of chromosomes known as XX, while males have XY. A few individuals are born with an unusual pattern of chromosomes; one such pattern occurs when males have an extra Y chromosome and is known as XYY. Early researchers reported that such individuals were more likely than the general population to be in prison, and there was a suggestion that the reason why they were incarcerated was because they were very aggressive. However, doubt was soon cast on these conclusions. XYY individuals tend to be slightly taller, less intelligent and more impulsive than the general population. Overall, prisoners with normal chromosomes also tend to be taller, less intelligent and more impulsive. Therefore it is quite possible that XYY individuals are more likely to be in prison for these reasons rather than because they are aggressive. Added to this, their crimes tended to be petty theft and offences involving cars, not crimes associated with violence.

Currently some researchers still maintain that having XYY chromosomes is liable to make these males more aggressive, but that the effects of this chromosome pattern are complex and subtle. Indeed, most XYY people behave in such an ordinary way that many are probably never tested and therefore remain undiagnosed. Others argue that there is no sound evidence that these men are more prone to aggression or violence than people with the normal number of chromosomes.

The psychodynamic explanation: Freud's theory of aggression

> **KEY TERM**
>
> **Psychodynamic**: the relationships between the mind and personality and mental or emotional consequences, especially at the unconscious level.

The famous psychologist, Freud (founder of the **psychodynamic** approach), believed that a lot of our mind is unconscious, so we are often not aware of the real reasons why we do things. Buried deep in this unconscious mind are some primitive instincts – we are born with them but we are not aware they are there. Freud believed that people have two conflicting instincts: a *life instinct* called eros, and a *death instinct* called thanatos. Thanatos is a profound unconscious desire to escape the tensions of living by being dead.

In the beginning this instinct towards self-destruction is turned inwards on ourselves, but eventually the life instinct fights this urge and, at least in most people, these destructive feelings are turned outwards onto other people or things. So, in essence, Freud believed that we are all instinctively aggressive. What's more, we cannot escape these aggressive urges and if they are not satisfied they can be dangerous.

Both the aggressive instinct and the life instinct are contained in part of the personality called the **id**. The id is the most primitive part of our personality and likes to have its own way and be satisfied immediately. However, there are two more parts to the personality. One of these is the ego, which tries to keep a balance and satisfy our urges in acceptable ways. Then there is the superego, which is the moral part of the personality that tries to control the urges of the id. The id and superego are always at loggerheads, and it is up to the ego to try to keep a reasonable balance between them. In order to do this, the ego uses ego defence mechanisms. There are several defence mechanisms that are used by the ego to satisfy our aggressive urges. Two of these are:

- *Displacement*: We can take out our aggressive urges on other people or on other things. We may, for example, shout at our parents when really it's our boyfriend or girlfriend who has upset us.
- *Sublimation*: Our aggressive urge can be expressed in a non-destructive way, for example by playing sport (especially contact sport), or alternatively by imagining being aggressive towards someone or something.

Freud believed that if these aggressive instincts are not discharged, then they build up, rather like steam in a boiler. If this "steam" is not vented from time to time by some display of anger or by sublimation, then the strain can cause psychological disorders. In the extreme it may result in sudden, unprovoked and extreme acts of violence.

The motivational explanation: The frustration–aggression hypothesis

Think about the circumstances in which you feel angry. One of these may well be that you feel frustrated because nothing is going right. There was no milk left for breakfast, you couldn't find your school tie, the bus was late and the teacher had a go at you for being unpunctual. You feel angry and want to yell at someone. Dollard et al. (1939) put forward an explanation of aggression that takes account of this. Known as the **frustration–aggression hypothesis** it suggests that frustration always leads to aggression, and that all aggression is caused by frustration.

According to these researchers, aggression is a biological drive in the same way that hunger and thirst are drives, and it "drives" you to react in a certain way. Just as hunger motivates you to look for food, so frustration motivates you to be aggressive. However, unlike hunger and thirst, which are triggered by feelings within your body (internal factors), frustration is triggered by external factors such as having to queue for ages for lunch or failure to win an important sports match. According to this view, aggression is either expressed directly, by, for example, punching someone who is annoying you, or it is displaced onto something or someone else, like kicking the desk when you feel angry.

It soon became evident that there are two major problems with this theory. First, frustration does not *always* lead to aggression: sometimes it makes you depressed, or exhausted. Second, frustration is not the *only* thing that causes aggression. For example, aggression can be caused by being in pain or in a very noisy environment.

The frustration–aggression hypothesis therefore became modified to take account of this. A more general hypothesis known as the arousal–aggression hypothesis was put forward. This suggests that when you feel frustrated you become aroused and this may lead you to be aggressive, but not always. Instead, you may channel your energies into having an energetic game of squash.

Social learning theory

One prominent theory that seeks to explain why people are aggressive is known as **social learning theory** (**SLT**), which is covered in further detail in Chapter 6. This is very different from the theories we've already looked at since it does not suggest that biology or instinctive drives are involved in aggression, just our experiences of the world. According to this theory one of the main reasons why people (especially children) behave the way they do is because they imitate the important people around them. If parents love watching football, their children may well watch it too. If parents are violent and aggressive, then children are likely to act in the same way.

In essence then, the general principle of social learning theory is that children and adults often learn by *observing* and then *imitating* the behaviour of other people.

ACTIVITY 4.4

Try to think of at least two important differences between the SLT approach to explaining aggression and the psychodynamic (Freudian) explanation.

ACTIVITY 4.5

How do you think SLT and Freud's theory of aggression would explain the two case studies at the beginning of the chapter? For each of them, write a paragraph explaining the roots of the individual's aggression from both of these points of view.

The people who are imitated are referred to as *models*. The most important models in a child's life are first their parents and later on their same-sex friends and media characters, especially celebrities. It follows that children are likely to be aggressive if their parents and friends are aggressive and/or the media characters they admire are also aggressive. These factors often link together: children brought up in aggressive households often choose aggressive children as their friends and are also attracted to role models who are violent.

A process called **monitoring** may increase or decrease the tendency of children to carry on behaving in the way they have learnt from their early role models. In monitoring, we look at our own behaviour. If we feel good about what we have done, this strengthens the behaviour and we are more likely to do it again. Whether or not we feel good about it depends to some extent on the role models. If, for example, a child imitates the behaviour of an aggressive person on TV and knows, from previous experience, that their dad would approve, they will feel proud and carry on. If on the other hand they know that dad would not like them behaving this way, then they feel rather ashamed and do not do it again. Of course, it is not necessarily dad who affects them, simply any role model who they admire and want to be like.

Social learning theory says that just as we are likely to copy some people more than others, so we are likely to copy certain actions more than others. In general, and hardly surprisingly, we copy actions that we believe will have good outcomes. If we see someone rewarded (or reinforced, to use the correct terminology), this increases the likelihood that we will copy them. If we see them punished, we are less likely to copy them. So if John sees his big brother thump another child and other children cheer him on, he's likely to copy him. If, on the other hand, an adult tells the brother off, John is less likely to copy him.

Notice that the child is not directly experiencing the punishment or reinforcement but is still affected by it. We use the terms **vicarious punishment** and **vicarious reinforcement** for punishment and reinforcement that have an effect on the individual but are received indirectly rather than directly.

ACTIVITY 4.6

Media figures are often reinforced for being violent. See if you can give examples of six media characters, two from TV, two from films, two from books, who are reinforced in some sort of way (by admiration, money, etc.) for being aggressive.

ACTIVITY 4.7

We have said that some people are more likely than others to be used as models. Name six people who may well be used as models by yourself and some of your classmates. On what grounds have you chosen these people?

AQA Studies of the development of aggression

STUDY ONE: BANDURA, ROSS AND ROSS (1961)

This study was the first of a series of similar studies carried out by the originator of social learning theory, Albert Bandura, together with his colleagues. In some cases the aggression was seen in real life (as in this study) while in others it was seen on film.

Children are exposed to violent images at an early age and often incorporate them into their play. How well do children distinguish between playful and real aggression in their lives?

Aim: Bandura et al. wanted to investigate whether young children will imitate an aggressive model.

Method: The basic design of the study was that an experimenter would take the young children, one at a time, into a room in which there were two tables in different corners. The child was seated at one table on which there were lots of attractive toys. The adult model was seated at the other table on which there was a Tinker Toy set, a mallet, and a 5-foot Bobo doll (an inflatable doll as shown in the picture opposite). The experimenter would then leave the child and model alone together.

Half of the children were in the *aggressive (experimental) condition* in which the model played with the Tinker Toy for a short while and then turned his or her attention to the Bobo doll. They used exactly the same sequence of actions each time. They would punch the doll, throw it to the ground on its side, and punch it repeatedly on the nose. They would then put the doll upright and use the mallet to hit the doll around the head. This sequence was repeated three times and while they were doing it the model would say things such as "Sock him in the nose", "Kick him", "Pow" (remember this is 1960s America!). The sequence, which lasted about 10 minutes, was deliberately designed to include unusual aggressive acts that the children were unlikely to have come across before. In this experimental condition, half the models were men and half were women.

The other half of the children were in the *non-aggressive condition*. In this case, the model sat and played with the toys, mainly the Tinker Toy, and completely ignored the Bobo doll. This also lasted for 10 minutes.

After the children had watched the model, they were taken, on their own, to another room with the experimenter (not the model). They were given various attractive toys to play with, including a smaller Bobo doll and a mallet. They were left there for about 20 minutes and their behaviour was observed through a one-way mirror.

Bandura was careful to look not only at effects of aggression as compared with non-aggression, but also at the effects of whether the model was the same or opposite sex as the child. So he had four different conditions:

- A group of girls and a group of boys who were exposed to a same-sex aggressive model.
- A group of boys and a group of girls who were exposed to an opposite-sex aggressive model.
- A group of girls and a group of boys who were exposed to a same-sex non-aggressive model.
- A group of boys and a group of girls who were exposed to an opposite-sex non-aggressive model.

Results:
The effect of watching an aggressive model: Children in the aggressive condition reproduced a great many of the physical and verbal aggressive

Adult "models" and children attack the Bobo doll

acts they had observed. In the non-aggressive (and control) condition, the children showed no aggression at all but simply played with the toys in a non-aggressive manner. Most of them did not play with the Bobo doll, but if they did, they did not treat it at all aggressively.

The effect of gender: Boys reproduced more physical aggression than did the girls but there was no difference in boys and girls with respect to verbal aggression.

The effect of the sex of the model compared with the child: Boys were more likely to be aggressive if they had seen a male model rather than a female one, and girls were more likely to be aggressive if they had seen a female model rather than a male one.

Other findings: Some of the children were surprised, even shocked, that a woman would behave so aggressively. One little boy commented, "That's not a way for a lady to behave." This was certainly not the case for the male aggressive model. A more typical remark about his behaviour was one made by a lad who said, "Al's a good socker, he beat up Bobo."

EXAM HINT

For the Bobo doll study, there is too much detail in the text for you to write it all in an exam. Summarise the study in your notebooks so you have an answer suitable for a question that asks you about evidence supporting the social learning theory of aggression. Do it in the following way:

Aim: one sentence

Method: two/three sentences (to include the two main conditions – watching aggressive/non-aggressive model)

Results: two sentences (don't be vague here – avoid sentences such as "all children showed aggression").

Conclusion: one sentence

KEY TERMS

Generalise: refers to whether a result/finding can be applied to the whole population (e.g. all the people in the world).

Longitudinal study: when the same participants are studied over a number of years, even a lifetime, in order to study changes over time (e.g. the TV programme *Child of Our Time*).

Ethical issues

As the evaluation suggests, there are ethical problems with this study. The children were too young to give informed consent, and were exposed to potentially upsetting experiences.

Conclusion: The results show strong evidence that children are likely to copy new types of behaviour that they would have been unlikely to produce otherwise.

EVALUATION

⊕ This study used an experimental design, with the children randomly split between aggressive and non-aggressive conditions, so it is reasonable to conclude that it was the aggressive model that caused the children to show aggressive behaviour rather than anything else. It shows that new aggressive responses can be acquired by observation and imitation.

⊕ The findings have important implications for everyday life, since children watch a lot of aggressive behaviour on television and in films (and sometimes in real life).

⊖ The experiment was carried out in artificial conditions (children are not usually left alone with a model who behaves in this way), therefore it does not necessarily tell us much about real-life behaviour of children. When studies are rather artificial and don't reflect everyday behaviour, we say that they lack ecological validity. Just because children copy an aggressive model in these circumstances does not mean that they would imitate aggression in more natural conditions. This means that we cannot be sure that the results **generalise** to real-life situations.

⊖ There are ethical concerns with this study. Very young children were placed alone in an unfamiliar room with a stranger who acted in a very aggressive manner. They may have been upset by the whole procedure. They also learnt new ways to be aggressive.

The second study uses a very different method from Bandura and looks in more detail at the effects of watching violence in the media.

STUDY TWO: HUESMANN ET AL. (2003)

Aim: To see if there is any relationship between watching violent TV when young and violent behaviour in adult life.

Method: Huesmann et al. (2003), in the USA, carried out a **longitudinal study** that involved a correlation. It was a longitudinal study because they looked at the same group of people over 15 years. It involved a correlation because they looked for a relationship between the amount of media violence the people had watched and the amount of aggression they showed.

Results: They found that the more violence a child watched, the more likely they were to become aggressive adults. This was true of children from all families regardless of the child's level of aggression when they were young, their intelligence, and the occupation of the parents. The type of aggression the participants showed included pushing, grabbing, and shoving their spouses, hitting their children, and driving aggressively. The men showed three times the average rate of crime.

Conclusion: The researchers believe that the amount of violence a person uses in adult life is related to the amount of violent media they experience during their childhood, not to how aggressive the children were at the start of the study.

EVALUATION

➕ One of the ways in which a study can be evaluated is in terms of how important the findings are for society as a whole. This study deals with a very important issue because children watch a great deal of television, much of which involves violence. In fact it is estimated that by the time a child is 18 years old, he or she will witness on TV about 200,000 acts of violence including 40,000 murders (Huston et al., 1992). It is therefore very important that we study its effects.

➖ The problem with any correlation is that it does not necessarily show cause and effect – it does not automatically follow that watching violent TV or playing violent games *causes* people to be aggressive. It could simply be that aggressive people like watching violent TV programmes and playing violent video games.

Why psychology matters

Television is a very important part of the lives of the vast majority of people, so it is very important to study its impact on people's behaviour. By doing this, we have research that can inform the debate on censorship of television and on controls such as the watershed.

The third study is different again and looks at the effect of testosterone on aggression.

STUDY THREE: KLINESMITH ET AL. (2006)

Aim: Klinesmith et al. had two related aims. One was to see if handling a gun increased testosterone levels, and then to see if it increased aggression levels.

Method: Thirty male students (aged 18–22) took part in the study. They were told that they were taking part in a study of taste sensitivity. A sample of saliva was taken from each of them and used to test their testosterone level. Then each man was led into a room where he sat at a table with an object on it. For half the men this was a pellet gun (that mimicked a Desert Eagle automatic handgun), while for the other half it was a child's game (called Mouse Trap). Each man was asked to take it apart and put it together again according to instructions. After 15 minutes, each student's testosterone level was measured again.

In the second part of the study the men were given a cup of water and a bottle of hot sauce. They were told that the water would be given to the next man in the study and they could put as much hot sauce in the water as they liked. This was used as a measure of aggression – the more sauce they added, the more aggressive they were considered to be.

Results: Testosterone went up about 100 times more in the men who handled the gun than in those who handled the toy. On average, they put three times as much sauce in the water. In essence, the more a man's testosterone went up after the gun handling, the more hot sauce he put in the water.

Conclusion: The researchers concluded that these results suggest that guns may increase aggressiveness by increasing the level of testosterone. (Interestingly, when they were debriefed, many of the men who had handled the gun said they were disappointed that no one had drunk the spiked water.)

ACTIVITY 4.8

Devise a story board (a series of illustrations, each one in a box) to describe the method of this study.

EVALUATION

➕ As this is an experimental design with a control group, it does provide evidence that testosterone levels may be raised by certain situations that people associate with violence and aggression.

➕ Klinesmith et al.'s study may have important implications. Gun crime is a serious problem in the USA and, increasingly so, in Britain. If handling a gun raises testosterone levels, then societies need to consider how wise it is for people to have easy access to guns.

➖ The sample size is not very large, nor is it representative as only college students were used. We cannot therefore assume that these findings would apply across the age range.

➖ It could be argued that the researchers did not use a very appropriate measure of aggression: giving someone a very spicy drink would not represent everyone's view of an aggressive act. The measure lacks ecological validity and therefore does not necessarily mean that these situations would result in more direct aggression such as thumping someone.

Methodology

This study, like many others, uses only college students as its sample. This means that the sample is not representative in several ways – the participants are all of a similar age and are well educated; they are also probably middle class.

AQA Ways of reducing aggression

Different theories of aggression lead to very different suggestions for controlling, reducing or even eliminating aggression.

The psychodynamic approach – catharsis

Recall that Freud (the founder of the psychodynamic approach) believed that aggression is instinctive and that if aggressive urges are not released in some way they can build up and be dangerous. Rather than bottling up feelings, Freud believed that a psychologically healthy way of controlling or reducing aggression is to release it by means of a process known as **catharsis**. Although catharsis can involve direct aggression, it can also be achieved by using indirect methods such as playing hard physical sport or watching a violent film. Freud even suggested that people are attracted to certain jobs because they provide a means of venting unconscious pent-up aggression.

> **KEY TERM**
>
> **Catharsis**: a psychodynamic principle that is simply an emotional release. The catharsis hypothesis maintains that aggressive urges are relieved by "releasing" aggressive energy, usually through action.

ACTIVITY 4.9

The examples above, of playing hard physical sport and watching violent films, are socially acceptable ways of achieving catharsis. Try to suggest other such ways. Which professions/jobs might, according to the psychodynamic approach, provide a means of releasing aggression?

EVALUATION

⊖ One of the biggest problems with catharsis is that watching such things as violent films, a boxing match, or real-life violence does not appear to reduce our aggressive urges. In fact, it tends to do the opposite and make us more violent. Social learning theory appears to be a better explanation for the way people respond to watching aggressive behaviour.

⊖ This problem with catharsis is supported by studies which demonstrate that playing sport can increase aggression. Patterson (1974) found that high-school football players were more aggressive after a season than before it, indicating that playing sport does not drain off aggressive urges.

⊕ Since there are instances in which people appear to need to express their aggression or it may "explode" in uncontrolled anger, it may be possible that Freud was partly right and that "safe" outlets are necessary. However, these safe outlets need to be carefully monitored to ensure that they do not increase aggression as media violence may do.

Does watching violence on television make people more aggressive?

Aggression, especially for boys, is often rewarded in much of the media, including video games

The social learning approach to reducing aggression

Social learning theory leads us to very different ways of reducing aggression from those implied by the psychodynamic approach. Bandura's work shows that children copy violence they see in real life and on film, especially if this violence is seen to be rewarded. Studies like that of Huesmann et al. support this conclusion. It follows that if significant models that children encounter in their everyday lives – parents, teachers, TV characters – acted in a non-violent manner, then aggression could be significantly reduced.

It is also important not to directly reward aggression. Eron (1980) states that "if we want to reduce the level of aggression in society, we should also discourage boys from aggression very early on in life and reward them too for other behaviours; in other words, we should socialize boys more like girls".

Most Western societies emphasise the importance of achievement, competition and success. Aggression, in one form or another, is a way to achieve these goals, especially in boys, so aggression is seen to be rewarded in much of the media including video games. In order to reduce aggression, television could be used to emphasise the value of cooperation and non-violence. With respect to video games, a challenge for the producers of these games is to provide exciting ones that do not centre around torture and killing.

It is also important to consider ways of reducing violence in already violent children. If children have learned by example or encouragement to respond to any aggression by escalating the violence (by, for example, hitting anyone who swears at them), then it is difficult for them to know how to respond in a non-violent way. The story at the beginning of this chapter illustrates this well. Such individuals need to be taught different ways of reacting to situations in which they are provoked. Role-playing of potentially aggressive situations in order to teach non-violent responses has been a method used successfully by psychologists with violent young offenders.

ACTIVITY 4.10

In a small group devise a situation in which one person provokes another (by, for example, being rude, arrogant, insulting). Write a short sketch of how this situation could escalate into violence. Then write an alternative in which the provocation is exactly the same but the situation is handled in a different way so that it ends up quite peacefully. Then act them out in front of the class.

EVALUATION

◑◐ Programmes using role play to teach young violent offenders non-aggressive ways of reacting to provocative situations have been partly successful. Quite often they reduce aggression in the young offenders' institute or prison, but it is not clear how well they teach people to respond once they leave the institution and return to ordinary living (Ireland, 2000).

⊕ There is evidence from many studies using different methods (such as laboratory experiments, field experiments and correlations over many years) that children are liable to be more aggressive if they see a lot of aggression around them. This supports the view that violence could be reduced by reducing the level of violence children see.

⊖ Although reducing the amount of media violence children experience is likely to reduce aggression, this can only ever be a partial solution. There are other important influences on children and these probably have a greater effect. Charlton et al. (2000), among others, emphasise that children are unlikely to be aggressive if they come from stable, loving homes in a culture that emphasises the importance of cooperation and caring, and that such children will not be greatly influenced by media violence.

Chapter summary

- Aggression can be defined as the intention to inflict some form of harm on others.
- Biological explanations point out that the hormone testosterone plays an important part in aggression. Aggression may also be caused by genetics, brain injury and chromosomal abnormalities such as XYY.
- Freud argues that aggression is an instinctive drive that is part of the id. Often our aggression forms part of the unconscious mind and is therefore disguised even from ourselves.

EXAM HINT

When you are discussing ways of reducing aggression, always mention how the theory relates to the means of reducing aggression. Do not, for example, simply say that people can reduce aggression by not watching violent TV. Instead, mention that this is based on SLT, which states that children imitate role models. Likewise with the opposite argument that watching violence can reduce aggressive urges, say that this is the Freudian view, based on the concept of catharsis.

- The frustration–aggression hypothesis states that all aggression results from frustrating experiences and not from any other source. A modified version of this, known as the arousal–aggression hypothesis, states that frustration leads us into a state of arousal that often but not always results in aggression.
- Social learning theory (SLT) argues that aggression arises from the imitation of aggressive models, especially those who are significant in a child's life, are powerful, are similar, and who are rewarded for behaving aggressively.
- Three important studies of aggression are:
  - Bandura et al. (1961), a laboratory experiment in which very young children watched an aggressive model (experimental group) and were compared on aggression to a group who had watched a non-aggressive model (control group). The experimental group were more aggressive than the control group.
  - Huesmann et al. (2003) carried out a longitudinal study measuring whether there was a correlation between the amount of violent TV watched in childhood and aggressive behaviour in adult life. They found that the more violent TV the children had watched, the more aggressive they were as adults, and the more likely they were to have a criminal record.
  - Klinesmith et al. (2006) found that playing with a toy gun increased levels of testosterone in male students and also made them more aggressive compared with a control group who played with a neutral toy. They concluded that it is possible that being in a situation associated with aggression makes people more violent because their testosterone levels increase, rather than there being a direct connection.
- The psychodynamic approach would suggest that one way of releasing pent-up aggression in a safe way is by means of catharsis. This can be done in such ways as by watching violence or by playing hard physical sports. However, this way of reducing aggression has been criticised on the grounds that such activities appear to increase rather than reduce aggression.
- Social learning theory implies that aggression would be reduced if children were not exposed to aggressive models and if they also had non-aggressive figures to admire. Already aggressive children may be helped to become less aggressive by social skills training in which they are taught non-aggressive ways of responding to provocation.

AQA Exam-style questions for AQA

1. (a) Describe **one** study of aggression. Include the aim, method, results, and conclusion. (4 marks)

   (b) Evaluate the study you have described in 1(a). (3 marks)

2. Explanations of aggression include:
   * Psychodynamic
   * Biological
   * Social learning

   Outline an explanation of aggression based on **one** of these theories. (4 marks)

3. Describe and evaluate the way in which the psychodynamic explanation would suggest that aggression could be reduced. (*Use continuous prose*) (6 marks)

EXAM HINT

Remember that with any question for which you are asked to use continuous prose, some of the marks will be decided on QWC (quality of written communication). Check the introductory chapter to ensure that you understand what is required to obtain good marks in this respect.

What you need to know AQA

The specification lists the following things that you will need to be able to do for the examination:

■ Distinguish between non-verbal and verbal communication, including paralinguistics

■ Describe types of non-verbal communication, including: functions of eye contact; facial expression and the hemispheres of the brain; body language; posture, gestures and touch

■ Describe and evaluate studies of non-verbal communication and verbal communication (including Argyle, Alkema & Gilmore, 1971)

■ Understand what is meant by personal space and the factors that affect it (cultural norms, sex differences, individual differences, status) and describe and evaluate studies of personal space

■ Understand contemporary implications of studies of non-verbal communication and their benefits and drawbacks

What you need to know OCR

The specification lists the following things that you will need to be able to do for the examination:

■ Outline examples of body language and facial expressions as a form of non-verbal communication (NVC)

■ Use social learning theory to be able to:
  ■ Explain the role of observation and imitation, and the role of reinforcement and punishment in learning NVC
  ■ Describe cultural variations in NVC
  ■ Explain criticisms of social learning theory of NVC
  ■ Consider evolutionary theory as an alternative theory, with specific reference to survival and reproduction.

■ Describe and outline the limitations of Yuki et al. (2007)

■ Explain how psychological research relates to social skills training

Non-verbal communication

■ ■ ■ ■ ■ ■ ■ ■ ■

Dear Linda,

I've been internet dating lately but don't seem to be getting anywhere. I can't understand what I'm doing wrong. I'm fairly good looking, presentable and in a good job. When I meet someone new, I'm always very attentive, look them in the eye, make comments on what they say. Yet none of them ever wants to see me again. I get the impression they feel uncomfortable. Please help!

Dear John,

Sounds like you might have a problem with your non-verbal communication! You particularly mention that you are attentive and make eye contact. Are you trying too hard? It's possible that they would say you are being too intense, and rather than looking you are devouring with your eyes and making your date really uncomfortable. When you meet someone new, do you lunge at them rather than take their hand? Are you leaning forward with too much enthusiasm and interrupting them in an attempt to show interest in what they have just said? My advice to you is to study your own body language and RELAX. Sit back and genuinely listen to what they have to say. Don't stare, try to be natural. I know this is difficult as we are not always aware of our own body language, but you do need to pay particular attention to it and you may do better next time. Good luck!

Dear Linda,

I'm going for an interview for a job I really, really want and I'm dead nervous. What can I do to make the most of this opportunity? Help!

Dear Emma,

How exciting! People often prepare well to answer interview questions but forget that they will be judged on non-verbal communication as well as on what they say.

One of the most important things about an interview is to remember that the image the interviewer has of you when he or she first meets you is the one that is going to last. If you're slouchy, sloppy or messy it won't matter how well you answer the interview questions, you are not going to

Our non-verbal communication influences how others perceive and respond to us.

get the job. When practising for an interview, work on your non-verbal communication as well as your other interviewing skills. It could be what clinches the job offer for you.

Think all the time about the impression you are making and get yourself into a "smart" frame of mind from the start. Think about the way you are sitting in the reception area, the way you greet the receptionist and the interviewer, and the way you wait. They will all have an impact on whether you are going to be considered for the job. Be friendly and pleasant, but not overbearing. Shake hands with the interviewer. Your handshake should be firm – not sticky or wimpy.

Try to sit upright, not leaning backwards or forwards. Leaning back makes you look too casual; leaning forwards can give the impression of aggression. Make eye contact frequently for a few seconds at a time, without staring. Smile and nod as appropriate; only laugh if the interviewer laughs first. Use an even tone of voice, not too loud or too quiet. Consider the questions before answering them. Above all, try to stay calm and relaxed.

Good luck!

NON-VERBAL COMMUNICATION

The whole of this chapter is concerned with **non-verbal communication (NVC)** but it is divided into two sections to cover both of the exam specifications. If you study AQA then use the first part of the chapter. If you study OCR, then, in the main, you need the second part. However, it would be helpful if you read through the first part as well as this provides some useful background. You do not need to know it in detail unless it's referred to in the second section, but you might find some of the activities interesting and relevant.

AQA Non-verbal and verbal communication (PART 1)

KEY TERM

Non-verbal communication (NVC): messages expressed by communication other than linguistic means.

Communication is essential to survival. In humans it is a very important part of their social behaviour, and humans spend a great deal of time communicating with each other. They also communicate with different species of animals. Within the non-human animal kingdom the same applies – there is communication both within members of the same species and across species.

The difference between verbal and non-verbal communication

An essential means of communication in humans is **verbal,** that is, it involves speech, and can also involve writing since this stands for language. But an additional and very important means of communicating is not by what we say but what we do. Communication that does not involve words is called "non-verbal communication" (NVC) and can be defined as "those messages expressed by other than linguistic means". NVC contributes enormously to the meaning of the message; indeed it has been shown to be more important, varied and intricate than we often assume it to be.

We can think of NVC as being divided into two types (although they are often used at the same time):

Our interaction with animals, and especially our pets, often involves non-verbal communication

- Communication during speech that does not come from the words themselves but from the way the message is conveyed – the tone of voice, the pausing, the "hums and haws" and the general pace of the speech.
- Communication that does not involve any speech at all, such as our posture or our facial expression.

We will start by looking at NVC that occurs when we are speaking.

Paralinguistics

Paralinguistics is the study of **paralanguage,** which in turn refers to *the non-verbal elements of communication that express emotion and the meaning of the message.*

When people have a conversation, the speech itself is full of non-verbal signals – the pitch of the voice, the urgency of expression, the speed of talking, and so on. For example, if someone responds to a comment such as "calm down" by saying "I'm perfectly calm", but there is a strain in their voice, their teeth are somewhat clenched and there is tension in their body, you know they are anything but calm. The NVC has given them away. Even in simple ordinary phrases such as "thank you" there is a wealth of additional meaning as well as the words themselves (see Activity 5.2).

ACTIVITY 5.1

Think about all the different means of communication there are between

- Humans and humans
- Humans and dogs
- Humans and cats
- Dogs and cats

Take each pair of these in turn and think about ways, other than by speech, that one of the pair could communicate the following emotions to the other: fear, threat, affection, anger, submission. For human–human you could try to act out the emotion in pairs (or alone) while the class guesses which one it is.

KEY TERMS

Verbal communication: involves speech, and can also involve writing since this stands for language.

Paralinguistics: the study of *how* something is said rather than *what* is said.

Paralanguage: the non-verbal elements of communication that express emotion and the meaning of the message.

Think of paralinguistics as the study of *how* something is said rather than *what* is said.

ACTIVITY 5.2

The importance of NVC can be seen in this simple activity. Think about how you would say the following

(a) if you were sincere
(b) if you didn't really care but thought you should
(c) if you were being sarcastic:
- Thanks a lot
- I had a really great time
- I love banana sandwiches

A huge amount of what you mean is conveyed by the way these phrases are said as well as what is said.

Important paralinguistics are tone, speed, pitch, volume, number and length of pauses. So, for example, if a high-pitched tone is used this often means the person is upset, angry or nervous; if there are a great many pauses, they lack confidence, and so on. Think of a witness giving evidence to the police about a crime – how would the paralinguistics affect the degree to which they were believed?

Researchers have investigated the power of paralinguistics by the use of something called "content-free speech". This is speech that has been electronically modified so the words are unintelligible but the paralinguistics (tone of voice, etc.) remain the same. It's rather like listening to a foreign language you've never heard before. Participants are quite capable of picking up the emotion being expressed and the strength of it (Starkweather, 1961). Paralinguistic cues are so influential that if a listener wants to determine a speaker's attitude he or she pays more attention to these cues than to what is said. Furthermore, if the way something is said contradicts what is said (such as someone shouting "I'm not angry") then we take more notice of the paralinguistics than we do of the words themselves.

ACTIVITY 5.3

The following exercise demonstrates how the emphasis on a word can change the meaning of a sentence. The simple sentence "I did not say you were stupid" can have six different meanings depending on which of six words is emphasised. So, for example, say:

"*I* didn't say you were stupid"
"I *didn't* say you were stupid"

and so on, changing the emphasis each time. Consider how different the meaning of each sentence is.

[AQA] Types of NVC other than paralinguistics

Now let's turn our attention to NVC that does not involve speech. This includes:

- **Eye contact**
- **Facial expression**
- **Body language**
- **Personal space** (the distance people keep between themselves and others).

Let us consider each of these in turn.

Eye contact

Eye contact has enormous social meaning. If we want to know how someone is really feeling, we look into their eyes. If we want to talk to someone, we "catch their eye". Conversely, if we want to avoid someone, we look away. In a classroom, if you don't want the teacher to ask you a question, you avoid looking at him or her (it doesn't work – teachers are wise to it).

Eye contact serves several functions:

- It provides feedback to others on our mood and personality.

We make judgements about people according to the amount of eye contact they make. We generally assume that people who avoid our eyes are embarrassed, ashamed or disinterested. A high level of eye contact or gaze implies interest, intimacy, attraction or respect. The amount of eye contact people make is also used to judge their personality. People who make frequent eye contact are judged as honest, straightforward, friendly and likeable (Kleinke et al., 1974) whereas people who avoid eye contact are seen as unfriendly, shifty or shy (Zimbardo, 1977). The following study looks at this.

> **KEY TERMS**
>
> **Eye contact**: a form of NVC that provides feedback to others on our mood and personality, regulates the flow of conversation, and expresses emotion to others.
>
> **Facial expression**: one of the most important forms of NVC because it conveys emotion. The six most recognised facial expressions are surprise, fear, anger, disgust, happiness, and sadness.
>
> **Body language**: a type of NVC involving posture, gestures, and touch. It is the way we stand and walk, and the gestures we use to convey information.
>
> **Personal space**: an invisible space around us that we allow people to whom we are close to enter, but if someone else comes into it we feel uncomfortable.

[AQA] A study into eye contact

EXLINE ET AL. (1967)

Aim: Exline et al. wanted to assess the effect of different amounts of eye contact on people's judgement of others.

Method: Confederates (people who worked for the researcher) interviewed the participants one at a time. During the interview they were asked to make eye contact either 15% of the time or 80% of the time.

The participants were then asked to describe their interviewer, using a checklist of words.

Results: The confederates who made eye contact only 15% of the time were described using such words as cold, defensive, immature, submissive. When they gazed for 80% of the time they were described using words such as friendly, self-confident, natural, mature and sincere.

Conclusion: The amount of eye contact can have a significant effect on how others are judged. If you want to make a positive impression on someone, you should maintain a high level of eye contact.

EVALUATION

⊖ Of course, this study uses rather an artificial situation with a deliberate attempt to use a certain amount of eye contact, so it cannot totally reflect all real-life encounters.

⊕ Nevertheless, it does demonstrate how differently we are likely to judge people who make different amounts of eye contact, and how negatively people are viewed when they make very little eye contact. It therefore has useful applications.

So, is it true that a lot of eye contact is always a good thing? No! Too much eye contact (staring) can have a very negative effect since staring, in humans and other animals, is used to communicate aggression and dominance. People describe someone who stares as tense, angry, embarrassed and unintelligent.

• It regulates the flow of conversation.

When we have a conversation with someone, we look at them intermittently: we make eye contact in bursts of about 3 seconds then we look away. Conversations involve "turn taking" (one person talks, then the other, and so on) and there are some interesting changes in eye contact that give clues to when it's someone else's turn to speak. We tend to look more at the end of what we are saying, but to look away at the start, especially if we are answering a question (Kendon 1967). It seems that the gaze is used by the speaker to gain feedback from the listener: at the beginning of what you are saying you do not need a response, but towards the end you want to know how what you have said has been received. Goodwin (1981) analysed 50 hours of conversation in settings such as parties, shopping and eating. He concluded that when someone is talking they want to know that others are listening, and they look at them in order to get a look in response.

There are other signals given by the eyes during conversation. An "eyeflash" (looking at the person directly then looking away again quickly) is used to emphasise a point, whereas ordinary glances are used to emphasise particular words or phrases. In a group of people engaged in conversation, a glance by the speaker in the direction of someone else can indicate who they want to speak next. In this way, eye contact is continually used to regulate the flow of a conversation.

• It expresses emotion.

You've probably heard the expression "their eyes were like saucers". When we are excited, interested or very frightened, the pupils of our eyes dilate (get larger). Hess et al. (1960) measured the pupil size of men and women while

Methodology

Analysing everyday behaviour, as done by Goodwin (1981), provides data high in ecological validity and gives valuable information as to the purpose that eye contact serves.

they viewed certain pictures. They found that a person's eyes grow larger in proportion to how interested they are. Men's pupils enlarged by about 18% when they viewed a picture of a naked woman, while a woman's pupils enlarged about 20% when she saw an image of a naked man. One of the largest increases occurred when women looked at a picture of a baby.

Subconsciously we take in this information and are affected by it. Without a word being said, people know if someone is interested in us and we respond accordingly.

Facial expression

One of the most important forms of NVC is facial expression because it conveys emotion. Darwin, the founder of evolutionary theory, concluded that all animals that live in groups, and who need to cooperate and reproduce, need to be able to express emotion as a means of communication. Ekman et al. (1976) showed people from many cultures different photographs of faces expressing emotion and found that there were six that were recognized everywhere most of the time, indicating that they are innate. These were:

- surprise
- fear
- anger
- disgust
- happiness
- sadness.

> **How psychology works**
>
> It is only by analysing behaviour in detail that psychologists understand how we can be subconsciously affected by certain stimuli, for example a baby. We are not consciously aware of our own reaction or those of others.

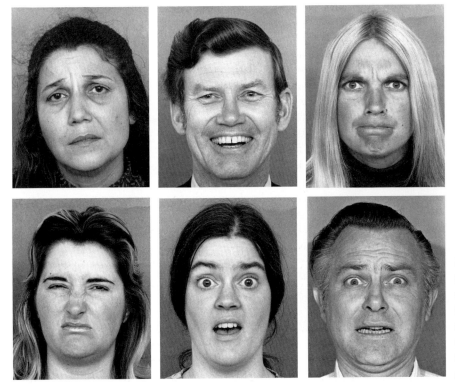

Paul Ekman tested a wide range of different cultures and concluded that there are six basic types of emotion expressed in faces. Copyright © Paul Ekman

Our faces do, of course, express many other emotions such as interest, amusement, boredom, impatience, and so on.

These emotions are recognised quite early in childhood, another indication that they are not learnt but innate. Between 3 and 5 months infants can discriminate first joy, then surprise, fear and sadness. By the time the child is 2 years old he or she can recognise all six main facial expressions for emotion. A child of 6 can begin to tell if the face and inner emotion do not match; in other words, they can tell that a sad person who is smiling is not really happy.

ACTIVITY 5.4

Think of each of the six emotions listed on the previous page. What parts of the face are used to express these emotions? You can probably do this exercise by just thinking about it, but it's more fun to make faces corresponding to each emotion into a mirror, or to pair up with someone who expresses each emotion in turn and you note the main facial features that express each one. Then change places.

What parts of the face express emotion? We are all familiar with the eyebrows being raised in surprise, with narrowed eyes to express annoyance and the lips being curled up for a smile or turned down for sadness.

Our face provides a window into what is happening in the brain. The brain can be considered to be in two "halves", the left and the right side, joined by a big bundle of fibres (called the corpus callosum). Research on the brain indicates that each "half", or hemisphere as it is known, has a different set of functions (although there is a lot of overlap). The left half, for example, is responsible for language. The right side has been associated with more "primitive" processes such as emotion. Since the right side of the brain controls the left side of the face and vice versa, one way in which it's possible to explore this idea is to see whether the left side of the face is more emotionally expressive than the other. This is investigated in the following study.

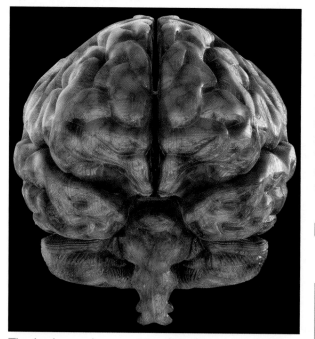

The brain can be considered an organ of two halves. Each half, or hemisphere, has a different set of functions

AQA A study into facial expressions

SACKEIM ET AL. (1978)

Aim: Sackeim et al. wanted to see whether one side of the face is more expressive than the other, and to infer from this whether one side of the brain is more involved in emotion than the other.

Method: The researchers photographed faces showing a variety of different emotions. They then cut the photos down the middle, through the nose, and reproduced a mirror image of each side. So what they now had was two pictures of each facial expression, one representing the left side of the face duplicated and one representing the right side duplicated (we call these faces *composites*: a composite is something made up of different parts). They then asked people to judge the intensity with which each face expressed emotion.

Results: The left side composite faces were judged as expressing a far more intense emotion than the right side composites. The researchers concluded that "emotions are expressed more intensely on the left side of the face".

Conclusion: Since the left hand side of the face is controlled mainly by the right hemisphere of the brain and it is this side of the face that is more emotionally expressive, it seems likely that basic emotions are controlled by the right hemisphere of the brain.

EVALUATION

➕ The Sackeim et al. study supports previous research which shows that the right hemisphere of the brain is largely responsible for basic emotions.

➕ The methodology was quite ingenious because it enabled one side of the face to be judged independently of the other. If a proper face had been used and each half covered up in turn, it would have been quite artificial because we don't look at half-faces when we judge emotions.

➖ This study has been criticised because the photos were posed and a photographer instructed the models to use particular muscles, such as "raise your upper lip". The only emotion that was spontaneously shown during the photo-shoot was happiness, and with this one there was no difference in the intensity of the left and right side composites.

Methodology

There are times when a contrived situation (in this case an artificial face) is very useful in psychological investigation. Even though it is not "natural", it reduces variables and allows us to see which cues affect our responses.

Body language

Our bodies constantly send messages to others. The way we stand, walk, the gestures we use all convey information.

Posture

The way you hold yourself makes a big contribution to your body language as a whole and often shows your level of self-confidence. When a person hunches their shoulders with their head down it indicates that they lack confidence; it may even indicate that they wish to hide away. In contrast, walking with

KEY TERMS

Status: level of social standing on a hierarchical scale. For example, an employer has higher status than an employee.

Postural echo: a type of NVC in which people are seen to "mirror" the postures of a partner that they are communicating with.

Everyday life

There are very many situations in which an awareness of body language is helpful in presenting the type of "image" we want to convey. Obvious examples are job interviews and meeting people. I'm sure you can think of others.

shoulders back and head held high gives a definite message of self-confidence and even authority. A relaxed body posture indicates exactly what it is – a relaxed and "at home" feeling.

Your posture when you are with other people also conveys certain messages. If you orientate your body towards someone it shows that you are paying attention to them. Leaning back indicates a lack of interest or that you are a rather reserved person. If people are feeling aggressive they, like some animals, puff themselves out; likewise if they want to show their high **status**.

In general, we can describe postures as "open" or "closed". An open posture is one in which we can see the body (the torso) with arms and legs uncrossed and shoulders back. This can convey one of several messages: self-confidence, a relaxed non-defensive state or even aggression. The closed position is one that closes up the body in a more stooped posture, with arms across the body, holding your arms and legs crossed if sitting down. It is a very defensive posture and shows a lack of self-confidence and nervousness.

It has sometimes been noticed that when people are together, perhaps having a conversation, they tend to adopt postures that are the mirror image of each other. For example, one person may cross their legs from right to left while the other crosses them left to right. As one leans forwards, so does the other. They may even synchronise hand positions and hair grooming. We refer to this as **postural echo** and it tends to demonstrate that the two people are getting along well, that they are "on the same wavelength".

Gestures

We are all familiar with how gestures are used to convey meaning. A beckoned finger for "come here", a wave to attract attention or to say "goodbye", a pointing figure to indicate something, a shake of the head to mean "no" and a nod to mean "yes".

Some gestures are universal (the same in every culture) but many vary from culture to culture and can be a source of confusion or embarrassment. Gregor (1993) reports the case of a newly employed Asian engineer in an American company. As he was leaving his office for his first meeting his secretary crossed her fingers in a gesture intended by her to wish him good luck. Unfortunately it rather confused and embarrassed him since in his country, crossing your fingers is a sexual proposition.

Some gestures, such as pointing, are universal

ACTIVITY 5.5

Investigate how a single gesture can have different meanings in different countries and give examples of how misunderstandings can arise from this. (You may wish to include an incident involving Winston Churchill.)

Nevertheless, as mentioned earlier, many gestures are universal (and some are even used by non-human animals). The following study demonstrates this.

AQA A study into gestures

SAITZ ET AL. (1972)

Aim: Saitz et al. wanted to compare the use of gestures in the USA, Colombia and four African countries.

Method: Observations were made of the gestures used in these cultures.

Results: The study showed that 65% of the gestures used in North America and 73% of those used in Colombia were also used by the four African countries. The following were very common: pointing, shrugging, nodding the head, clapping, beckoning, waving, patting on the back, thumbs down.

Conclusion: Many gestures are universal or, at least, are the same in a wide variety of cultures. They may have evolved to serve a certain function, for example, Darwin suggested that head shaking (meaning "no") may have evolved from babies at the breast shaking their heads away when they have had enough.

> **Diversity**
> It is important for people to show awareness of other people's cultures, but it is equally important to be aware that gestures can be misinterpreted and may not be intended as offensive. We need to appreciate cultural diversity and not be quick to take offence or draw hasty conclusions.

EVALUATION

➕ Cross-cultural studies are extremely useful for investigating the origins of behaviour and in judging whether they are innate or learned.

➖ There are many different cultures and subcultures world wide, so looking at a small number does not always indicate whether behaviour is universal. Many isolated cultures have not been looked at in detail.

Touch

Touch is the most primitive form of social communication, as indicated by the fact that it is used by many species of animal and by very young children. It is perhaps surprising then that touch is one of the most rule-bound of all NVC and can easily cause offence if used inappropriately. Among adults in Britain, various kinds of greetings and farewell touches are allowed. Females shake hands or embrace, perhaps kiss on the cheek when they greet a friend, but men in Britain will only shake hands. This is different in other countries. In France, for example, men kiss each other. When male politicians from Britain and France meet each other there is sometimes obvious discomfort from the

British man when being embraced by his French counterpart, however hard he tries to hide it. The study by Willis and Rawdon (1994) mentioned later in this section (see page 116) looks at the cultural differences in the use of touch.

Interestingly, touch is an important part of many games (think of wrestling and rugby football) as well as a lot of ceremonies (such as weddings, christenings and funerals).

Touch serves many functions. Jones et al. (1985) analysed 1500 touches and found 18 types of touch, which could be grouped as follows:

- Positive affect, such as reassurance or during sex
- Playful
- Control
- Ritual (especially greetings and partings)
- Mixed, for example both greeting and affection
- Task-related, such as a nurse touching a patient
- Accidental.

Methodology
Field studies are studies carried out in a natural environment, so the findings are high in ecological validity. This means that they tell us something about behaviour in everyday situations.

In relationships, touch has two basic meanings: it is used to express warmth or to assert dominance. If one person touches another (rather than both touching each other) then it is a sign of dominance, assertiveness and higher status.

Touch can be very persuasive and people use it, deliberately or subconsciously, to persuade others to do something for them. When asking a favour, people are far more likely to agree to it if you touch them while asking than if you don't. Several field experiments have demonstrated this, including the following.

AQA A field study into the effects of gaze and touch on compliance

KLEINKE (1977)

Aim: Kleinke wanted to see if touch increased compliance with a request (increased the likelihood that a person would do as asked).

Method: One researcher left a coin in a public phone box, waited until someone used the phone then, when they came out, approached the person, explained that they had left the money and asked if they would give it back. Sometimes they would gently put their hand on the person's arm when making the request; sometimes they would not.

Results: The money was far more likely to be returned if the individual was touched on the arm while making the request than if they were not touched.

Conclusion: Touch is interpreted by people as a positive gesture, as a gesture indicating that the person who touches is friendly and honest.

ACTIVITY 5.9

With the Middlemist et al. study, what ethical guidelines were broken?

Cultural norms and personal space

Personal space is very much affected by culture. Different cultures have very different **cultural norms** for how close they stand to others and how much they touch each other. Little (1968) examined cultural differences over 19 different social situations in a sample of Americans, Swedes, Greeks, Italians and Scots. They had to place dolls at distances that reflected where they would stand in real social situations. The situations they had to assess included two good friends talking about a pleasant topic, a shop owner discussing the weather with his assistant, two people talking about the best place to shop, and two strangers talking about an unpleasant topic. The findings showed considerable differences between cultures. The Greeks stood closest, the Americans next closest and the Scots the furthest away. Interestingly, there were considerable male–female differences with the Greeks and Scots but with the Greeks it was the women who stood closer than the men; with the Scots, women stood further away than did men. On average, across all nations there was only a small gender difference, the men standing slightly closer than the women.

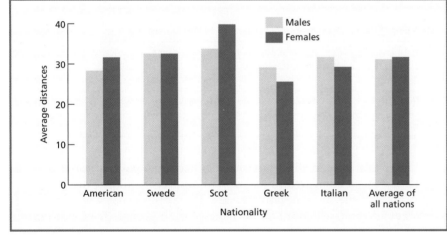

Results from Little's (1968) study

ACTIVITY 5.10

In the exam, it is best to describe studies in terms of aim, method, results, conclusion. Do this yourselves for the study by Little (1968). Then attempt to evaluate it (you can do this by the good and bad points in the method).

ACTIVITY 5.11

How did Little measure personal space in this study? Was it by **simulation**, **questionnaire**, or field experiment?

AQA A study into gender, culture and personal space

WILLIS AND RAWDON (1994)

Aim: Willis and Rawdon wanted to study differences between female and male students from Chile, Spain, Malaysia and the United States.

Method: Participants all completed the Same-Sex Touch Scale, which measures the importance we place on touch in interactions with the same sex. The higher the score, the more importance was placed on touch in same-sex interactions.

Results: The average scores for each gender in each nationality are shown in the table below.

Nationality	Female	Male
United States	70.6	58.3
Malaysia	54.3	46.1
Chile	64.6	56.8
Spain	69.8	61.9

As can be seen, in all cultures females had more positive scores towards same-sex touch compared to males. With respect to culture, the Malaysian students had the most negative scores. The Spanish males were the most tolerant of same-sex touch of all males. Of all groups, females from the United States had the most positive scores.

Conclusion: Personal space is affected by culture and gender.

Where would you sit...

...to work quietly?

...to chat to a friend?

EVALUATION

The research has limitations in that the measure was via a questionnaire and not *actual* observation of interactions.

However, it does note cultural and gender differences in personal space. It would be useful for you to read the section on culture and NVC (page 123).

ACTIVITY 5.12

You are at a business conference and you are to meet the following people: an American female, a Malaysian female and a Spanish male. Based on the findings from the Willis and Rawdon study, how are you going to approach each one?

ACTIVITY 5.13

Look at the diagram below. Imagine you have been asked to go and talk to the person already seated. It is a person of the same sex who you don't know. Where would you sit?

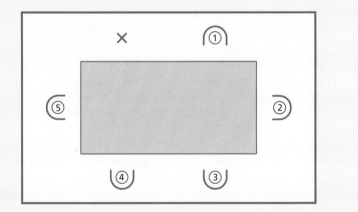

Do the same if it is:

- A same-sex friend who you know well and you are just going to chat to.
- A same-sex friend who you know well and you are going to eat with.
- An opposite sex person from your class.
- A familiar adult such as your mum.
- A person who you know and are cross with – you see them sitting at the table and you want to have it out with them.

Compare your results with others in the class. Particularly consider whether there are any gender differences, especially in the first and second situations.

Sex differences in personal space

You've probably noticed that, at least in Britain, women are far more likely to hug each other than are men. Not only are there **sex differences** in physical touching but also in personal space. The following classic study demonstrates this.

AQA A study into sex differences in personal space

FISHER AND BYRNE (1975)

Aim: Fisher and Byrne had two main aims in this study:

1. To examine gender differences in the invasion of personal space.
2. To examine how gender affects the putting up of barriers to indicate to others where our personal space is.

Method: For the first aim, Fisher and Byrne's confederates (people who knew what the experiment was about) went into a university library and sat near someone who was sitting on a table on their own. They either sat opposite them, one seat away or next to them. In all, they invaded the personal space of 62 males and 63 females. After the invasion had taken place, Fisher and Byrne asked the participant to complete a questionnaire about the experience. It asked questions about how the participant felt during the invasion of their personal space (e.g. how happy they felt, how attracted they were to the confederate, their perceived level of crowding, etc.).

For the second aim, a different researcher was used who was not told the aim of the research (called the single-blind technique). They had to observe 33 males and 33 females and record where they placed their personal belongings on a library table.

Results: From the first study, distinct gender differences emerged. Males disliked being invaded by someone approaching from opposite them, but did not mind someone invading the space next to them. For females, the opposite results arose; they did not mind people invading the space opposite to them, but disliked invasion when someone sat next to them.

For the second study, the results backed up those reported in the first study. Males were more likely to place their personal belongings in front of them, while females were more likely to place personal belongings next to them – both males and females were placing barriers to defend against people invading from their least preferred direction. The table on the left shows the number of "barrier placements" observed on the table where participants were sitting.

	Barrier next to person	Barrier opposite person
Male	9	15
Female	17	6

Conclusion: From this study it is clear that males do not like to have their space invaded from the front. Females do not like to have their space invaded from the side. Both genders defend this invasion by placing barriers to stop people getting too close.

EVALUATION

➕ The study was thorough in that it investigated both *feelings* towards invasion of personal space and actual *behaviour* of participants, so it provides two valid measures of reactions to invasions of personal space.

➖ The study involved mainly students in a university library so it does not tell us a great deal about gender differences in other age groups or in other situations (e.g. a social gathering).

➖ There are ethical issues with this study. The participants had not been consulted; in addition they may well have experienced a little embarrassment and discomfort.

ACTIVITY 5.14

How did Fisher and Byrne measure personal space in this study? Was it by simulation, questionnaire, or field experiment?

Individual differences in personal space

Personality is another factor that influences personal space, with people showing **individual differences** in the way they react. Some studies, but not all, have shown than extraverts (outgoing people) stand closer to others than do people with a quieter, inward temperament. People who are very confident, assertive and self-assured also stand closer than average.

Unsurprisingly, anxious people tend to keep a greater distance between themselves and others and this applies even more clearly to mentally ill people. Another group who keep a very large distance between themselves and others is disruptive and aggressive teenagers.

Interestingly, the stage of the menstrual cycle also appears to have some effect on personal space. Sanders (1978) found that women aged 17–27 years of age tended to have a larger personal space during the menstrual period compared to the middle of the cycle.

Despite the above, personality on its own is difficult to relate to personal space. Generally, we need to take account both of the personality *and* other factors. For example, we need to consider the relationship between the people and the situation (is it a friendly encounter, an interview, an argument?).

Status and personal space

People of unequal status (boss and employee; teacher and pupil) tend to stand further apart than do equals. The person of higher status uses personal space as

KEY TERM

Individual differences: differences between people that are not specific to a given social category such as sex, gender, ethnic group, etc.

well as other non-verbal communication to exert their higher status. They tend to face the other person rather than stand next to them, put their shoulders back, pull their body up to maximum height, fix their gaze on the eyes of the other person: all ways of emphasising their higher status.

Status is also shown in terms of the amount of looking (gazing) people do. Lower status people tend to gaze at higher status people far more than the other way around, perhaps because the lower status person needs to know what is expected of them by the higher status person. However, as you might expect, it is a different story when it comes to staring down another person. Strogman et al. (1968) investigated this by putting people in pairs, one of a higher status than the other, and seeing which could outstare the other (who could stare whom down). They found that the higher status person could usually outstare the lower status one. They concluded that this demonstrated a "pecking order" in terms of gaze.

AQA Contemporary practical implications of studies of NVC

Lie detection

How do people get away with telling lies to such an extent that they can con someone out of their life savings? And why is it that when you tell a small lie (my dog chewed up my homework – but, honestly, I *did* do it) you get a withering look and perhaps a detention from your teacher? Maybe the answer is in NVC.

Ekman et al. (1974) suggested that liars often give themselves away with non-verbal cues, but usually the listener is not paying attention to these so the lies go undetected. Imagine a situation in which someone wants to know if another person is lying – they listen to what the person has to say and they look at their face and into their eyes. However, it's fairly easy to "lie" not only with words but with your face, so the liar gets away with it. What the listener should be looking for is other give-away signs – signs such as fidgety movements of hands and feet, a high pitched tone or a quiver in the voice. People who pay attention to these non-verbal cues are often quite good at telling whether or not someone is lying. Conversely, the best liars are those who can train themselves in these cues as well as the more obvious ones (think about that if you ever want to be a successful contestant on a quiz show that depends on deception, such as *Golden Balls*).

Obviously the ability to detect lying is quite important for the criminal justice system. In order to investigate whether people could be trained to detect lying Ekman et al. (1991) compared four groups of professionals: police detectives, agents from US customs, people working for the CIA (Central Intelligence Agency) and people working for the Secret Service. The four groups were asked to watch a videotape and judge who was lying. The Secret Service agents were better than all of the other three who were, in fact, no better at lie detection than ordinary members of the public. Perhaps the Secret Service agents, who are used to scanning crowds in order to detect threats to the high ranking politicians they are guarding, are better trained to look for cues other than those found in the face.

What other factors affect lie detection? At first glance, it may seem strange that the less information people receive the better they are at detecting lies. For example, people can detect deception better if they only see the body of someone (on a videotape) than if they see the face as well. But on further consideration, this is perhaps unsurprising given what we have already said – that people find it easier to lie with their face than with their body. With only the body to go by, the detection of a lie becomes easier – the waters are not muddied by seeing someone who is making a real facial effort to look as if they are not lying.

So next time you are trying to convince your teacher that the dog really did eat your homework, you know what you need to do!

Chapter summary (Part 1)

- Non-verbal communication can be defined as "those messages expressed by other than linguistic means". One type of NVC is known as paralinguistics, which involves the way something is said rather than what is said (the tone of voice, etc.). Other forms of NVC include eye contact, facial expression and body language.
- Functions of eye contact include: providing feedback to others on our mood and personality; regulating the flow of conversation; expressing emotion.
- Facial expressions express many emotions including the basic ones of surprise, fear, anger, disgust, happiness and sadness. Sackeim et al. (1978) concluded that these basic emotions are controlled by the right hemisphere of the brain and expressed more on the left hand than the right hand side of the face.
- Body language includes posture, gestures and touch. All of these convey information to others and affect our relationships. Argyle et al. (1971) concluded that non-verbal messages convey more information than the actual verbal content of the message, so if you say something friendly in a hostile manner, you will be seen as hostile.
- Personal space is another form of NVC.
  - It can be defined as a portable, invisible boundary surrounding us, into which others may not trespass. It regulates how closely we interact with others, moves with us, and expands and contracts according to the situation in which we find ourselves (Bell et al., 1996).
  - There are cultural differences in personal space. The study by Little showed that Swedish and Scottish people require more personal space compared to Italians or Greeks.
  - There are also sex differences in personal space. Fisher and Byrne, in their library-based study, reported that males do not like to have their space invaded from the front, whereas females do not like to have their space invaded from the side.
  - There are individual differences in personal space. People's personality and status influence the distance they stand from others.

- A contemporary practical implication of NVC is lie detection. Liars tend to give themselves away by body language such as fidgety movements of the hands and feet. This has implications for the criminal justice system.

AQA Exam-style questions for AQA

1. When we communicate with other people, for example when we mingle at a party, we use both conversation and non-verbal means of communication to interact.
   a. What is meant by *non-verbal communication*? Use an example from interaction at a party to illustrate your answer. (3 marks)
   b. What is meant by *verbal communication*? Use an example from interaction at a party to illustrate your answer. (3 marks)

2. a. What is meant by *personal space*? (2 marks)
   b. List three factors that might affect personal space. (3 marks)

3. Describe **one** study of non-verbal communication. Include the aim, the method, the results and a brief conclusion. (4 marks)

OCR Non-verbal communication (PART 2)

This part of the chapter is concerned with the specification as applied to those taking OCR. First of all you will need to cover some of the work in the very first part of this chapter. You will need to know the following sections:

- The difference between verbal and non-verbal communication, including the definition of NVC (pages 100–101).
- Eye contact (pages 103–104).
- Facial expression (pages 105–106) but not including the study by Sackeim.
- Body language (pages 107–111).

OCR Social learning theory as an explanation for NVC

The role of imitation and observation

In Chapter 4 you learnt about social learning theory. According to this theory, one of the main reasons why people (especially children) behave the way they do is because they imitate the important people around them. In essence, the general principle of social learning theory is that children and adults often learn by *observing* and then *imitating* the behaviour of other people.

The people who are imitated are referred to as *models*. The most important models in a child's life are first their parents and later on their same-sex friends and media characters, especially celebrities.

From a very early age, children will observe their parents and other carers and begin to imitate the non-verbal means by which they communicate – often long before they imitate the verbal means of communication. They are likely to copy gestures, body language and intonations in speech. As they get older and their sense of gender develops, boys are more likely to imitate their fathers and other male role models, while girls will be more inclined to imitate their mothers and other female role models. All of this is, of course, done quite unconsciously, just as the use of much NVC is itself done quite unconsciously. Eventually children begin to resemble their parents in ways other than in their physical appearance because they use the same hand gestures or ways of emphasising certain words. It has been noted that children often have very similar facial expressions or gestures to their parents, suggesting that the parents act as models whom the children imitate.

Other important NVC that is observed and imitated is how closely you stand or sit to others, how much touching, hugging and kissing goes on, and so on. This is the reason why there are such differences between cultures (and subcultures, such as social classes) in the amount of contact that occurs. The fact that there are considerable differences between cultures in the degree to which people stand close, touch, hug, kiss and so on is accounted for by social learning theory. Quite simply, we observe and imitate the behaviour of the culture in which we are brought up. We shall return to these cultural variations shortly.

The role of reinforcement and punishment

Social learning theory states that we tend to imitate behaviour that is reinforced (or rewarded) but avoid imitating behaviour that is punished. These reinforcements and punishments can be quite subtle. In the case of reinforcers, they involve anything that is pleasant, and would include a feeling of well-being, of being loved or respected. In the case of punishments, they include anything unpleasant, such as a feeling of rejection or of discomfort. With respect to NVC, suppose you observed your parents smile at someone so you did the same and received a return smile, you would be likely to smile at that person (or, indeed, at other people) on other occasions. The opposite is true if you observed them being rejected: you would not imitate their behaviour, however subtle that rejection was.

Cultural differences in NVC

Before going on, read the section entitled 'Cultural norms and personal space' earlier in the chapter (page 115). As mentioned there, people from different cultures have very different social norms for how close they stand, how much touching they do, and so on. Hall (1966) studied cultural differences in personal space and distinguished between "contact" and "non-contact" cultures. Contact cultures are those in which there is a lot of social mixing, people enjoy the company of others and there is a lot of physical contact between them. These include many Mediterranean countries such as Italy and Spain, Latin American countries and many countries in the Middle East. In contrast, in non-contact cultures people are far more inclined to keep themselves to themselves and limit the amount of physical contact they have. These countries include Britain, other northern European countries and the United States. Unsurprisingly, these cultures have different notions of what is appropriate behaviour in terms of personal

Diversity

Research like this helps us to understand why people from some cultures may appear standoffish and snobby (as the British are often considered to be), and why others are considered to be "in your face".

space so their notions of what is reinforcing and what is punishing are also very different. When people from non-contact countries, such as Britain, visit a contact country, such as France, they often feel uncomfortable because a stranger might approach so closely that they touch them, breathe in their face and stare right in their eyes. These actions make the British person very uncomfortable and they are likely to instinctively move back and avoid eye contact. This, in turn, can be viewed by a French person as an attitude of stand-offishness and snobbery and they feel offended. Their different experiences of appropriate behaviour in terms of NVC can therefore lead to misunderstanding. This emphasises the important role that reinforcement and punishment have in NVC.

ACTIVITY 5.15

Investigate different greetings around the world. In Britain we traditionally shake hands or kiss but in other cultures there are different means of greeting people. Find out as many different ones as you can.

Criticisms of social learning theory of NVC

Social learning theory is useful in being able to account for cultural (and subcultural) differences in NVC. It follows that if behaviour is different between cultures then it must be learnt, not innate. However, there are many aspects of NVC that are *universal*, in other words, the same across the world. This includes the facial expression for certain emotions: happiness and sadness, for example, are recognised in all cultures, as mentioned earlier. Critics of the social learning theory of non-verbal communication argue that it underestimates the extent to which NVC is innate and "hard wired" into us and overemphasises the role of learning in such behaviour.

Evolutionary theory and NVC

In 1967 Desmond Morris wrote a controversial and fascinating book entitled *The Naked Ape* in which he pointed out the similarity between humans and apes and argued that much human behaviour is the result of evolution. This leads us on to an alternative approach to social learning as an explanation of NVC that comes from evolutionary theory. Evolutionary psychologists such as Morris point out that there are certain similarities between human and monkey NVC. The following are some of these similarities:

- certain facial expressions, especially in showing emotion
- the use of gaze as a social signal
- the use of touch in order to greet
- the use of the same gestures such as pointing and beckoning
- certain postures for dominance and submission.

Some human signals (e.g. smiling) are innate rather than learnt. We know this because as well as some of them appearing in apes and monkeys, they also appear in all cultures (however isolated) and in blind children who obviously cannot observe them. This implies that evolution plays at least some part in shaping human NVC.

Do these apes' facial expressions look similar to those a human would make?

Nevertheless, it is very important to emphasise that NVC is not entirely innate. We have already noted the cultural differences. In addition, although there are similarities between monkey and human NVC, there are also important differences. For example, from quite an early age children do not express their emotions in an automatic way but learn to control them. Furthermore, all of the NVC that occurs during speech is likely to be learnt by imitation rather than being innate since it is learnt from interaction with parents.

To sum up, NVC cannot entirely be accounted for by evolution, nor is it entirely learnt, and we need both social learning theory and evolution to give an explanation that best fits the evidence.

The following core study illustrates some of the important differences between Japanese and American NVC and how this has been expressed in modern forms of communication such as emoticons.

ACTIVITY 5.16

Draw up a table of the differences between social learning theory (SLT) and evolutionary theory in explaining NVC. Use two columns, one headed SLT and the other evolutionary theory, and list the evidence in favour of each (try to find three pieces for each). This is a good revision exercise.

OCR **A study into facial expressions**

OCR CORE STUDY: YUKI ET AL. (2007)

Aim: Yuki et al. wanted to see if there is any difference in the way in which Japanese and American people judge whether a face is happy or sad.

Method: Groups of Japanese and American students were asked to rate how happy or sad various computer-generated emoticons seemed to them (see the next page for some examples of emoticons).

The researchers then did the same using photographs of real faces that they manipulated in order to control the degree to which the eyes and mouth were happy, sad or neutral.

Results: The Japanese gave more weight to the emoticons' eyes when gauging emotions, whereas Americans gave more weight to the mouth. For example, American participants rated smiling emoticons with sad-looking eyes as happier than the Japanese participants did.
   Likewise with the photographs of real faces: the Americans looked to the mouth while the Japanese looked to the eyes.

Conclusion: The way we express emotion varies from culture to culture and therefore must, to a certain extent, be learnt rather than innate.

Limitations

- Obviously emoticons are only a very approximate representation of a real face. Since there are far more features in a real face than in an emoticon, the study does not necessarily tell us about other features that might be important in judging emotion in a face.
- Even with the photographs of real faces, there is no movement in the face at all and no cues from body language, so the viewer is forced to use only those limited cues to judge happiness or sadness. It's possible that with a real-life face the differences between Japanese and American individuals would not be so noticeable.
- Only students were used in this study so they may not be representative of the target population. It's possible, for example, that older people do not judge facial expressions in the same way.

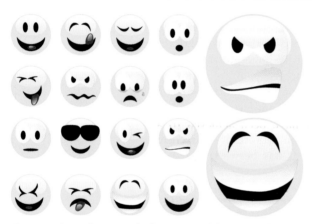

An emoticon is a symbol or a combination of symbols used to convey emotional content in written or message form

OCR How psychological research relates to social skills training

Social skills training as a treatment for offenders

Earlier in the chapter we learnt that from a very early age people acquire social skills such as making appropriate eye contact (not staring or not meeting someone's eye) and standing a certain distance from others. However, some people never acquire these skills and they make others very uncomfortable. Among the people who lack these skills are many offenders, and one of the programmes that is offered to some young offenders in particular is known as social skills training. This training is aimed at improving the ability to cope with ordinary social interactions.

   Some courses start by teaching certain non-verbal skills, known as micro-skills, such as eye contact, gesture and posture. It may seem strange that these skills need to be taught to adults but if they have not been learnt in childhood, then they will not come automatically. They are extremely important because people react quite negatively to those who lack these skills. Just think how you and others may react to someone who is stooped, who shuffles rather than walks, who doesn't make eye contact during a conversation, who stands too close, who stares, and so on.

Once these micro-skills have been learnt the course goes on to teach all-round skills such as how to maintain a good conversation, how to interact with members of the opposite sex or how to negotiate. The type of situation that might be practised is how to enter a room full of strangers, how to return faulty goods to a shop and courteously ask for a refund or exchange, how to politely refuse to get involved in a drinking binge when you've already had enough and how to say what you want to say without being embarrassed and "tongue-tied".

There are a variety of these programmes, all of which use the following basic techniques in order to teach people these basic skills. The common elements are that the skills are taught by a combination of:

- Modelling
- Instruction
- Role play
- Rehearsal.

Modelling involves an actor (or more than one actor) showing people how to behave in certain situations. Instruction involves being directly coached on what to do. Role play involves being placed in a certain situation (e.g. imagining you are being interviewed for a job or that you are going on a first date) and being advised about how to play the part. Rehearsal, as the name implies, involves rehearsing these skills until they have been achieved to a reasonable standard. The offenders then attempt to use these skills in various situations and receive feedback on their performance, the emphasis being on encouragement and praise rather than criticism.

The success of such programmes is not always easy to measure and is mixed. Spence et al. (1981) reported that several programmes improved the self-esteem of those taking part and gave them a feeling of greater control over their lives. However, other studies indicate that only about 10–15% of trainees could use these skills in real-life situations outside the training programmes. Nevertheless, 50% could do so once given additional help (Goldstein et al. 1989).

It would be fair to say that social skills training programmes appear to help people acquire these skills in the short term, but whether this helps them in the long term in the "real world" is less certain.

> **How psychology works**
>
> It may not seem obvious that this would be a useful exercise for offenders, but some of them have had an upbringing in which ordinary social skills that most people take for granted have not been learnt.

Chapter summary (Part 2)

- From Part 1 of this chapter:
  - Non-verbal communication can be defined as "those messages expressed by other than linguistic means". One type of NVC is known as paralinguistics, which involves the way something is said rather than what is said (the tone of voice, etc.). Other forms of NVC include eye contact, facial expression and body language.
  - Facial expressions convey many emotions including basic ones of surprise, fear, anger, disgust, happiness and sadness.

- Body language includes posture, gestures and touch. All of these convey information to others and affect our relationships. Argyle et al. (1971) concluded that non-verbal messages convey more information than the actual verbal content of the message, so if you say something friendly in a hostile manner, you will be seen as hostile.
- Social learning theory states that NVC is learnt by observation and imitation. Children imitate models, the most important of which are parents. They imitate NVC that they or others are rewarded for, but are unlikely to imitate NVC for which they or others receive disapproval (a form of punishment).
- There are considerable differences in NVC between cultures. Generally, cultures can be divided into "contact" or "non-contact". Contact cultures are those in which there is a lot of touching between people, while non-contact cultures engage in a lot less physical contact. These differences show that at least some aspects of NVC are learnt.
- Social learning theory of NVC has been criticised for overemphasising the role of learning, and for underestimating the importance of innate factors and the role of evolution in shaping our non-verbal behaviour.
- Evolutionary theorists believe that much NVC is innate and has evolved to best adapt us to the environment. In support of this, they point out similarities in the behaviour of apes and humans, and the similarity in the expression of certain emotions between cultures.
- The core study by Yuki et al. (2007) showed that there are important differences between the way Japanese and American people judge whether a face is happy or sad. Japanese people tend to judge by the eyes, whereas the Americans tend to judge by the mouth. This demonstrates the importance of learning in the expression and interpretation of NVC.
- Social skills training has been used to improve the NVC of offenders. The programmes include teaching micro-skills such as eye contact, gesture and posture, followed by teaching more all-round skills such as how to maintain a good conversation. They use modelling, instruction, role play and rehearsal in order to do this.

OCR Exam-style questions for OCR

1. a. Describe the research study of Yuki et al. (2007). Do this in terms of aim, method, results and conclusion. (4 marks) [OCR, 2008, Specimen Paper 2]
   b. Give **one** limitation of the Yuki et al. (2007) study. (1 mark)

2. a. Outline **one** criticism of the social learning theory of non-verbal communication. (2 marks)
   b. Outline the evolutionary approach as an alternative theory of non-verbal communication. (3 marks)

3. Describe **one** application of research into non-verbal communication. (4 marks)

Part 3

Biological psychology

Biological psychology is an approach to psychology that emphasises the role of biological factors such as genetics, evolution, and our body systems (physiology) in the study of behaviour. So, for example, it would investigate the relationship between a feeling of anxiety (a psychological response) and the bodily responses associated with such a feeling, including an increase in heart rate, sweating and trembling.

Chapter 6 • Sex and gender

We will look at the role of biology in explaining the differences in behaviour between boys and girls, men and women. We will then consider alternative, psychological explanations for gender differences. Included in this section is a consideration of androgyny – the tendency to show both personality traits associated with masculine behaviour and those associated with feminine behaviour. We will also investigate a condition known as gender dysphoria – a condition in which people are unhappy with their gender role and may, in some cases, wish to change sex.

Chapter 7 • Criminal behaviour

Criminal behaviour fascinates us and has been the topic of many television programmes and films. Real-life crime is also the mainstay of newspapers. In this chapter we consider research showing a link between certain criminal activities and biological processes such as brain disorders. We will also look at other possible causes of crime such as upbringing, and consider research into crime reduction.

What you need to know OCR

The specification lists the following things that you will need to be able to do for the examination:

- Distinguish between sex and gender
- Outline concepts of masculinity, femininity and androgyny
- Outline the role of chromosomes in typical gender development
- Outline the role of gonads and hormone production in typical gender development
- Describe basic evolutionary sex differences in human behaviour
- Explain the criticisms of the biological theory of gender development
- Consider psychoanalytical theory as an alternative theory with specific reference to the role of the Oedipus/Electra complex in gender development
- Describe and outline limitations of the Diamond and Sigmundson (1997) study
- Outline an application of research into sex and gender: Single-sex schooling

What you need to know AQA

The specification lists the following things that you will need to be able to do for the examination:

- Outline definitions of sex identity and gender identity and distinctions between them
- Describe biological differences between males and females (chromosomes and hormones)
- Outline and evaluate the psychodynamic theory of gender development including Oedipus and Electra
- Outline and evaluate the social learning theory of gender development including imitation, modelling and vicarious reinforcement
- Outline and evaluate the gender schema theory of gender development

as she feels that she has already been castrated. She is envious of her father's penis, hence this conflict happens during the *phallic stage*. In order to reduce her fears and envy, she then introjects her mother's personality and adopts many gender roles attached to being a female.

Critical thinking

Can you think of any aspects of Freud's theory or research that make it non-scientific?

EVALUATION

➕ Freud's study of a boy called Little Hans gives support to the theory. The boy had a fear of horses as they reminded him of his father. Once he had identified with his father by resolving the Oedipus conflict, the phobia disappeared and he began to act in a sex-typed way.

➖ As we are dealing with unconscious mechanisms, it is virtually impossible to test out the theory directly. This means it is unfalsifiable (cannot be shown to be incorrect) and unscientific. How can you test something out when you do not know where it is?

➖ There are alternative more plausible theories that can explain gender-appropriate behaviour, such as social leaning theory and gender schema theory, which have much more evidence.

EXAM HINT

If a question asks you about alternative *psychological* theories of gender development then it really does mean you have to mention a psychological theory. You cannot simply use the biological argument of testosterone, as this is not a purely psychological theory. You should use Freud and/or social learning theory.

AQA Social learning theory of gender

We can apply this theory to how we develop our gender identity.

ACTIVITY 6.8

Before reading on, can you remember some of the key terms linked to social learning theory? Can you use them to explain how we could develop our gender identity?

Remember the **ARRM approach to social learning** and the fact that we also **observe, imitate a role model** and may see **vicarious reinforcement**. All of these can be applied to the development of our gender identity.

Using the ARRM approach we can clearly explain how gender roles could be developed:

Attention
The child pays attention to the same-sex parent's behaviours and attitudes. This may be "accidental" (e.g. just happening to see Dad fixing a car or Mum baking) or motivated by the parent (e.g. Dad takes his son to the football or Mum takes her daughter shopping to the supermarket).

KEY TERMS

ARRM approach to social learning: the component processes involved in observational learning: Attention, Retention, Reproduction, Motivation.

Observation: watching people's reactions, responses, or behaviours.

Imitation of a role model: adopting the values, attitudes, and/or behaviours associated with a significant person. This can be a parent, a popular peer, or even a celebrity.

Vicarious reinforcement: learning through observing the consequences of a given behaviour when acted out by someone else.

Retention

After observing the same-sex parent, the child retains the information for future use. This may come out when the child is placed in a similar situation as to when they first paid attention to it.

Reproduction

The child has to be capable of reproducing the behaviour they paid attention to and retained. Sometimes this can be very difficult to do (e.g. fixing a car or using an oven). However, such behaviour can easily be acted out "safely" using games and toys. For instance, the boy can be bought a car that can be taken apart and rebuilt. Also, the girl can be given a toy kitchen to cook and prepare meals with.

Motivation

This can be both internal and external. Internal motivation can come from the child getting satisfaction from what they have done (e.g. taken the car apart and then rebuilt it successfully, or helping Mum make a cake). External motivation can come from the child being *reinforced* for showing gender-appropriate behaviour. This usually comes from the parents who praise the child for helping with the washing up or winning a football match. Remember that if the child observes their same-sex parent getting rewarded for gender-appropriate behaviour then this is a third type of reinforcement called *vicarious reinforcement*.

Therefore the idea is that we *imitate* the behaviour of a role model in terms of *modelling* their behaviour, and are more likely to do this if we see them getting a reward (given the term vicarious reinforcement).

ACTIVITY 6.9

Create your own examples of how a boy and a girl can learn one behaviour that is gender appropriate using SLT. Make sure you use terms like observe, imitate, and role model in your example.

Parents may play a major role in the development of sex-typed behaviour in their children

EVALUATION

➕ There is much evidence to suggest that we learn gender roles via social learning. For example, Fagot and Leinbach (1989) reported that parents do encourage **gender-typical** or gender-appropriate behaviour in children as young as 2 years, and Perry and Bussy (1979) demonstrated that children will even play with gender-neutral objects if a same-sex model does so beforehand.

➖ The theory cannot explain how some gender-appropriate behaviour that is shown in children appears spontaneous, that is, they show behaviour that they simply have *not* observed.

➖ Some psychologists believe that this theory portrays children as being passive and easily manipulated by models. Children are quite active in their behaviour and seek out new opportunities to learn rather than being shown what to do all the time.

> **How psychology works**
>
> With SLT and the biological approach to sex and gender there are clear ways to measure the variables (such as hormone levels or the role models offered to both sexes). The problem with the psychodynamic approach is that it is difficult to see whether such things as desire for the opposite-sex parent or penis envy really exist.
>
> This is one of the reasons why the psychodynamic approach is accused of being non-scientific.

AQA Gender schema theory

Bem (1981) then Martin and Halverson (1987) created another explanation for gender development that was different from the biological, psychoanalytical and social learning theories. *Schemas* or schemata are pockets of information that people have about certain things in the world. For example, we all have a schema for a tree and we can mentally picture one to help us understand the world and that it has trees in it. Martin and Halverson thought that we have gender schemas to help us understand the complex nature of sex and gender.

The gender schemas contain information similar to sex-typing: they are an organised set of beliefs about how each gender *should* behave. They help the child make sense of situations and make gender-appropriate decisions. These schemas develop in three stages:

- **Stage 1:** Initially children learn what things are associated with their own gender. This usually takes the form of toy choice, so then it can be used to decide on what to play with. In addition, the schema includes ways in which they should behave based on their own gender (e.g. boys should know how to use toy guns and girls should know how to brush the hair of their doll).
- **Stage 2:** A new type of schema begins to emerge at the age of 4 or 5 years old. The child begins to make links between existing schemas to allow a more complex understanding of the world. For example, they begin to register that boys who play with guns tend to make lots of noise and also like football. All of this is based on their own gender only.
- **Stage 3:** From around the age of 8 the final schemas begin to emerge. So far, all schemas have been based on their own gender in the first two stages. In this final stage, the child begins to formulate new schemas based on the opposite sex to get a more complete view of the world based on sex and gender.

> **KEY TERM**
>
> **Gender-typical behaviour:** any behaviour that is considered appropriate for males or for females, according to the cultural expectations of the society on upbringing.

Methodology

Sometimes psychologists cleverly use rather artificial conditions so that they can separate out the factors that influence children. In this case, if they had used conventional "gender" toys such as dolls, they would not have been able to tell whether the girls preferred them and the boys avoided them simply because that's what they were used to. By using "gender-neutral" toys and labelling them with a particular gender (which varied between conditions, so the same toy was sometimes for girls and sometimes for boys), they know that it is the label that affects the children and nothing else.

EVALUATION

➕ There is evidence to support the theory. For example, Bradbard et al. (1986) assigned gender to gender-neutral objects (so were told some were boy and some were girl objects). Children spent more time playing with the "gender-appropriate" objects. This also happened a week later when the children were re-tested. The objects had fitted into their gender schemas.

➖ As we have seen with social learning theory and the psychoanalytical approach to gender, parents are important in the development of gender. Gender schema theory ignores this.

➖ Some psychologists have noted that the theory does not explain why gender schemas develop in the way they do and why we need them to make sense of the world. The theory simply states that we have them.

OCR A study into psychosexual development

OCR CORE STUDY: DIAMOND AND SIGMUNDSON (1997)

This case study is a long-term follow-up of a child who underwent sex reassignment at birth.

Background to the case: The penis of an 8-month-old boy was accidentally damaged during an operation and he was then subsequently raised as a female. The literature at the time stated that the individual had developed into a normally functioning female. Standard medical texts and clinical advice had always advocated surgery to help a child develop psychosexually. According to these texts, the common theory is that it is easier to make a good vagina than a good penis. Therefore, if in doubt, conduct surgery to construct a vagina and raise the child as a girl. This is what happened to John (the name given to the child when he was a male) and Joan (the name given to the same child when she became anatomically female). This long-term follow-up attempted to assess if Joan was a normally functioning female.

The follow-up: *John* was interviewed along with his parents to see how *he* had developed after the reconstructive surgery to build a vagina. Diamond and Sigmundson wanted to investigate two ideas linked to the development of John and Joan: (1) individuals are psychosexually neutral at birth, and

(2) healthy psychosexual development is intimately related to the appearance of genitals.

(1) Individuals are psychosexually neutral at birth: One of the strongest memories reported by John's mother was post-surgery. She was told to treat him like a girl. But this was a disaster – as soon as she put a dress on Joan she ripped it off. At times Joan could act feminine, being neat and tidy. However, in one incident, she and her twin brother would rather mimic their father shaving than their mother applying make-up. Her mother tried to "correct" the behaviour but this was unsuccessful. Girl's toys, clothes and activities were mainly rejected by Joan; she had little interest in dolls or sewing. She was seen as a tomboy, playing soldiers and getting involved in rough and tumble play. Joan never liked the clothes she was expected to wear and never thought she looked like a girl physically. She had no friends and no one would play with her. Joan was expelled from school as one girl taunted her so much that Joan attacked her. Even though Joan had no penis she would still try to urinate standing up. At the age of 12, Joan was supposed to take oestrogen to feminise her. She would often throw away her daily dosage. At the age of 14 Joan told one of her doctors that she had suspected she was a boy for a long time. Her psychiatric team had noticed Joan's marked preference for male activities. Shortly after this, Joan decided to switch to living as a male. John recalls that all of a sudden everything clicked and he felt he finally understood who he truly was. She had a mastectomy at the age of 14 and phallus construction at the ages of 15 and 16. John adjusted well to being a boy and those girls who had taunted him for being Joan became sexually attracted to him! John was reluctant to have erotic moments with the girls and when one such girl gossiped about this it was she who was rejected as John's new, understanding, friends rallied to his support.

(2) Healthy psychosexual development is intimately related to the appearance of genitals: When Joan expressed feelings about not wanting to be a girl she was ridiculed by her therapists. She felt that she could not really argue with "doctors in white coats" so simply went along with the procedures. When she turned 7, Joan began to rebel about all things linked to the procedures. She continually felt embarrassed as she was forced to expose her vagina repeatedly in check-ups to make sure everything was all right and to see whether more repairs were needed. She had meetings with male-to-female **transsexuals** to convince her of the advantages of being a girl. After one such meeting when she was aged 13, Joan ran away from the hospital and was found hiding on a nearby roof. She always felt that the doctors were much more concerned about the appearance of her genitals than herself. Even after all this Joan knew she wasn't a girl. She kept trying to say this to her doctors but no one appeared interested. During middle school she had difficulty making friends and was often called cave man or gorilla. With continued therapy to help her generate a female identity, Joan kept thinking that she was being treated as a "freak". At the age of 14, Joan could take no more and

> **KEY TERM**
>
> **Transsexuals**: individuals who have a strong desire to be the opposite sex and undergo surgery to change their sex.

refused to live as a girl. She began to wear gender-neutral clothes like jeans and shirts and had night dreams about being a muscular man with a slick car and lots of friends. Inkblot tests showed that Joan was thinking more like a boy than a girl. She convinced local therapists that there had been a "mistake" and she underwent penile construction that was partially successful. John had his first sexual partner at the age of 18 and he now has a wife. He still cannot believe the narrow-mindedness of people for thinking that his entire personality was linked to the presence or absence of a penis.

Conclusion: It would appear that individuals are *not* psychosexually neutral at birth (so we cannot simply make them switch sex). Also, there is more to healthy psychosexual development than what genitals a person has. Diamond and Sigmundson also wanted to highlight the absolute necessity to have long-term follow-ups for cases like this as all of the initial (and only) documented evidence for this case was that the whole thing had been a success.

Limitations: As this is a case study of one boy it could be difficult to generalise to other children who have had similar experiences. There may be something unique about John and his experiences. Also, long-term follow-ups like this one have to rely on the participants' memories. These may not be as accurate as if they had been followed during the process (see Chapter 10 on memory and forgetting). Therefore, we cannot be fully sure that the recollection of key events happened as described in this case study. Finally, with interviews there may be interviewer bias, where questions are worded in a particular way to generate answers that researchers want to hear rather than what the participant truly wants to say. Some psychologists could criticise Diamond and Sigmundson for this as they were attempting to show that the procedures were not effective.

ACTIVITY 6.10

As you will be aware, there is no way in which you could write all of the Diamond and Sigmundson study in the examination. Therefore, try to summarise the study in no more than 10 sentences. You must be able to get the study across to a person who knows nothing about it. This is great examination practice!

OCR Application: Equal opportunities for the sexes

This section focuses on equal opportunities for the sexes in the classroom. Sadker and Sadker (1995) noted that girls tend to receive less attention and less encouragement from teachers compared with boys. This is seen when they ask boys more complex questions and listen to boys' responses for longer. However, some psychologists note these differences may be because of the boys themselves. That is, boys tend to be more assertive and disruptive and they will try to dominate the use of resources such as computers and science equipment, so the teacher has no choice but to pay more attention to them.

> **ACTIVITY 6.11**
>
> Before reading any further, get into pairs and create a school that should be able to cater for the needs of boys and girls. Think about the layout, resources needed and anything else you feel is necessary to educate boys and girls together. Can it be done? Have a look at the responses of your classmates. Are you designing the same thing or are there many differences?

If you found it difficult to create a school that could cater for boys and girls, then one option could be same-sex schooling. Therefore the rest of this application discusses the positives and negatives of such places. Lippa (2005) noted the following recommendations about educating boys and girls:

- *Boys*: Use after-school tutoring, create workshops to help boys with social skills and find ways for boys to channel aggression more effectively (e.g. sports leagues at lunchtime or after school).
- *Girls*: Create workshops to encourage maths and science, use field trips to expose girls to female role models and teach women's studies.

Theory behind differences in education
This could be about nature and nurture (nature – born with certain abilities; nurture – learn certain abilities through experience). If nature accounts for sex differences in education, then programmes at school should be tailored for each sex separately. If nurture accounts for sex differences in education, then programmes at school should account for this and change to reduce any differences (e.g. use of appropriate role models).

Is single-sex schooling the answer?
There is some evidence to suggest that all-girls schools do encourage more interest in maths and science. Also, girls experience more social support in their classes and these classes have better order and discipline. However, some psychologists argue that the girls who *choose* to attend same-sex schools bring about these effects rather than the school itself. Girls who choose same-sex schools tend to be better motivated, have higher academic abilities and have less interest in less academic social activities. Therefore it is difficult to assess if same-sex schooling is the cause of improved academic success.

Why psychology matters
In everyday life it is not always easy to see what particular factors influence a school to produce high achievers, but it is important that we look at these factors very carefully in order to try to maximise the potential of every child.

ACTIVITY 6.12

In small groups, design a study that assesses whether same-sex schooling brings about better academic and social abilities in its students. Think about how you would run this and take into account ethics.

So, what about the boys? Research shows that same-sex schools for boys provide higher levels of structure and discipline, which reduces behavioural problems. This could also be a result of boys not having to behave in such a way as to impress the girls in the class. However, being in a same-sex environment may just enhance things like toughness, hierarchies in terms of dominance and ingroup–outgroup conflict. Also, with boys being separated from girls, some research has shown that the boys are *more* likely to see girls as sex objects and not intellectually equal because they have not had sufficient interactions with girls at school.

Overall, it appears difficult to conclude whether same-sex schooling is an equal opportunity for both sexes to be educated positively. Some psychologists see it as an opportunity to get the best out of children, while others believe it is a wasted opportunity to encourage interactions between the sexes. You decide!

Chapter summary

- Sex refers to the biological status of a person, while gender refers to the psychological status of a person.
- Masculinity refers to the behaviours and ideas that are considered to be a characteristic of being male. It is an example of sex typing.
- Femininity refers to the behaviours and ideas that are considered to be a characteristic of being female. It is also an example of sex typing.
- Androgyny refers to a set of behaviours that include high levels of both masculine and feminine characteristics.
- The chromosomes that make a female are XX. For males they are XY. People also have sex hormones – for males this is testosterone and for females it is oestrogen.
- Basic evolutionary differences between the sexes can be based on mate selection, aggression and ability to care for children.
- One explanation for gender development is from Freud. Males go through an Oedipus complex whereby they take on their father's roles and ideas to gain the affections of their mother. Females go through the same process, but Jung called it the Electra complex. They wish to gain the affections of their father so adopt the mother's roles and ideas.
- Another explanation is social learning theory. A child pays attention to the same-sex parent's behaviours, retains the information in memory, and decides to reproduce that behaviour but only when motivated to do so.
- A further explanation is gender schema theory. The gender schemas (mental representations of things) contain information similar to sex typing: they are an organised set of beliefs about how each gender *should* behave. They help the child to make sense of situations and make gender-appropriate decisions.
- Diamond and Sigmundson (1997) reported on the case of John–Joan. During an operation John's penis was damaged and it was decided to

turn him into a girl and construct a vagina. Originally it was reported that everything was fine and Joan was happy being Joan. However, this follow-up revealed that Joan had never really been happy being a female and wanted to be a man again. This happened after reconstructive surgery and now John is living happily as a male.

• One application of research into sex and gender is same-sex schooling. This is about equal opportunities in education, and some psychologists believe that we can only achieve this via single-sex schooling. There is some evidence to suggest that children do achieve more in single-sex schools, but other psychologists argue that it just promotes more *issues* between the sexes.

OCR Exam-style questions for OCR

1. Define the term androgyny. (2 marks)

2. Outline how hormones play a role in typical gender development. (3 marks)

3. Outline **one** criticism of the biological approach theory of gender development. (2 marks)

4. What is the Oedipus complex? How is it related to gender development? (3 marks)

5. Outline **two** things about the Diamond and Sigmundson (1997) case study. (4 marks)

6. Outline **one** limitation of the Diamond and Sigmundson (1997) case study. (2 marks)

7. You will have studied an application of research into sex and gender. Describe and assess the application. (6 marks)

AQA Exam-style questions for AQA

1. Define gender identity. (2 marks)

2. What is the chromosome difference between males and females? (2 marks)

3. What is the Oedipus complex? (2 marks)

4. In social learning what is meant by the terms (a) modelling and (b) vicarious reinforcement? (4 marks)

5. Describe and evaluate the gender schema theory of gender development. (6 marks)

What you need to know OCR

The specification lists the following things that you need to be able to do for the examination:

■ Outline the problems of defining and measuring crime

■ Explain the concept of a criminal personality

■ Explain the role of heritability in criminal behaviour

■ Explain the role of brain dysfunction in criminal behaviour

■ Describe the facial features associated with criminals

■ Explain the criticisms of the biological theory of criminal behaviour

■ Consider social learning theory as an alternative theory

■ Describe Mednick et al.'s (1984) adoption study into the genetic basis of criminal behaviour

■ Outline the limitations of Mednick et al.'s study

■ Explain how psychological research relates to crime reduction

Criminal behaviour 7

Stephen "Tony" Mobley has all the attributes of a natural born killer. Nobody could blame his upbringing – he came from an affluent, white, middle-class American family and he was not abused or mistreated as a child. Yet as he grew up he became increasingly violent, and at the age of 25 he walked into a pizza store and casually shot the manager in the neck after robbing the till and joking that he would apply for the job vacancy when the man was dead.

That was in 1991. Now Mobley is waiting on Death Row in Georgia to hear whether his appointment with the electric chair is to be confirmed. His last chance of a reprieve rests with a plea from his lawyer that the murder was not the evil result of free will but the tragic consequence of a genetic predisposition. The genes of Tony Mobley, his lawyers argue, meant he was born to kill.

"There is no legal defence to his crime," says Daniel Summer, Mobley's attorney. "There is only the mitigating factor of his family history. His actions may not have been a product of totally free will. Murder, rape, robbery, suicide, 'you name it', the Mobley family has had it," he says.

There is nothing new about the notion that criminals are born rather than made; it has cropped up repeatedly over the past century in the continuing debate over nature versus nurture.

Over the past 10 to 15 years, new techniques in molecular biology have enabled scientists to identify specific inherited defects in DNA, the genetic blueprint. One of the most startling pieces of research into the genetics of violence has come out of the Department of Human Genetics at the University Hospital in Nijmegen. This was the work that inspired the unusual plea of mitigation from Tony Mobley's lawyers.

The scientists at Nijmegen studied the apparent inherited aggression of the Dutch family. Han Brunner, who led the research team has, however, distanced himself from suggestions that he has found a "gene for aggression". "The notion of an 'aggression gene' does not make sense," he says, "and it would be wrong to suggest that any one gene or collection of genes can account for something as complex as aggressive human behaviour." He emphasises that his research has only demonstrated how a very specific genetic defect can result in a fairly specific behavioural abnormality in one particular family, not society at large. The family spanned four generations and almost a century in time. He found that at various times 14 men in the family had displayed mental retardation combined with unusually aggressive posturing, verbal abuse and sometimes physical violence.

However, other work directly contradicts these findings. Such contradictions serve to reinforce the difficulties of explaining complex emotions in biological terms.

Even if there does appear to be a genetic basis to some types of behaviour that lead to criminality, psychologists are almost unanimous in their belief that it does not mean some children are doomed to a life of crime. "Just because it's genetic it doesn't mean to say it's not amenable to environmental intervention," says a clinical psychologist. "If weapons are available and you have kids with, say, attention deficit disorder, it's a set-up. You're setting up a situation to happen."

Nevertheless, some psychologists may be persuaded that cold-blooded murderers such as Tony Mobley can have a genetic predisposition to violence and antisocial behaviour which they are born with.

Stephen Mobley was eventually executed by lethal injection at the Georgia Diagnostic and Classification Prison in Jackson, Georgia on March 1st, 2005.

ACTIVITY 7.1

Imagine you are a member of a small group in charge of people who are stranded on an island, living in a basic way while you wait to be rescued. It is up to the group to decide on a list of behaviours that you will consider criminal. Discuss the reasons why you choose some actions and not others.

Results: The adoptees whose parents were persistent offenders were also more likely to be arrested repeatedly as adults than those whose biological parents had clean records.

The percentage of crimes committed by the adoptees was higher if both their biological and their adoptive parents were criminals.

Conclusion: The researchers concluded that genetic factors did contribute to criminal behaviour. However, they did not believe they were the only cause. The fact that the likelihood of adopted children being criminal was increased if both their adoptive and biological parents were criminal indicated that environmental factors also have an effect on criminality.

Adoption studies seek to distinguish between genetic and environmental factors, such as the type of neighbourhood the family lived in, in determining the influences of criminal behaviour

Limitations of Mednick et al.'s (1984) study

- There was no account taken of the neighbourhood in which the adopted children grew up. If they grew up in a similar environment to their biological parents, then it is possible that environment rather than genetics was responsible for their behaviour.
- Some of the adopted children may have spent some time with their biological parents in early life and this could have influenced them.
- If the family who adopted the children knew they came from a criminal family, they may have treated them in such a way that increased the likelihood of them becoming criminal. They could, for example, have assumed that if anything wrong happened the child was responsible, and accuse them. This, in turn, could lead to resentment and the child becoming "bad" in response (known as a self-fulfilling prophecy).
- It is possible that some of the adoptive parents had a criminal record before adopting children and kept this hidden. It may be this that influenced the children rather than their biological parents.

OCR Brain dysfunction

The work of Raine et al. (1997) is covered in Chapter 13. *This study is very important, so make sure you read it before going any further*. They found that the murderers in their study who were pleading guilty by reason of insanity had less activity than the controls in the prefrontal cortex, an area linked to self-control. They also found differences in the amygdala, which is one of the structures in the brain that helps control violent behaviour.

Of course this study only looks at a relatively small number of people who have committed one type of crime (and who are pleading insanity), so the findings do not generalise to all types of crime or even to all murderers.

EXAM HINT

For this section make sure you can summarise Raine et al. (1997) in terms of Aim, Method, Findings, Conclusion.

OCR Criticisms of the biological theory of criminal behaviour

• The main problem with biological theories is that they do not take account of environmental factors. Other factors almost certainly have an influence. These include:

  • Socialisation: The way you are brought up within the family and the values you are given.
  • The culture and subculture: The values transmitted by influences other than the family, such as the school, peer group and area in which you live.

• The studies supporting the biological approach have been criticised. Walters (1992) has analysed a fairly large number of family studies (including adoption studies) and found a small relationship between crime and genes, but a greater one between environment and crime. He points out that some of the older studies were quite poorly designed.

Biological factors may play a part in crime, but they can never totally account for it. Even if some individuals have a genetic temperament that makes them aggressive, impulsive and inconsiderate, these personality characteristics can be, and usually are, channelled into legal activities depending on the environment. If the environment discourages criminal activities, then such individuals will be unlikely to commit crimes. On the other hand, if the environment is one in which, for example, there is poor discipline, violence, poverty and a chaotic family life, then a criminal lifestyle becomes more probable in those whose genes dispose them to be aggressive and impulsive. It is necessary to look at the *interaction* between biology and the environment in order to get a fuller understanding of the causes of crime.

We will now look at an alternative theory, that of social learning theory, in order to consider a very different approach to explaining criminal behaviour.

OCR Social learning theory and crime

Social learning theory was considered in Chapter 4. It would be useful to read this before we go on to look at how it explains criminal behaviour.

Bandura (1963), the founder of social learning theory, believed that people, especially young children, observe behaviour and imitate it, especially if it is the behaviour of powerful role models such as parents, same-sex peers (friends), older same-sex siblings and the media.

Not all behaviour or all role models are imitated. One of the factors that makes behaviour more likely to be imitated is if the role models are seen to be reinforced (rewarded) for their behaviour. The process of being indirectly reinforced is known as **vicarious reinforcement**. Vicarious reinforcement involves learning by watching other people being rewarded rather than being rewarded directly. This means that if one child sees, for example, a child snatch an attractive toy from another child and get away with it, he or she may well do the same. The behaviour of snatching a toy has been seen to be rewarded because the child now has the toy, and this increases the likelihood that other children will copy. If criminal and/or violent behaviour is seen to be rewarded, then children are likely to copy it. On the other hand, if it is seen to be punished it is unlikely to be copied. This process is known as **vicarious punishment** and it discourages crime.

In addition, children will copy acts that they are themselves directly rewarded for. If they watch someone stealing and they do the same and get away with it, they are likely to do it again. The converse is obviously true: if they get caught and punished, they are far less likely to carry on doing it. Obviously when crimes are committed one of the main reinforcers is material gain – if you steal something and get away with it, you keep what you've stolen. It is important to note, however, that admiration, attention and respect are also powerful reinforcers and those people who are admired and feared within their group for being criminal gain from this as well.

This theory easily accounts for why crime may run in families. The children of criminals see a powerful role model (their father, or, less often, their mother) commit a crime, and copy it, especially if the parent is a respected or feared member of the local community who is obeyed by others.

ACTIVITY 7.4

With respect to criminal or antisocial behaviour, think of three of each of the following:

• Direct reinforcements
• Vicarious reinforcements
• Direct punishments
• Vicarious punishments

You could use a variety of types of crime and think about why they are committed. Is it for direct reinforcement (such as money) or because of vicarious reinforcement (such as following a successful gang member)? You could also use TV crime programmes to get some ideas.

OCR Application of research into criminal behaviour: Crime reduction

Every society wants to prevent and reduce crime, and has laws in place to punish criminals. In this section, we will consider ways in which crime can be prevented or reduced.

If we take the extreme view that crime is biological in origin, then there is little that can be done to reduce crime or to prevent it other than sterilise criminals (so they cannot produce children) or imprison them for life. There is a history of sterilisation in many countries including the USA, but in modern society this is not considered desirable or necessary. As mentioned already, most researchers into criminal behaviour agree that the environment interacts with biology to produce criminal behaviour, so we need to look at how programmes of rehabilitation and of punishment can reduce the likelihood that people will reoffend.

The prospect of being imprisoned for a crime serves as a vicarious punishment, and thereby a deterrent

Imprisonment

Imprisonment is one way of coping with crime. Prisons serve a variety of purposes:

- They *punish* criminals by depriving them of their liberty.
- They *deter* the criminals themselves and others from reoffending. If this puts off others from committing crimes it serves as a form of vicarious punishment.
- They *prevent* the criminals reoffending during the time they are in prison.
- They provide *rehabilitation* – education, training and treatment to restore offenders to a useful life on the "outside".

How effectively do they do this? Unfortunately, being in prison can have some very unwanted effects. It teaches the young new ways of offending and is often a hotbed of aggression and serious bullying. Some research indicates that for many offenders, especially first-time ones, probation is better at preventing reoffending than is prison. This is not, however, true for people who have committed a series of offences (Glaser 1983).

> **Everyday life**
> It is important to recognise that prisons may not always prevent crime; there are circumstances in which they may increase the likelihood of individuals continuing to offend because of the role models, examples and "advice" provided by other prisoners that affect young offenders. It is therefore desirable to use programmes such as the Token Economy so prisoners are not only "rewarded" for antisocial behaviour but for appropriate behaviour as well.

Behaviour modification

Behaviour modification is another way of tackling crime, both to prevent and to reduce it. Behaviour modification involves using the theories of learning to change behaviour, and has been used in many real-life settings. We will now consider ways it can be used with criminals (and will consider its use further in Chapter 12). Many behaviour modification programmes in prisons and young offenders' institutions depend on a technique called the **token economy**. This works on a fairly simple basis of rewarding good behaviour. Every time a prisoner (or young offender) shows desirable behaviour, such as cooperation or doing as they're told, they are given a token. Tokens can be collected and exchanged for rewards such as leisure activities, sweets, passes home. The system is quite successful at controlling behaviour within the institution; whether it improves behaviour in the long term in the outside world is less certain.

> **KEY TERMS**
>
> **Behaviour modification:** involves using the theories of learning to change behaviour.
>
> **Token economy:** a method of behaviour shaping that rewards appropriate (desired) behaviours with secondary reinforcers (tokens) that can be collected and exchanged for primary reinforcers (something that is wanted).

Short sharp shock

A system based very much on punishment rather than reward is a "short sharp shock" regime for young offenders, based on the belief that a short, highly unpleasant custodial sentence will "shock" young offenders and deter them from committing future crimes. A Home Office Report in 1984 reported that these regimes were no better or worse than any other regime at influencing behaviour once the offenders were released, and the same applies in the US.

Some psychologists believe that this is because young offenders often come from very chaotic, unpleasant, unloving and abusive environments, and they need to learn new behaviours and ways of responding to provocation if their behaviour is to become more socially acceptable. Learning theory states that punishment may decrease the likelihood of certain behaviours occurring, but does not teach new ways of behaving. If people who do not know alternative ways of responding are punished harshly for their behaviour this simply increases anxiety and frustration and can be counter-productive.

> **EXAM HINT**
>
> If answering questions on crime reduction/ prevention using the learning approach, make sure you use psychological language (such as behaviour modification, token economy, vicarious punishment, secondary reinforcement). This is the only way you will get full credit for your answer.

Chapter summary

- Crime can be defined as anything that is forbidden by the criminal justice system, in other words, any behaviour that breaks the law. There is no agreed way in which a society decides what should be criminal, but age and intention are taken into account. One way of deciding is by the consensus view – that a behaviour is considered a crime if the majority of people believe it should be.
- Crime is measured in two ways:

  - Police records.
  - Information from surveys of householders asking them about being victims of crime.

  Police records can be inaccurate because:

  - Crimes are not reported because they are considered too trivial.
  - Crimes are not reported because the victims are afraid.
  - Crimes are not detected.

  Survey information can be inaccurate because:

  - People may have forgotten.
  - People may be too embarrassed to say.
  - People may not tell the truth.
  - Some crimes are not detected.
  - Only household and personal crimes are included.

- Biological explanations of the causes of crime include the idea that crime is inherited. Family studies do indicate that crime runs in families, but this could be a result of upbringing.
- Adoption studies are useful in that children are not brought up by their biological parents, so it separates out the influence of genes from the influence of upbringing. The study of Mednick et al. (1984) supports the view that genes do influence criminal behaviour, but also demonstrates that the family upbringing also has some influence.
- Brain dysfunction is another biological explanation of crime. Raine et al. (1997) conducted brain scans of murderers and found dysfunction in the prefrontal cortex or the amygdala of the brain. This study does not necessarily indicate that crimes other than murder are caused by brain dysfunction.

- Biological explanations of crime can be criticised on the grounds that the evidence in favour of them is not always convincing, and because they underestimate environmental factors such as upbringing.
- An alternative to biological theories in explaining criminal behaviour is social learning theory. This states that if children see criminal behaviour in role models such as fathers, older siblings and media figures, they are liable to imitate it. They are particularly likely to imitate behaviour that is vicariously reinforced, that is, reinforced in the role model.
- Ways of reducing, controlling and preventing crime include the use of prisons, behaviour modification programmes (including the token economy) and short sharp shock.

OCR Exam-style questions for OCR

1. (a) Briefly define what is meant by the term "crime". (1 mark) [OCR, 2008, Specimen Paper 2]

   (b) Outline **two** problems of defining crime. (2 marks)

2. Discuss the role of heritability in explaining criminal behaviour. (4 marks)

3. Describe how social learning theory accounts for criminal behaviour. (4 marks)

4. Describe and evaluate Mednick et al.'s (1984) study into the genetic basis of criminal behaviour. (10 marks)

Part 4

Developmental psychology

Developmental psychology looks at the way people change as they get older. Developmental psychologists aim to describe how children and adults develop, and to explain why they develop as they do. They look at the influence of factors such as our genes, our experiences, and the environment we live in. In this section we will focus on children's social development and how they form their first relationships. We will also look at how their mental abilities develop to be able to process increasingly complex information as they get older.

Chapter 8 • Attachment

We will look at how and why an infant bonds with their caregiver and what the effects are if a child does not have an opportunity to form this bond.

Chapter 9 • Cognitive development

We will examine the work of the psychologist Piaget who identified the stages of development in mental processes that all children seem to follow. We will also consider an alternative theory of cognitive development – that of Vygotsky. In addition, we will look at the ways in which the work of these two theorists has influenced educational practice in schools.

What you need to know OCR

The specification lists the following things that you will need to be able to do for the examination:

- Key concepts
  - Describe separation protest and stranger anxiety as measures of attachment
  - Distinguish between different types of attachment: secure, insecure-avoidant, insecure-ambivalent.
- Core theory: Bowlby's theory
  - Explain the concept of monotropy
  - Explain the concept of a critical period in attachment
  - Describe the effects of attachment, deprivation and privation
  - Explain the criticisms of Bowlby's theory of attachment
  - Consider behaviourist theory as an alternative theory, with specific reference to reinforcement in attachment as opposed to instinct
- Core study: Hazan and Shaver (1987)
  - Describe Hazan and Shaver's survey of the relationship between attachment types and adult relationships
  - Outline limitations of Hazan and Shaver's study.
- Application of research into attachment: Care of children
  - Explain how psychological research relates to care of children, e.g. dealing with separation in nurseries, encouraging secure attachments through parenting classes, dealing with stranger anxiety in hospitalised children

Attachment

8

The following is a true account of what can happen when attachments are disrupted in early life. Only names have been changed.

Lesley was the daughter of Val and David who were both from middle-class backgrounds and had met at university. Just before her finals Val discovered she was pregnant and she and David decided to marry. Because of a shortage of money they lived with David's mother and sister, both of whom helped with childcare. Val took a few part-time jobs but decided not to pursue a career until Lesley was older. When Val was working, Lesley was looked after within the family and was greatly loved.

When Lesley was 2½ years old, David and Val separated. Val could not afford to live alone with Lesley. She was persuaded (mainly by David's mother and sister) to leave Lesley with David in the mother's home so her home and carer arrangements could have some continuity. It soon became apparent that Lesley's main attachment was to her grandmother and that she felt unhappy when separated from her.

About 6 months later, David's new girlfriend Mary, who was pregnant, moved into the mother's house. She and Lesley virtually ignored each other; Lesley continued to be cared for by her grandmother with the help of the aunt. She saw Val intermittently but did not like leaving her grandma's house to visit her. Val was now leading her own life and as long as Lesley was well cared for and loved, she saw no reason to disrupt this arrangement. They were virtually strangers now. Within a year, David and Mary bought a house some distance from David's mother's home and even further from Val's. Lesley went to live there; it was not an arrangement that anyone was happy with but no one discussed it.

It was then that serious problems started. Lesley changed almost overnight from a contented, easy-going child into a desperately unhappy aggressive one. She hated Mary, whom she saw as responsible for removing her from all she knew and loved, and simply would not cooperate. As Mary commented, it was hard to believe that a 4-year-old could be so difficult. Lesley missed her grandmother, and Mary, pregnant again, was concerned only for her own son and the new baby. Lesley's behaviour became so uncontrolled that she was rejected by two nursery schools and the teacher at her new primary school could not control her. The other parents complained and the local authority stepped in. Lesley was sent to a boarding school, which she hated. She also hated school holidays, which were spent at David and Mary's. The relationship Lesley had with her three brothers from her father's second marriage was very poor.

When Lesley was 12, David left this marriage to live with another woman who had two small children. Lesley was faced with a dilemma – who to stay with in school holidays. She knew that David's third wife did not want her nor, in truth, did her father, so she continued going to Mary's house. They had an uneasy relationship but Mary felt guilty about what had happened to her step-daughter and tried to be supportive. Lesley, on her part, wanted some familiarity in her life. On her 16th birthday she took an overdose of painkillers. She was found in time and offered counselling, but her problems were by now far too deep-seated to be sorted out easily. Lesley lived with Mary and had a series of boyfriends, all of whom she treated badly. Eventually she moved out and lived alone, suffering from serious bouts of depression. At 25 she deliberately got pregnant, thinking that if she had a baby to love, all would be well. It wasn't. She feels guilty, but she doesn't love the baby and his crying drives her mad. It's beginning to look as though her problems of attachment, rooted in her early childhood, will continue on to the next generation.

ACTIVITY 8.1

Gather in groups of four to six, mixed in terms of boys and girls if possible, to discuss the following:

It is 1941, 2 years after the start of the Second World War. You are a married couple living in London, which is being heavily bombed. You regularly have to go into the air-raid shelters and the situation is frightening. The husband has been conscripted into the army, so he is away a good deal. You have three children: a girl aged 8, a boy aged 6, and a boy aged 11 months. The government is encouraging everyone to have their children evacuated and, in your case, they would go to Wales. The arrangement is as follows: all the children will live in the same family and the authorities will ensure that they are well fed, clothed, cared for, and educated. You can send any or none of the children. Once they are there, you are permitted one visit for a weekend every month (no more). Although it is for a weekend, with travelling etc. you will be with the children for approximately 24 hours. Obviously you have no idea when the war will end, but certainly there is no end in sight at present.

The task: As a group, you must come to a unanimous decision as to which, if any, of the children you will allow to be evacuated. Discuss the reasons for your decision and let everyone have a say. Once your decision has been made, consider its effect on all of the children, whether or not they have been evacuated. For example, if you decide to send the older two but not the baby, what effect might this have on sibling relationships once the family is reunited?

Once the groups have made a decision, discuss the topic as a class.

In this chapter we will look at the early relationships that children form and the effect these have on them in later life.

OCR The development of attachment

Anyone who has had anything to do with a young baby will be aware that babies are extremely **sociable** beings right from birth. They stare intently at human faces (particularly when being fed), they smile from about 6 weeks of age and they crave human company. If they do not receive much human attention they will not thrive, however well they are fed and otherwise cared for.

Babies appear to have an inborn tendency to enjoy the company of others

Babies appear to have an **innate** (inborn) tendency to be sociable, that is, to enjoy the company of others and to be willing to engage in social interaction. Sociability is shown by the following behaviour of babies:

- crying in order to attract attention;
- turning their heads towards human speech and moving their head and arms to the rhythm of speech;
- staring intently at faces.

Infants start life by being happy to interact with anyone who pays them attention. By age 6 weeks they begin to smile. At first they will smile at anyone but by about 3 months they will smile more and generally be more friendly towards familiar people than towards unfamiliar ones. However, they are not distressed by strangers.

A milestone occurs at around 8–9 months when this behaviour changes quite suddenly. Children now get very distressed if their primary caregiver figure (who we will call "mother" for convenience sake, but who is not necessarily the mother) leaves the room and they cannot see her. They will cry and, if they are mobile, will crawl towards the door through which she left. This distress on being parted from their main attachment figure is known as **separation protest**. They also become very wary of strangers. If a stranger tries to interact with them while they are with the mother, they will ignore them or look away. If they are approached by a stranger when they are within the vicinity of the mother, they will move towards her quickly. If they are unable to crawl, they will put out their hands for her. This wariness of unfamiliar people is called **stranger anxiety**. These two behaviour patterns – separation protest and stranger anxiety – are indications that the first specific attachment has occurred. These behaviours get more intense as the child gets older and will

KEY TERMS

Sociability: the human desire to seek companionship with others.

Innate: characteristics that are natural rather than learnt and are present at birth, although they may not become active until later life.

Separation protest: the distress that young children experience when they are separated from their primary caregiver.

Stranger anxiety: the distress that young children experience when they are exposed to people who are unfamiliar to them.

peak at around 18 months. These stages of attachment are shown in the table opposite.

OCR What is attachment?

An attachment is a *long-enduring, emotionally meaningful tie to a particular individual* (Schaffer, 1996).

Attachments in young children have the following characteristics:

1. They are *selective* – they are directed towards specific individuals who are preferred above all others.
2. They involve the *desire to be near* the person they are attached to.
3. They provide *comfort* and *security* and are particularly important when the child is upset, ill, or tired.
4. They involve *separation protest* – the child gets really upset if they become separated from the person to whom they are attached.

SCHAFFER AND EMERSON (1964)

There has been an enormous amount of research done on attachment (much of it in Britain). One of the major studies by Schaffer and Emerson (1964) is as follows:

Aim: Schaffer and Emerson wanted to study the attachment behaviour of a group of infants from their early life (this varied from 5 weeks old to 23 weeks) until they were 18 months old.

Method: This was a *naturalistic observation* (an observation study in an everyday setting) of 60 children from working-class homes in Glasgow. The researchers visited the infants' homes every 4 weeks until they were a year old and then again when they were 18 months old. Mothers were also asked to keep records of the children's behaviour.

Results: The infants all followed the same stages of attachment, which are shown in the table opposite. Important observations were:

- By about 7 months most of them were showing separation protest and stranger anxiety, indicating that they had formed a *specific attachment*.
- The person with whom the child formed the first attachment was the one who appeared most responsive to their needs; for example, the one who would offer comfort if they were upset. It was not necessarily the person who fed the child or the one who spent most time with them.
- By 18 months of age, the vast majority (52 of the 60) showed multiple attachments and 20 had attachments to five or more people, such as their father, grandparents, and older brothers and sisters.

Conclusion: Children usually develop attachments to more than one person, although the first attachment is to one particular individual. Children appear to attach to those people who are most responsive to their needs.

Methodology

A naturalistic observation provides data (information) that are very high in ecological validity because the observation is done in the natural environment (in this case in the children's own home).

Stages of attachment

Based on the research they had done, Schaffer and Emerson suggest that attachment takes place in the stages shown in the table below (the ages are just a rough guide, they will vary from child to child).

Stages of attachment		
Stage	**Age**	**Response**
Asocial phase	0–6 weeks	Very young infants smile and cry but not at any special individuals.
Stage of indiscriminate attachments	6 weeks to 7 months	Infants greatly enjoy human company. They smile more at people than at lifelike objects such as puppets (Ellsworth et al., 1993). They get upset when an adult stops interacting with them, regardless of who the adult is. From about 3 months, however, they smile more at familiar than unfamiliar faces and are more easily comforted by a regular caregiver than by a stranger.
Stage of specific attachment – the first true attachment	7–9 months	Infants show two main signs that they formed a specific attachment to one person: stranger anxiety and separation protest.
Stage of multiple attachments	10 months onwards	Children begin to be attached to others, such as grandparents, siblings, and other regular caregivers. By 18 months, the majority of infants have formed multiple attachments.

OCR Individual differences: Insecure and secure attachment

The Strange Situation studies

Once the concept of an attachment bond had been suggested, researchers began to look at how attachment behaviour varies between children and how these individual differences arise. One particular researcher, Mary Ainsworth, investigated attachment behaviour using a set-up known as the "Strange Situation". This is a situation in which a mother and a child are placed in an unfamiliar room containing interesting toys and observed through a one-way mirror. After a short while a stranger enters and soon after that the mother leaves. The mother then returns and the stranger leaves. The mother then leaves again, so the child is now alone. The mother then returns. At all stages the reactions of the child are recorded carefully by observers. This method, in which behaviour is recorded in a very controlled setting, is known as a **controlled observation** (or structured observation). The exact procedure is shown in the table below.

The Strange Situation procedure	
Episode	What happens
1	The mother (or caregiver) takes the infant into the laboratory room and sits quietly in a chair. She does not interact with the infant unless the child tries to attract her attention.
2	A stranger enters, talks to the mother and then approaches the baby with a toy.
3	The mother leaves quietly without drawing attention to herself. If the infant does seem bothered, the stranger tries to interact by talking to him or her and playing. If the child shows distress, the stranger attempts to comfort him or her.
4	The mother returns and greets the infant. The stranger leaves. The mother tries to get the infant to play, then leaves, waving and saying "bye-bye".
5	The baby is left alone.
6	The stranger enters and interacts with the infant, offering comfort if the child is upset or a toy if the child is passive.
7	The mother returns, greets the infant and picks him/her up. The stranger leaves quietly.

KEY TERMS

Controlled observation: an observational research method carried out in conditions in which the researcher has some control, such as a laboratory or a specially designed room. This is also called a structured observation.

Secure attachment: a style of attachment that is formed when caregivers respond sensitively to the infant's needs.

Secure base: a concept formulated by John Bowlby to describe the role of the primary caregiver as being a "safe" point to which the child can return when feeling anxiety, fear, or distress.

The measures taken during the Strange Situation are as follows:

1. The infant's willingness to explore and play with new toys.
2. Stranger anxiety – the response of the child to the stranger.
3. Separation protest – the response of the child when the mother leaves.
4. Reunion behaviour – how the child reacts when the mother returns.

Ainsworth found considerable differences in these measures between children and, on the basis of this, she classified attachment into three types:

• **Secure attachment** infants happily explore the new toys when their mother is with them and they use her as a **secure base** for exploration. When the stranger appears, the child moves closer to the mother but will carry on exploring the environment while keeping a wary eye on the stranger. As long as Mum is there, they feel safe. They show distress when the mother leaves and are delighted to see her when she returns. Their distress quickly disappears and they cuddle contentedly with her. They clearly prefer her over the stranger. This is considered to be the optimal (best) form of attachment.

The concept of a secure base is an important one. It provides children with the security they need to venture forth and learn about the world. In everyday life this might be seen by the child scrambling down from the caregiver's lap to play with a toy, but every now and then looking back and sometimes returning for a hug.

- **Insecure-ambivalent attachment** (sometimes referred to as insecure-resistant attachment) children do not explore the new toys with such confidence. Compared to secure infants, they remain closer to their mother, showing signs of insecurity even in her presence, such as clinging behaviour. They become very distressed when she leaves. When she returns they may cling to her but show ambivalent (mixed) reactions such as hitting her while still clinging. They are clearly angry and anxious. She does not provide a secure base.
- **Insecure-avoidant attachment** children show very little or no reaction when the mother leaves them or when she comes back. They are unconcerned about a stranger being there and show little, if any, preference for the mother over the stranger, often avoiding both.

In studies in the USA, Ainsworth et al. found approximately 65% of children were securely attached, 21% were insecure-avoidant and 14% were insecure-ambivalent.

> ### KEY TERMS
>
> **Insecure-ambivalent attachment**: an insecure attachment style characterised by behaviours such as clinging to the primary caregiver and extreme distress on separation from the primary caregiver.
>
> **Insecure-avoidant attachment**: an insecure attachment style characterised by behaviours that avoid contact with the primary caregiver.

> ### Ethical issues
>
> When using young children in psychological research, it is important that they are not caused too much stress. Here, if the children were really upset by their mother's departure, the study was cut short.

ACTIVITY 8.2

Pair up the type of attachment with the appropriate response:

Insecure/avoidant   "What's happening here? One minute you're here, the next you're gone. I need you but I'm very angry that you treat me like this."

Secure attachment   "You've left me *again*. I'll just have to face the fact that I need to take care of myself – no one else will."

Insecure/ambivalent   "I've missed you; I'm so pleased you're back; now I can get on with what I was doing."

ACTIVITY 8.3

In groups of three, enact a short play for the rest of the class. One of you is the infant, one is the caregiver, one is a stranger. Decide which type of attachment is going to be shown by the baby and then carry out the Strange Situation scenario and behave as the infant would if they were attached in that way. If you prefer, create your own scenario based at home or even in a public place such as a shop. The class has to guess which type of attachment is being shown by the infant.

EVALUATION OF THE STRANGE SITUATION STUDIES

⊕ The studies look at an important aspect of human behaviour. Separations do happen in real life and it is important that we investigate their consequences.

⊕ Because the procedure is identical for all infants, the studies are replicable (can be repeated) and we are therefore able to compare different children's responses in similar situations and generalise from the results.

⊖ The studies are done in an artificial environment and therefore lack ecological validity. This means that the behaviour shown is not necessarily a true reflection of ordinary everyday behaviour.

⊖ Some researchers argue that this is not an appropriate way to assess attachment in all children. If children have been in regular daycare from an early age, they are used to separations and their apparent lack of concern when the mother leaves could just reflect independence and self-reliance, not insecurity.

OCR What determines attachment behaviour?

How can we explain the fact that some babies are securely attached while others are insecure? We will look at two main reasons why babies show these individual differences:

• the temperament (personality) of the baby;
• the behaviour of the main caregiver.

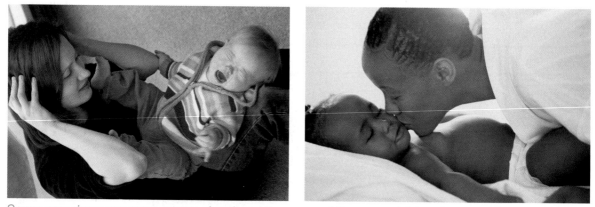

Some caregivers are more responsive than others . . . while some children have much easier temperaments than others

The **temperament hypothesis** suggests that it is the innate personality of a child that makes him or her attach securely or insecurely. Some babies are irritable, or simply very quiet and passive, and it is therefore difficult to form attachments. Others are alert, cheerful, and smile a great deal; with them it is much easier to form an attachment.

A different explanation is offered by the **caregiver sensitivity hypothesis**, which argues that it is the behaviour of the main caregiver that determines whether the child is securely or insecurely attached. Ainsworth (who did the Strange Situation studies) put forward this hypothesis. She carried out a series of **longitudinal studies** and found that the mothers of securely attached infants were, right from the start, more effective at soothing them, gave them more cuddles, and were more likely to talk to them face-to-face than other mothers.

OCR Bowlby's theory of attachment

Why do attachments occur in young children? What purpose do they serve? We are going to consider the work and theory of a very influential man in the field of attachment – John Bowlby. His theory covers two important aspects of attachment formation and although it is a single theory, it is convenient to look at it in two parts:

- The way in which children form attachment bonds and the nature of these bonds.
- What happens if these bonds are not formed properly, that is, the effects of deprivation and privation on a child.

Bowlby's theory of how attachment bonds are formed

Bowlby proposed that children have an instinctive need to attach to one person and that they are biologically "pre-programmed" to make such an

KEY TERMS

Temperament hypothesis: the view that a child's temperament is responsible for the quality of attachment between the child and its caregiver, as opposed to the view that experience is more important.

Caregiver sensitivity hypothesis: the view that it is the behaviour of the main caregiver that determines whether the child is securely or insecurely attached.

Longitudinal studies: studies in which the same participants take part over a number of years, even a lifetime, in order to examine changes over time. For example, the BBC TV programme *Child of Our Time*.

Goslings usually imprint on their mother but the scientist Konrad Lorenz arranged it so that he would be the first thing these goslings saw. From then on they followed him everywhere and showed no recognition of their actual mother

attachment. This happens in some of the animal kingdom as well. You may have noticed how, in the spring, a mother duck waddles along followed by a string of ducklings. These birds attach very soon after hatching by a process called imprinting. They are pre-wired to follow any object that moves near them soon after hatching. This is usually the mother duck but could be any animal, including a human being. (You may have seen an episode of Tom and Jerry in which, when an egg ends up in Jerry's bed and hatches there, a baby woodpecker thinks Jerry is his Mum and follows him everywhere.)

Bowlby compared attachment in human infants to the process of imprinting in ground-nesting birds. He believed that *the impulse to attach and then stay close is innate; the actual attachment figure is learnt*. The imprinting or attachment process keeps the youngsters safe. In humans, this attachment does not need to start as early as in ducklings because newborn infants cannot move away and get lost, but after about 7 months they learn to crawl. According to Bowlby, this is the reason why attachment occurs at this age – it prevents the infant from crawling away into danger.

Let's consider some of the most important aspects of Bowlby's theory:

1. The tendency to form an attachment bond is *instinctive*. Humans are born with the instinct to bond with another person.
2. The bond that a child develops with its main caregiver (often the mother) is a very special one, different from other bonds that a child develops. Other bonds are good to have but they are not, as Bowlby said, the "tops". He believed there is one main attachment figure and no one else is as important. The tendency to bond with one main person is called **monotropy**.
3. There is a **critical period**, from 7 months to 3 years, during which the baby is most likely to form this attachment bond. If it is not formed by the age of about 3 it is unlikely to form at all and the child may never attach to anyone.
4. The first attachment serves as an **internal working model**, which is the basis of our expectations and rules regarding relationships in later life. If, for example, we have been let down in early life, we may not be very trusting when we grow up, or even easily able to relate to our own children. On the other hand, children who are securely attached are likely to be loving, caring adults. (Later in this chapter we will look at the effects of attachment on romantic relationships.)

ACTIVITY 8.4

Children often use the various people with whom they have a bond in different ways – typically, Mum if they are hurt or afraid, Dad if they want to play, Grandma if they want to be indulged!

Think of three individuals who were important in your early life and write down what your memories are concerning the activities you did with each of them. Were they quite different from one another?

OCR Bowlby's theory of what happens if the bond is not formed properly: The effects of deprivation and privation

Given that the attachment process is so important in a child's life, what happens if it is disrupted or if the opportunity for attachment is limited? We will look at both the short-term and the long-term effects of **deprivation** and **privation**.

Short-term effects: The work of Robertson and Robertson

In the late 1960s, James and Joyce Robertson, colleagues of Bowlby, looked at the effects on young children of being separated from their parents in circumstances such as the child spending time in hospital or being sent to a residential nursery while the mother or main caregiver was in hospital. You may be surprised that a very young child would be left in hospital and rarely visited by his or her parents, or be sent to a residential nursery while the mother was having another baby, but in those days it was common practice. People believed that as long as children were physically well cared for, they would be fine. However the Robertsons, having looked at how children react in these circumstances, felt that a lot of harm was being done and believed it was important that the medical profession and other caring professions recognised this. What exactly did they believe happened?

They suggested that when children are first separated from their mother or mother substitute they go through three stages of reaction, known as *the syndrome of distress*:

1. protest
2. despair
3. detachment.

During the *protest* stage children attempt to follow the mother, scream, and do everything they can to recover her. They will continue looking for her long after she has gone.

During the *despair* stage they will often sob but in a more "helpless" way, making far fewer attempts to find the mother. They tend to show a distinct loss of hope.

Separation from the caregiver can have severe emotional effects on a child

During *detachment* they appear calm and even "settled". However, this apparent calm often masks underlying distress. The child appears to be emotionally "flat", not really responding very much to anything.

After reunion with the mother, this detachment may persist for a while but it is then likely to be followed by ambivalence (contradictory emotional reactions) to the mother. The child may be "clingy" and anxious, yet hostile whenever the mother leaves. It may be months, or even longer, before children separated for several days or more without good substitute care stop being extremely anxious.

Robertson and Robertson (1967–73) made a series of extremely moving films that vividly showed these stages. They argued that this type of distress was not necessary and that the short-term consequences of separation can be greatly improved by careful handling of the separation. They put psychological theory into practice, and took into their own home children who had to undergo temporary separation from their families. They recommended that children should be introduced to their new home beforehand while they were still securely with mother and be given a daily routine as close as possible to their familiar one, and that the carer should talk to them about their mother. They demonstrated that these children fared much better than those who were not given such care.

ACTIVITY 8.5

Josh is a 3-year-old boy whose mother Sue, a single parent, has to go into hospital for at least 2 weeks. She is very worried about Josh because he has never been looked after by anyone else. Sue has always been a single parent and has no relatives close by.

In groups, consider what advice you would give Sue as to how to cope in the best possible way with the situation. It may be best to divide it up into "before", "during", and "after". The "after" is very important as, however well prepared Josh is, he may feel upset and insecure when he returns home. What kind of behaviour might he show and how would it be best for Sue to respond to this behaviour?

Long-term effects: John Bowlby's maternal deprivation hypothesis

For many years John Bowlby worked with delinquent and disturbed children and was especially concerned with children he described as "affectionless". Such individuals seem unable to form close bonds with anyone, show any real consideration for others, or appreciate the needs and feelings of other people. Bowlby carried out many studies of disturbed children and consulted many other psychologists whose work he used in an attempt to formulate the reasons for this affectionless type of personality.

Children who do not have this need satisfactorily met may suffer from what Bowlby termed **maternal deprivation**. Maternal deprivation is said to occur when a child under the age of 3 is deprived of his or her mother figure for a period of at least 3 months, or has a number of changes of mother figure.

Bowlby argued that research, mainly in orphanages and hospitals, showed that maternal deprivation of this kind has the following effects:

- Emotionally disturbed behaviour such as bed-wetting.
- Dwarfism in children (not growing properly).
- Depression.
- Intellectual retardation.
- A crippling in the capacity to make relationships with other people – a so-called *affectionless psychopathy*.

Bowlby believed that there is a serious risk (around 25%) of the damage being *permanent* unless the situation can be reversed in the first 3 years of life.

The following study is one of several on which Bowlby's maternal deprivation hypothesis is based.

BOWLBY (1944): 44 JUVENILE THIEVES

Aim: Bowlby wanted to investigate the causes of delinquency in adolescence and assess whether it was related to separation in early life.

Method: From the clinic for disturbed adolescents where he worked, Bowlby selected two groups of boys:

- 44 juveniles who had a criminal record for theft
- 44 adolescents with emotional problems who had never been in trouble with the law.

Bowlby interviewed them all to assess whether they showed signs of affectionless psychopathy. He assessed this by seeing if, among other things, they showed a lack of affection for others and felt very little if any guilt over their actions. He also interviewed the families to see if the boys had had any significant separations from their main carers in the first 2 years of their lives. He studied the background and personality of the young thieves over 3 years.

Results: Bowlby found that 17 (39%) of the criminals had been separated from their mothers for 6 months or more before they were 5 years old. In practice this meant that the children had repeatedly or continually been in foster homes or hospital, often not visited by their families. Of these 17, 14 (89%) were cold and uncaring, felt no shame for what they had done, and seemed quite detached from ordinary standards of decency. They were what Bowlby termed "affectionless psychopaths".

Of the second group, only two had been separated as children and only two appeared affectionless.

Conclusion: Bowlby concluded that "there is a very strong case indeed for believing that prolonged separation of a child from his mother (or mother substitute) during the first five years of life stands foremost among the causes of delinquent character development."

> **Critical thinking**
>
> One way in which Bowlby obtained his information about the separation experiences of the boys in their early life was by interviewing the parents. See if you can think of two reasons why this information might not be accurate.

The monkeys in Harlow's study appeared to be more attached to the cloth-covered artificial "mother" than to a wire version that provided milk

The work of Harlow

Research on the damaging effects of disrupting the attachment bonds also comes from work with animals. One of the most famous studies (although controversial, for ethical reasons) comes from Harlow (1959). He kept newborn monkeys in total isolation and put them in a cage with a wire surrogate "mother" and a cloth one. He found that, regardless of which surrogate mother "fed" them (had the bottle attached to her), they preferred the cloth mother. They would cling to her, especially when frightened, and would only go to the wire mother for food.

The long-term consequences for these poor monkeys were dire. After about 6 months in isolation, they showed signs of serious disturbance such as biting themselves, curling up in a ball and rocking back and forth, and making facial grimaces. Adult female monkeys raised in this way were extremely poor mothers who neglected or abused their babies.

Bowlby cited the work of Harlow in demonstrating the enormous psychological damage that can occur in monkeys, a species close to humans, if they are deprived of love in early life.

Why psychology matters

The work of Bowlby, the Robertsons (mentioned earlier) and several other theorists in this field has had an enormous impact on the way in which children are treated. Not all of these are considered positive, but most of them are. Psychology matters because it has led to a huge improvement in childcare practices overall and has reduced the short-term misery and long-term harm to children.

EVALUATION OF BOWLBY'S THEORY OF ATTACHMENT

➕ There is evidence to support Bowlby's idea that certain species have evolved an attachment mechanism so that they are kept nurtured and safe. Imprinting studies and other results from natural animal studies support this.

➕ One positive aspect of any theory is how useful it is. Bowlby's theory, with its emphasis on the possible damage to children if they are not cared for adequately in early life, has been very important. His theory has been fundamental in changing certain practices, such as encouraging parents to visit (or stay with) children in hospital and the abandonment of large-scale orphanages in favour of smaller homes or foster care.

➖ The study by Schaffer and Emerson (discussed earlier on page 166) showed that most children form attachments with more than one person. Some psychologists believe that, although these attachments may be different, no single one is more important than another. They therefore doubt that attachment involves monotropy.

Some psychologists believe that Bowlby exaggerated the importance of the critical period. They believe that bonding can occur in later childhood.

There is some evidence to support the maternal deprivation hypothesis, including his study of the 44 juvenile thieves (1944).

However, there are several problems with using this study as evidence for the long-term effects of separation. First, the information obtained by Bowlby only shows a *correlation* between separation and later personality problems. Correlational studies cannot be used to assume that one factor *causes* another, so it is not possible to conclude that separation necessarily caused the later problems. It is quite possible that a third factor, such as a very stressful family life, had caused both the separations and the personality problems. Second, since Bowlby only studied adolescents from a clinic for disturbed boys, you cannot tell how many adolescents from the ordinary community who were separated as children did *not* develop problem behaviour. It would be a more valid study if his original sample had been adolescents who had been separated, rather than those from a clinic. Third, there is no way of knowing just how accurate the recall of the boys and their carers was with respect to the amount and number of separations they had experienced. And finally, the sample is very small – only 17 of his sample were separated – and this is a rather inadequate number from which to generalise.

ACTIVITY 8.6

Go back to the **case study** at the beginning of the chapter and list the reasons why, according to Bowlby's theory, Lesley might have problems forming attachments.

OCR ## The distinction between privation and deprivation

Rutter (1972) conducted his own research into maternal deprivation. He agreed with certain aspects of Bowlby's maternal deprivation hypothesis but disagreed with others, and believed it needed to be modified. Here are some of the important points he made:

- It's very important to distinguish between the effects of *never* forming a bond (as in the case of children raised in orphanages) and *breaking* a bond, that is,

KEY TERM

Case study: a research method involving a detailed investigation of a single individual or a small group of individuals.

Children in Romanian orphanages are liable to have suffered privation

being separated from the mother. Rutter used the term "privation" to describe a situation in which a bond is never formed and "deprivation" to describe the circumstances that occur if there are constant separations.

- The *circumstances of separation* could be very important. There is a huge difference between a child remaining with familiar people while the mother goes into hospital and a child being removed from everything she or he knows to stay in an unfamiliar place with strangers. It also makes a significant difference whether the separation is related to problematic family circumstances. Rutter suspected that many problems are related to stress rather than separation. Of course separations are often stressful, but it is possible to experience separations that are not overly stressful and, crucially, it is quite possible to experience stress within a family environment without ever experiencing physical separation from the mother.

In terms of *long-term effects*, Rutter's work led him to believe that there were separate effects from the different types of deprivation or discord that children had experienced. He concluded that:

- The failure to develop bonds with anyone (privation) in early childhood is the main factor in the development of affectionless psychopathy.
- Intellectual retardation is a result of lack of stimulation in early life, but is not necessarily as a result of separation – children can be under-stimulated in their own home.
- It is family discord and the lack of a stable relationship with a parent that are associated with later antisocial behaviour, delinquency, and criminal behaviour.

OCR Behaviourist theory of attachment: The "cupboard love" theory

The behaviourist theory, or learning theory, approach to why an attachment bond is formed sees it in a rather different way from Bowlby. This theory sees the attachment bond as the result of learning rather than a natural instinct. According to the behaviourist theory, children attach to their main caregiver because this person provides enormous amounts of positive reinforcement.

Early learning theorists tended to emphasise the role of feeding – after all, a child is fed about 2000 times in its first year and food is a powerful reinforcer. Nevertheless, it soon became clear that this was not the only reinforcer involved in attachment behaviour. If you remember, Harlow's studies with monkeys demonstrated that they will attach to the cloth "mother" regardless of who feeds them. Modern learning theories of attachment do not place such great emphasis on the role of feeding, but they do emphasise the importance of other reinforcement such as attention, loving care, responsiveness. They believe that the strongest reinforcers for infants are not associated with food but with social interaction. This, in turn, implies that children are innately predisposed to enjoy the company of others and the comfort and attention they receive from them.

EVALUATION OF THE BEHAVIOURIST THEORY OF ATTACHMENT

➕ The theory is supported by the research of Schaffer and Emerson (1964) who found that infants most readily attach to those who are responsive to the infant's needs rather than those people who care for them most of the time. This supports the behaviourist view because it is these people who provide the most reinforcement.

➖ On the negative side, it does appear that attachment is an instinctual need rather than a learned preference. Even when children do not receive reinforcement from any individual, they make desperate (sometimes heart-breaking) attempts to try to form an attachment bond to someone – anyone. Indeed, many children become attached to parents who ignore, neglect or even maltreat them. This implies that children have a need to attach, and that it is not simply the incidental result of reinforcement and something the child can easily do without.

➖ It is difficult for this theory to account for the suddenness with which certain reactions in the attachment process occur and, indeed, the reason for them. It is difficult, for example, to see why children suddenly develop stranger anxiety. This does not fit with a behaviourist approach because it occurs quite suddenly and without any unpleasant experiences being associated with unfamiliar individuals.

➖ Another important shortcoming of this theory is that it does not explain the emotional intensity that attachments involve; it seems doubtful that extremely strong emotions can depend simply on learning (Durkin, 1995).

OCR Types of love and attachment styles

At the beginning of this chapter we looked at three types of attachment: secure, insecure-ambivalent and insecure-avoidant. Now we are going to look at research on the effects of these attachment styles to relationships later in life.

Hazan and Shaver (1987, 1990) argue that the kinds of attachment bonds we form in childhood influence the style of loving we experience as an adult, in other words that securely attached infants are likely to have secure romantic relationships in adult life and so on. The following core study was used as support for this theory.

OCR CORE STUDY: HAZAN AND SHAVER (1987)

Aim: Hazan and Shaver wanted to see if there is a relationship between attachment type and later experiences in romantic relationships.

Method: The researchers placed a "Love Quiz" in a local newspaper (the *Rocky Mountain News*) and analysed the replies of the 620 adults who responded. Their ages ranged from 14 and 82 years.

Later, they also did the study using responses from 108 students.

Respondents to the quiz were first asked to read the following descriptions:

A. I find it relatively easy to get close to others and am comfortable depending on them and having them depend on me. I don't often worry about being abandoned or about someone getting too close to me. (This corresponded to secure attachment.)
B. I am somewhat uncomfortable being close to others. I find it difficult to trust them completely, difficult to allow myself to depend on them. I am nervous when anyone gets too close, and love partners often want me to be more intimate than I feel comfortable being. (This corresponded to insecure-avoidant attachment.)
C. I find that others are reluctant to get as close as I would like. I often worry that my partner doesn't really love me or won't want to stay with me. I want to merge completely with another person, and this desire sometimes scares people away. (This corresponds to insecure-ambivalent attachment.)

They were then asked to rate each one to indicate how well or poorly each description corresponded to how they felt in romantic relationships, using the following grid and ticking the relevant box.

Style A	1 ☐	2 ☐	3 ☐	4 ☐	5 ☐	6 ☐	7 ☐
	Disagree Strongly			Neutral/ Mixed			Agree Strongly
Style B	1 ☐	2 ☐	3 ☐	4 ☐	5 ☐	6 ☐	7 ☐
	Disagree Strongly			Neutral/ Mixed			Agree Strongly
Style C	1 ☐	2 ☐	3 ☐	4 ☐	5 ☐	6 ☐	7 ☐
	Disagree Strongly			Neutral/ Mixed			Agree Strongly

The participants also answered a variety of specific questions about their experiences in romantic relationships. They were also asked about their relationship with parents (their attachment history).

Findings: Hazan and Shaver compared the type of experiences that the participants had with their parents (and therefore their supposed attachment styles) with their reported experiences of adult relationships.

Generally they found a correspondence between the two. They found that:

* Those people who showed *secure attachment* in infancy were confident in their adult relationships, found it easy to get close to people and were not unduly worried about being rejected. They were quite happy to be dependent and have people depend on them; they were trusting and stable. In their childhood they had had a loving relationship with their parents.
* Those who were *avoidant* in infancy tended to become nervous when people got too close to them and were unwilling to depend on others. They feared that a potential partner may expect to become more intimate than they themselves would like. They were detached and unresponsive. These people reported having difficulties with their mother in childhood, generally finding her cold and unresponsive.
* Those who showed *ambivalent (anxious or insecure) attachment* in early childhood worried that their partners did not really love them, at least with the intensity they would like. These people were anxious, uncertain of their partners and often obsessively jealous. They reported a childhood that involved difficulties with their father, reporting him to be unfair.

In both groups (the adults and students) there were very similar percentages of attachment styles: 56% secure; 24% insecure-avoidant; 20% insecure-ambivalent. Hazan and Shaver pointed out that these were similar to the percentages found in infant attachment (which, if you recall, were 65% secure; 21% insecure-avoidant; 14% insecure-ambivalent). This supports the view that adult attachments are related to infant ones.

ACTIVITY 8.7

Copy out and complete the following table:

	Type of attachment in adult romantic relationships		
	Secure	**Insecure-avoidant**	**Insecure-ambivalent**
Proportions of each attachment type in adulthood, according to Hazan and Shaver (1987)	56%		
Relationships with parents			Father was unfair
Love experience		Fear of intimacy	

EVALUATION

➕ The fact that the percentages of secure, avoidant and ambivalent attachment were similar in Ainsworth's Strange Situation studies and the adult Love Quiz responses supports the theory that infant attachment experiences are related to adult romantic ones.

➕ The sample of people used was large and, in the first study, involved a very wide age range. Their experiences in childhood would not therefore have been simply a result of a particular type of upbringing that was popular in one generation. Similarly, their experiences of adult romantic relationships would not just reflect the social norms for conducting relationships that were current at the time.

➖ The sample of adults used, although large, could have been biased in several ways. First, they were all readers of one particular newspaper from one area of one country. Second, they chose to complete a "Love Quiz" in a newspaper and therefore may have been particularly interested in adult romantic relationships. It's possible, for example, that they were having a difficult time in their relationship and wanted to find out why. For both of these reasons, their responses may not have been *representative* of those of the general public.

➖ Their recall of their childhood experiences with their parents may not have been accurate. It's often difficult to remember what happened in early infancy, and later recall can be affected by adult experiences.

➖ The categorisation of adult romantic experiences into three broad categories is rather crude and may not reflect the subtleties of people's experiences.

➖ The relationship between infant attachment experiences and adult romantic ones is only a correlation and therefore does not necessarily show that the childhood experiences *caused* the adult ones as suggested by the theory.

OCR Application of research into attachment: Care of children

The research on attachment has had a significant effect on the way children are treated. It has helped to inform childcare practices in many walks of life such as nurseries, hospitals and foster homes. In addition, it has given guidance as to how to help parents to form secure attachments with their children. We will look at a small but important sample of these applications.

Dealing with separation in nurseries

Some parents worry that if their children are placed in a nursery in their early years, this may result in poor attachment. However, research shows that this is not necessarily the case. The National Institute of Child Health and Human Development (NICHD) is conducting a longitudinal study of 1300 children, looking at their development as they grow up. This research is published every few years. It takes into account the family circumstances and the type of daycare the child receives (e.g. whether the child is brought up entirely within the family or attends a nursery before school). It also considers such factors as physical growth, language development, reading development and sibling structure (brothers and sisters). The most significant finding so far is that whether or not the child attends a nursery or is brought up at home is not important to their well-being. The most important factor is the family environment. Basically, if mothers (and fathers) are happy, especially if they are happy about returning to work and about the childcare arrangements, then so are the children.

When children are well cared for at home and at nursery, they show secure attachment even if they are in nursery for a lot of the time. The *quality* of care that a child receives is the most important factor.

> **How psychology works**
>
> One of the most valuable ways in which psychologists can acquire knowledge of developmental trends is by conducting longitudinal studies, especially when information is gathered from a large number of people, as in the NICHD research.
>
> In this study, a great many factors are taken into account, so we can consider how they *interact* with one another.

A good nursery

In order for children to show good social and emotional development nurseries need to have:

- a low child-to-adult ratio
- small numbers of children
- a sensitive, stimulating, and warm relationship between carers and children.

Ways of dealing with separation in nurseries

It is important that parents and carers liaise closely to ensure that there is consistent care for each child and that any problems can be sorted out at an early stage.

- If the nursery is large, then each child should be looked after by the minimum number of people so they are not encountering strangers on a regular basis.
- Carers need to speak to children in a sensitive and caring manner.
- The nursery needs to be of good quality, showing the characteristics listed above.

In conclusion, when the quality of care is good both at home and at the nursery, children should be able to develop secure attachments and develop well both socially and intellectually.

A sensitive, stimulating, and warm relationship between carers and nursery children is an important factor in terms of positive social and emotional development.

Children in hospital

It goes without saying that hospital can be a frightening place for children and, if they have to stay for a period of time, could disrupt the attachment bond if the situation is not handled well. The work of Robertson and Robertson, mentioned on page 173, showed how a child may go through the stages of distress, despair and detachment if their experiences of separation are not handled in a sensitive way. Earlier Spitz and Wolf (1946) had also carried out a series of studies of hospitalised children and found that even the previously happy, contented and secure ones soon became quiet, apathetic and sad when they were left in hospital for some time without regular visits from parents. In those days, this was not infrequent for several reasons, including the fact that children sometimes had to be kept in isolation if they had a serious infectious disease such as tuberculosis. Of course these days such diseases are rare as children are inoculated against them.

How to cope with children in hospital

- Before: If the child is old enough and there is advance notice that they have to go into hospital, prepare them by talking to them about what will happen. There are also books written especially for the purpose of describing to children what happens when people go to hospital. It's very important to tell them that they will return home. (You can never take for granted what to adults is obvious – children may think they are never coming home and have "moved" to a new place. They won't necessarily express these fears openly.)
- During: While in hospital, regular visiting is obviously important and some parents may even be able to stay.

   Many hospitals now ensure that a child has a "special" nurse who is "their" nurse and whom they can become attached to. This is particularly important if the stay is a long one.

   For children whose parents, for whatever reason, cannot visit very often, there is a voluntary group of hospital visitors and, again, children are often given their "own" friend to visit them.

   Other contact with the home is important: regular phone calls and postcards for example. Again, constant reassurance that they will go home eventually is important.

- Afterwards: Parents need to be tolerant of tantrums, upset sleep patterns, bed-wetting, childish behaviour and such like. Children will take a while to re-settle after a period away from home.

Parenting classes

Many people find parenting quite a challenging task. As I'm sure some readers of this textbook will understand, children can be difficult at times!

   Parenting classes provide support and advice to parents on how to cope with children and ensure that they are well adjusted and happy – that they develop secure attachment bonds.

EXAM HINT

When answering questions on how to cope with stays in hospital (or any question concerning this section on application of research into attachment), be careful to include some psychological theory and research in your answer. If you could simply have written your answer without any psychological knowledge (i.e. just using common sense), it is very unlikely to be awarded full marks. So, for example, mention the Robertsons' research and say that regular visiting is important so the child does not go through the stages of distress, despair and detachment. Likewise, mention the types of attachment and say that careful preparation and regular visiting will prevent attachment becoming insecure.

   Along similar lines, think psychologically when discussing nursery care. Mention, for example, the NICHD research.

A typical course, entitled "Mothering on Solid Ground", puts at the top of its list of descriptions that it is "designed to help" mothers develop a secure attachment with their babies. It recognises that women often feel physically, emotionally and/or mentally exhausted after childbirth and that this can lead to insecure attachments with their babies as well as other problems. It also emphasises that, because of society's expectations, mothers feel that they should be able to be a good parent without any help or respite. The course provides a great deal of practical help in managing toddler behaviour in such a way as to make parenting an enjoyable experience and the relationship between parent and child a secure and happy one. It also tackles fundamental issues that can lead to unhappiness and insecurity, such as self-doubt, the disapproval of others and conflict between parents as to how children should be treated.

ACTIVITY 8.8

Go to www.aparentconnection.com/parentingclasses.htm or Google "parenting classes secure attachment" and summarise the programme of classes that such a course covers.

A major (British) government project known as Parent Support Advisers (PSAs) was started in 2006. It aims to provide early intervention and support in a school setting to parents who appear to be in need of help. Although primarily aimed at improving children's school achievement, this inevitably improves relationships between parents and children, leading to more secure relationships. The project is widespread, involving over 3500 parents in 2008. An interim report on the progress of this scheme found these classes to be extremely helpful. The parents, all of whom have children between the ages of 8 and 13 with behavioural or psychological difficulties, told researchers they were calmer and more confident with their children, and spent more time listening and talking to them. Researchers reported that the courses do have benefits in reducing antisocial behaviour in children and in improving the parents' ability to cope with their children (Lindsay et al. 2008).

In conclusion, parenting classes do appear to help foster good relationships between parents and children. Since such relationships are the foundation of well-adjusted, happy children they are of great benefit to society as a whole.

Everyday life

This is yet another example of the way in which psychology has made an important contribution to improving the everyday lives of people – not just of the children and their families, but of society as a whole.

Chapter summary

- An attachment can be defined as a long-enduring, emotionally meaningful tie to a particular individual (Schaffer, 1996).
- According to Schaffer and Emerson, the stages of attachment are (1) asocial stage, (2) stage of indiscriminate attachments, (3) stage of specific attachment, (4) stage of multiple attachments.

- Ainsworth investigated attachment using the "Strange Situation", which was a structured observation. From this and other research, three types of attachment were identified: secure attachment, insecure-ambivalent attachment, and insecure-avoidant attachment.
- Bowlby's theory of attachment states that attachment is an innate, biological process that needs to occur during a critical period (roughly 7 months to 3 years) or it is unlikely to develop satisfactorily. The tendency to bond is monotropic (to one main person).
- Bowlby's maternal deprivation hypothesis states that long-term or frequent deprivation can result in several adverse effects in later life, including a failure to form satisfactory relationships, a characteristic known as affectionless psychopathy.
- Rutter distinguished between deprivation and privation. Deprivation occurs when an already formed bond is disrupted or broken; privation occurs when the child never has the opportunity to attach. It is privation rather than deprivation that tends to result in affectionless psychopathy.
- Behaviourist theory sees attachment as the result of learning rather than a natural instinct. Attachment is seen as the result of enormous amounts of positive reinforcement given to the child by the carer. These reinforcements (rewards) not only include physical ones (such as food) but social ones (such as love and attention). However, this theory does not account for why attachment behaviour, such as separation protest and stranger anxiety, develops so suddenly at a certain age, nor does it account for why some neglected children still attach to their carers.
- Hazan and Shaver believe that attachment patterns established in early childhood may affect adult romantic relationships. They carried out research using a "Love Quiz" and found three types of romantic relationships, which they believe reflect the secure, insecure-avoidant and insecure-ambivalent attachment found in infancy. They found similar percentages of each type of attachment in adults as had been found by Ainsworth in infants. However, this categorization of adult relationships into these three types is rather crude. Another criticism is that there is no conclusive proof that these infant relationships necessarily caused the attitude to relationships in later life.
- The work on attachment has some very important implications for the care of children. We looked at three such applications. First, the best way of handling hospitalisation so that it does not damage the attachment bond. Second, dealing with separation in pre-school nurseries. Third, the use of parenting classes to encourage secure attachment.

OCR Exam-style questions for OCR

1. (a) Describe Bowlby's theory of attachment. (4 marks)

   (b) Outline **two** limitations of this theory. (4 marks)

2. In attachment theory, describe what is meant by:

   (a) Separation protest. (2 marks)

   (b) Stranger anxiety. (2 marks)

3. Outline **two** limitations of Hazan and Shaver's study into attachment. (4 marks) [OCR, 2008, Specimen Paper 1]

4. Outline **two** ways in which the care of children has been influenced by research into attachment (4 marks).

What you need to know `OCR`

The specification lists the following things that you will need to be able to do for the examination:

- Describe how cognitive development occurs in invariant and universal stages
- Outline the stages of cognitive development: sensorimotor, pre-operational, concrete operational and formal operational
- Describe the concept of object permanence
- Describe the concept of egocentrism and the process of decentring
- Describe the concept of conservation
- Explain the criticisms of Piaget's theory of cognitive development
- Consider Vygotsky's theory as an alternative theory, with specific reference to the zone of proximal development
- Describe Piaget's (1952) experiment into the conservation of number
- Outline the limitations of Piaget's study
- Explain how psychological research relates to educating children

Cognitive development

The following conversation occurs between George (aged 4), whose much-loved granddad has been staying, and his mother:

George: "How long is 500 days?"
(Mother hesitates, puzzled by such a question from so young a child, and
    before she has a chance to answer...)
George: "Is it longer than a year?"
Mother: "Yes."
George: "That's OK then." (Contentedly turns away.)
Mother (still confused): "Why did you want to know?"
George: "Because granddad says he has to take an aspirin every day for the
    rest of his life. He's got a jar of 500 and says that will last him."

Sometimes, you have to be careful what you say to children, as they tend to take you literally! The interesting thing is that, to George, once he knew that 500 days was longer than a year, he was quite content because that, presumably, was forever!

There are any number of fascinating misconceptions that children have. Mary, aged 3, thinks the sky is blue because God painted it that colour, that when it rains it's because God is crying, and when it thunders it's because he is crashing saucepans together (although quite why God would do that is another mystery!). Omair, aged 6, thinks that when his mum got points on her driving licence, pencil points were drawn on it. Lucy, aged 5, told by a cross dad to "pull her socks up" when she was slow at finishing a task, did precisely that. Dan, aged 5, when asked the difference between 6 and 8, says that 8 has two rings and 6 has only one (which rather serves the adult right for asking a 5-year-old an arithmetic question in such a silly way).

ACTIVITY 9.1

You can probably think of some strange ideas you had as a child. As members of a class, collect some together. If you can't think of any, ask your parents or older brothers and sisters if they can think of examples of early childhood misconceptions either from you or from other members of your family. The words of nursery rhymes, hymns, and Christmas carols are good sources of these, as they contain many unfamiliar words that children simply translate in their own way.

People used to think that the main difference between children and adults was that children knew less than adults. However, we now recognise that this is not true. As the above examples show, children actually think differently from the way in which adults think. In this chapter we will look at the work of one of the most important developmental psychologists, Jean Piaget (who, despite the forename, was a man – his name is Swiss and the equivalent of John). He studied a great many children and developed a theory to describe the way in which children's thinking changes as they grow older and the means by which this happens.

ACTIVITY 9.2

When you were very young you may have believed in Father Christmas (or another similar figure who brought presents). Think of the reason why you eventually stopped believing in him. Get into groups and exchange and discuss these reasons. What does that tell us about the differences in the way younger and older children think?

ACTIVITY 9.3

Try to guess the answer a very young child (one about 3 years old) would give to the following questions:

Why is the sky blue?
Why are the branches of that tree moving?
Can a plant feel the prick of a pin?
Who were the first people to play hopscotch?
What makes the sun shine?
Is the moon alive?

OCR Piaget's theory

Jean Piaget

Piaget believed that as children get older, they go through several stages of thinking. There are four of these stages:

- The **sensorimotor stage**
- The **pre-operational stage**
- The **concrete operational stage**
- The **formal operational stage**

The sensorimotor stage (birth to 2 years)

Learning through senses and actions

Just think about how a tiny baby learns about the world. They explore with their hands and their mouth. They crawl around and touch things. They learn everything via their senses (touch, taste, hearing, sight) and through actions (grasping, sucking). This is how this stage gets its name: "sensori" = through the senses, "motor" = by doing.

Living in the "here and now"

Small children are limited to thinking about the here and now; they have no concept of the future or the past. If you tell a small child "we will do that tomorrow" he or she will not understand you, but gradually, as this stage advances, they will gain a little bit of understanding about the future and the past. Nevertheless, to promise to do something "next week" to a child under 2 years old is a rather pointless exercise!

In the sensorimotor stage, babies learn by crawling around and exploring the environment

Lack of object permanence

One important feature of the sensorimotor stage is the lack of **object permanence**. If you wave a bright toy in front of a 5-month-old, he or she will reach for it. If you then put it out of sight, say, behind your back, while the baby is watching, he or she acts as if it was never there, doesn't try to look for it, and doesn't get upset that it's no longer there. As far as the baby is concerned, *if I cannot see it, it does not exist.*

If you do the same thing with a 10-month-old, the baby will look for the toy and be upset that it has disappeared. They have begun to realise that the object still exists and must be somewhere around but they can't see it. Object permanence has begun to develop.

KEY TERMS

Sensorimotor stage: the first developmental stage, characterised by children learning to coordinate their sensory experiences (sights, sounds) with their motor behaviours.

Pre-operational stage: the second developmental stage, characterised by children learning to visualise objects and events mentally (in their heads).

Concrete operational stage: the third developmental stage, characterised by children learning to think logically about concrete events (e.g. maths equations, science experiments).

Formal operational stage: the final developmental stage, characterised by children learning to think logically about abstract (unseen) events.

Object permanence: the ability to understand that an object continues to exist even when it is out of sight.

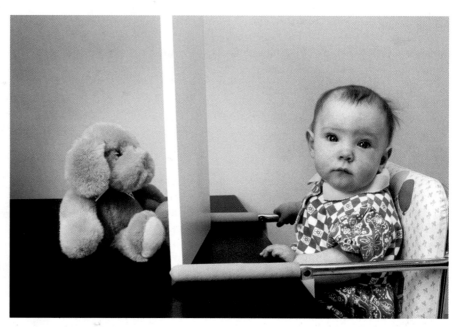

Object permanence is the term used to describe the awareness that objects continue to exist even when they are not visible

However, it has not developed completely. If you regularly hide an object behind the same screen, a baby of 10 months will search behind the screen for it. If you then, in clear view of the child, transfer the object to the back of another screen, the baby will look behind the *original* screen. This demonstrates that, although the child has begun to develop a concept of object permanence, a full understanding of it does not develop until the end of the sensorimotor stage. By that time, there's no fooling the child – if an object is hidden while they look on, they can quite easily find it.

The pre-operational stage (2–7 years)
The main achievement: Symbolic thought

Why did Piaget think that a new stage started at around 18 months to 2 years of age? Well, he believed that a significant change occurred in the child's thinking at this age: a new ability emerged, an ability known as **symbolic thought**. Let's use a simple example to explain what this is.

If someone said the word "table" to you, you would immediately conjure up a set of pictures in your mind: kitchen table, dining table, side table, picnic table, and so on. You have an image in your head of what the concept "table" means; in other words, you have an *internal representation* of it. Children in the sensorimotor stage do not have this. This is because they lack symbolic thought; symbolic thought involves the ability to have an internal representation of a concept. There are various ways in which a young child begins to demonstrate that they have symbolic thought:

- First, the child begins to talk. In order to use language, you have to be able to understand that a word, an arbitrary sound like "table", *represents* the object that constitutes a table. Not only do children in the pre-operational

KEY TERM

Symbolic thought: the ability to have an internal representation (a mental image) of a concept.

stage understand and use words that represent objects, they can also cope with abstract concepts such as "more". Indeed, this is one of the first words many children learn, applying it first to one concept, such as asking for "more" when given cake, but soon generalising it to other concepts, such as asking for "more" when playing a fun game. They must understand the symbolic meaning of the word "more" in order to do this.

In the pre-operational stage, children engage in pretend play

- Second, the child now enjoys *pretend play*. This starts with simple games like using one object to represent another, such as a stick to represent a spoon to stir your tea. Children of this age love to have their own tea set and play out a whole scenario from adult life, like pouring out "tea" for visitors. They then move on to games like "shop keepers", "cops and robbers", "doctors and nurses", and "schools" in which each child pretends to occupy a particular role.

- Third, children begin, in a simple way, to understand ideas of the past and future. Their thinking is no longer limited by the here and now.

ACTIVITY 9.4

Without using the examples above, think of four types of pretend play that you used to do. How complex were they? Did they involve other people playing different roles?

Limitations: Egocentrism and lack of conservation skills

So far, we have discussed the major achievement of this stage, but there are still many limitations in the way children in the pre-operational stage think. We'll now look at two of the most important of these: **egocentrism** and the inability to conserve.

Egocentrism

Suppose you were standing at one end of a room with your back to the wall looking at a picture on the opposite wall. A friend, Bill, is standing underneath the picture facing in your direction. It's easy for you to know that Bill cannot see the picture you are looking at, and that if there were another picture above *your* head, he could see it and you couldn't. In other words, you can appreciate what the room looks like from Bill's perspective. Young children in the pre-operational stage cannot do this. They are egocentric, which means they are not able to see things from anyone else's point of view. Let's now look at a famous study by Piaget that demonstrates egocentrism.

> **KEY TERM**
>
> **Egocentrism:** the inability to see things from anyone else's point of view.

THE THREE MOUNTAINS STUDY: PIAGET AND INHELDER (1956)

Aim: Piaget and Inhelder wanted to test the theory that children in the pre-operational stage (under about 7 years old) are *egocentric* and cannot view things from another person's point of view.

Method: A model showing three mountains was placed on a table. These mountains were different colours, with snow on top of one, a house on another, and a cross on the third. The child was invited to walk around the table and look at the model from all angles. He or she then sat down on one side while a doll was placed in front of another of the mountains, and the child was asked to say *what the doll could see*. In order to do this, they were shown a set of 10 pictures, each showing a different view of the model, and asked to choose the one that represented what the doll could see. The doll was then moved to another position and the child was asked the same question again.

Findings: The 4-year-olds were totally unable to choose the picture that represented what the doll could see, and always chose a picture that matched how they themselves saw the model. The 6-year-olds were a little more successful but often chose the wrong picture. Only 7- to 8-year-olds consistently chose the one that represented the doll's view.

Conclusion: According to Piaget, egocentrism is a characteristic of the pre-operational stage. Children in this stage fail to understand that what they see is relative to their own position. Instead they assume that what they themselves see is the "world as it really is". This demonstrates an inability to **decentre**, to step outside their own viewpoint and see things from another's point of view.

Lack of conservation

If you poured orange juice from a short stubby glass into a tall thin one, you might be surprised how far up the second glass it came, you might even think that

---

Diversity

It was reasonable for Piaget to use a model of three mountains when testing children who were used to such an environment, but it may be necessary to use a different model if you are testing young children who are not familiar with mountains. Older children should not be affected: they should be able to cope just as well with an unfamiliar environment as with a familiar one.

KEY TERM

Decentre: the ability to step outside one's own viewpoint and see things from another's point of view.

it looks as if there's more juice now it's gone into a different container. Despite appearances, however, you would know there's the same amount there. This is known as **conservation**. If, on the other hand, you were to do the same in front of a child in the pre-operational stage, and then asked if there was now more juice than before (pointing to the tall thin container), the most common answer would be that yes, there was. The fact that they'd seen you pour the liquid from one glass into another has no effect on their thinking – if it *looks* more it *is* more.

Children in the pre-operational stage are unable to conserve: they cannot appreciate that things remain the same even when their appearance changes. The inability of younger children to conserve was demonstrated by a series of experiments conducted by Piaget and his co-researchers. Typically, they would present the child with two identical quantities (such as glasses of juice, rows of counters, balls of modelling clay) and get the child to agree that they were the same. They would then rearrange one of the quantities (such as spreading out the counters, pouring the orange juice into a different shaped glass, making one ball of modelling clay into a sausage shape) and ask them again if the two quantities were the same.

The core study demonstrates the type of study done.

> **KEY TERM**
>
> **Conservation**: the ability to understand that changing the form of a substance or object does not change its amount, overall volume, or mass.

OCR A study into the conservation of number

OCR CORE STUDY: PIAGET (1952)

Aim: To see if children of various ages can conserve number.

Method: Two identical rows of counters are laid out on a table in front of the child, who is asked if the two rows contain the same number of counters. Once the child has agreed that they are the same, the adult spreads out the counters in one of the rows, so the row is longer:

• • • • • • •   • • • • • • •

• • • • • • •   • • • • • • •

The adult then asks the child if the rows contain the same number of counters.

Findings: Children in the pre-operational stage will usually say that there are more counters in the longer row. Very few children under the age of six (16%) could answer the second question correctly.

Conclusions: Younger children fail to conserve because they base their judgement on appearances.

A child performing the conservation of number task

rather than the fact that the quantity cannot have changed because nothing has been added or taken away. Adults know that the amount has stayed the same and that the reason why the row looks longer is that there is more space between each counter. However, pre-operational children pay attention to a single dimension only, the length of the row. This is another example of the young child's inability to decentre: they can only concentrate on one aspect of a problem at once – in this case the length of the row.

They think that if the row is longer, there must be more counters; they ignore the increased gap between them.

Pre-operational children also lack *reversibility*, that is the ability to mentally undo or reverse an action. They do not understand that if the counters in the second row were pushed back together, they would look the same as they did before; that is, the same as the other row.

Limitations of the study

Piaget has been criticised for the way in which conservation tasks were presented to the children.

First, we cannot be sure that young children use and interpret words in the same way as adults do. It is possible that young children's failure in the task may, in some cases, be caused by the fact that children do not really understand "more than" or "less than".

Second, in all the conservation tasks, the younger children may not understand what is expected of them and become confused. The children were asked the same question twice (are there the same number of counters in each row?), once before the change and again afterwards. A younger child may assume that a different answer is required the second time around. Other researchers (e.g. Rose & Blank, 1974; Samuel & Bryant, 1984) have used the same type of method but only asked the question once, after the counters had been rearranged. They found that many younger children could conserve. There were still age differences, but the age at which children started to be able to conserve was younger.

Third, as we will see later (page 205), McGarrigle and Donaldson (1974) repeated these studies but used a glove puppet called "naughty teddy" to rearrange the counters accidentally while fooling about. They found that 62% of 6-year-olds could now conserve compared with 16% in the original study. The researchers argue that younger children may have thought that because a grown-up had rearranged the counters it was fair to assume that something must have changed, but that this was not the case when the counters were rearranged by an incidental (rather than deliberate) action. (Nevertheless, as discussed later, there are criticisms of this study too.)

The core study investigated *conservation of number* but there are other types of conservation including *volume* (liquid), *substance* (solid quantity, such as amount of modelling clay), and *area*.

Conservation of volume

The procedure here is to start with two identical glass beakers containing exactly the same amount of a liquid such as orange juice. The adult, after

Ethical issues

When psychologists work with children, they must ensure that they are not upset or caused undue stress. One way of doing this is to present these research studies as games. Children then enjoy the experience and do not find it stressful.

EXAM HINT

The study of conservation of number is a "Core study", which means that you may be asked to describe it in terms of aim, method, results (findings) and conclusion in the exam.

getting the child to agree that the amounts are the same, pours the liquid from one of the glasses into a taller, thinner glass. The pre-operational child fails to conserve and thinks there is more juice in the tall thin glass. Again, they judge on the basis of one dimension – in this case, they judge by the height of the liquid in the beaker and don't take account of the shorter beaker's larger circumference. It's yet another example of their failure to *decentre*, to take account of more than one aspect at a time.

Conservation of mass (substance/solid quantity)

Children are shown two identical sausage-shaped lumps of modelling clay. As before, they are asked to agree that they are the same. One is then rolled into a longer, thinner shape. The pre-operational child usually says that the longer thinner one is bigger.

The age at which children can conserve differs depending on the type of conservation. Conservation of number comes first (usually around age 6), then conservation of mass and length, then weight and finally volume.

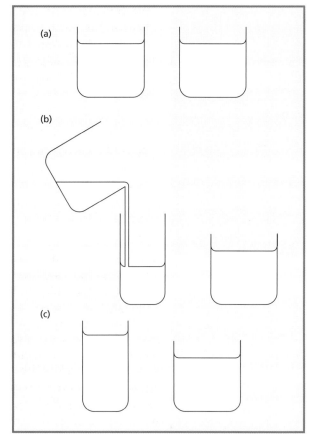

Why is it called the pre-operational stage?

The main characteristic of this stage, which is shown in egocentrism and in the inability to conserve, is that the child *cannot perform logical* **operations** (hence the name of the stage: *pre*-operational). An operation is not easy to define, but essentially it involves the ability to form a mental rule for manipulating objects or ideas into new forms and back to the original. For example, if an adult is told that 45 × 51 = 2295, they would know that 2295 ÷ 45 = 51 without calculating it. Young children do not have this ability. As mentioned earlier, pre-operational children lack reversibility; they are unable to *mentally reverse* operations. In the conservation studies, they cannot mentally put the counters back into their original position or mentally pour liquid back into the original container and thereby recognise that it is the same.

The characteristic that marks the beginning of the next stage is that children now begin to be able to think logically.

The concrete operational stage (7–11 years)

Children now begin to perform logical operations, so they can conserve. They now understand that if nothing is added or taken away, things must remain the same, despite appearances.

However, they can only manage logical thinking if concepts are presented in a "concrete" way, that is, by use of familiar objects. Take the following as an example: If I said to you, "All daffodils are yellow flowers (proposition A). Does this therefore mean that all yellow flowers are daffodils (proposition B)?", you would know that statement B was not true and was not a logical conclusion to draw from statement A. This is because you probably know of lots of yellow flowers that aren't daffodils. However, suppose I said to you:

A. *All xs are ys. Is it therefore true that*
B. *All ys are xs?*

You would find this much more difficult to work out, because x and y are *abstract* concepts and ones that are not easy to relate to. However, the two sets of arguments are identical – it's just that one is presented in a "concrete" form (using familiar objects) whereas the other is abstract and unfamiliar.

Many concepts are easier to understand if they are presented in a "concrete" way. Think about working out the surface area of a cube. If you make a two-dimensional cardboard model (one that you can lay flat), it's much easier to work out the surface area than by trying to use a formula that you have been given but have not worked out for yourself.

ACTIVITY 9.5

Try to solve the following puzzle with or without props (e.g. model characters or cardboard cut-outs). Even those people in the formal operational stage will find it much easier with props!

Three cannibals and three travellers are on one side of the river, and they want to get to the other side of it. They have a boat that will only carry two people. All the travellers and one of the cannibals can row. However, under no circumstances must the number of cannibals outnumber the number of travellers, or travellers will be eaten. Devise a method of getting all of them safely across the river in the fewest number of trips.

So, to sum up, children in the concrete operational stage:

• can think logically but only if the concepts are familiar and involve real objects
• can now *conserve*, although some forms of conservation (such as area) will not be achieved until well into the concrete operational stage
• are no longer egocentric, so they can now understand things from a variety of angles and viewpoints.

ACTIVITY 9.6

Here is another example of how much easier it is to solve problems using props.

Consider the following question: "If Mandeep is shorter than Simon, and Mandeep is taller than Chris, who is the tallest?"

Children in the concrete operational stage may struggle with this unless they are provided with visual props that help them work it out. Try to solve the problem in your head, without writing anything down. Now try to do it in the following way.

Draw a vertical line. Put a notch somewhere on the line to represent Mandeep. Put her name by it. Now, because Simon is taller than Mandeep, put a notch above Mandeep (not too close) and label it Simon. Now make a notch for Chris below Mandeep (because he's shorter than her). Now that you have everyone in place you can easily tell who is shortest, tallest, and who is in between.

Now make up a similar puzzle using four items and give it to another person in the class. Make sure they have sufficient information to do it properly. When you work with four or more items, you can appreciate how much difference it makes to have "concrete props".

However, children at this stage *cannot deal with abstract concepts or hypothetical tasks*. In order to solve problems, a child needs to be able to refer to real objects.

The formal operational stage (11 years +)
Once children reach adolescence, Piaget believed that they move into the *formal operational stage* in which they acquire two related skills that they did not have before:

- They can now deal with hypothetical situations – they can move beyond the actual states of the world and think of the possible ones.
- They will solve problems in a systematic, logical manner in which all possible combinations of factors are considered.

Let's look at examples of these new skills.

The pendulum task
One task Piaget used in order to show the difference between the stage of concrete operations and that of formal operations was the pendulum task. Children are given a set of different weights

that can be tied to a piece of string, a ball of string, and a stand. They are asked to make a pendulum.

Now they have to work out what determines the speed of the swing of the pendulum. The factors that they tend to consider are how hard the pendulum is pushed, how long the string is, and how heavy the weight is.

Because children in the formal operational stage think systematically, they try to solve the problem by systematically varying one factor at a time to see if it makes a difference. Then they test a second factor while keeping the other two the same, and so on. For example, they might keep the "push" and the length of the string constant while varying the weight. However, concrete operational children are quite likely to vary two or even three factors at once, so they may change the weight and shorten the string. They don't understand that this confuses the issue because they still can't tell which factor influenced the speed of the swing.

The test tube task

A second problem-solving exercise that demonstrates systematic thinking is the following: Imagine you are given a set of six test tubes (labelled A B C D E F), each containing a quantity of colourless liquid, no two of which are the same. You are told that there are two of these liquids that, if combined, make a blue solution. It is your task to work out, as quickly as possible, which two liquids they are.

The typical approach of concrete operational children is to mix any two liquids at random hoping to happen upon the solution. Children in the formal operational stage will systematically try every combination (A+B, A+C, A+D, and so on) until they find the answer.

ACTIVITY 9.7

This is based on an exercise by Piaget. Ask the following question to children of various ages, from about 9 years to 15 years:

"Suppose that you were given a third eye and that you could choose to place this eye anywhere on your body. Draw me a picture to show where you would place your 'extra' eye, and then tell me why you would put it there."

Typically, younger children in the concrete operational stage will add the third eye between the existing eyes. They cannot think beyond the familiar. In contrast, formal operational children give a wide variety of responses, using the eye so that they have a distinct advantage, such as at the back of their head, on the palm of the hand. They can see the advantages of the hypothetical situation and enjoy the challenge, while the younger children cannot think beyond the familiar and find the task rather silly.

Summary of Piaget's stages	
Sensorimotor	• learning through senses and action • lives in the here and now • full object permanence lacking
Pre-operational	• has symbolic thought • egocentrism • inability to conserve
Concrete operational	• can perform operations with familiar material • no longer egocentric • can conserve • cannot deal with abstract concepts or hypothetical tasks
Formal operational	• can deal with hypothetical concepts • can solve problems in a systematic, logical way

OCR The nature of cognitive development

It is important to note two aspects of the stages of cognitive development:

- They are *invariant*: This means that they are always in the same order, and none of the stages can be skipped because each successive stage builds on the previous stage and represents a more complex way of thinking.
- They are *universal*: This means that they apply to all children the world over, regardless of culture.

EXAM HINT

The specification requires you to describe how cognitive development occurs in invariant and universal stages, so make sure you understand the meaning of these terms.

OCR The processes used in cognitive development

Piaget did not just describe the stages through which children's thinking passed; he attempted to explain what processes were operating in order for this to happen. He suggested that the mind contains two types of mental structures: **schemas** and operations.

Schemas
As children explore their environment and interact with it, they gradually organise everything that they know about a particular object or activity into a *schema*. A schema contains all the information, experience, ideas and memories an individual has about an object or sequence of events.

Schemas used by young children are simple and practical. According to Piaget, children are born with a ready-made set of very simple schemas, such as grasping and sucking, and these he called *action schemas*. Over time, they

KEY TERM

Schema: an internalised mental representation that contains all the information, experience, ideas, and memories an individual has about an object or a sequence of events.

become more complex. A newborn sucks everything in the same way; an older child can adapt their sucking to suit the characteristics of the object, such as its hardness, size and shape.

Many early schemas are inaccurate. For example, a young child's thinking is characterised by **animism**, the belief that all natural phenomena and inanimate objects, such as rocks, are alive. If a child falls over a chair he or she may smack it! Another example of an incorrect schema is as follows. If a child has a pet dog called by a particular name, such as Alexander, it is not unusual for the child to believe that all dogs are called Alexander. Their schema for dogs does not allow for the fact that they each have individual names, and that the word "dog" is a collective name for all dogs but "Alexander" is the chosen name for their particular dog.

A further example of oversimplified schemas came from my daughter, then aged 4, during a stay by my father. The following conversation took place:

Siobhan: "Why do you call granddad 'dad'?"
Me: "Because he is my dad. He's your granddad, but he's my dad."
Siobhan (puzzled): "But daddy is dad, granddad is granddad."

I tried to explain further, but knew I was largely wasting my time – she simply did not have the schemas to understand relationships, or that some names (granddad, dad, mummy) are relationship names that are only appropriate for use by some people, while other names (Siobhan) belong to an individual regardless of who's using them.

As the child matures and their cognitive abilities develop, so their schemas are modified: they become more complex and more accurate. We will now look at how this occurs.

The state of disequilibrium

Children constantly come across information that does not quite fit into their existing schemas. To use the example from earlier, they may become aware that the neighbour's dog is called Woof and that Uncle Bill's dog is called Katie. This does not fit the schema that all dogs are called Alexander. This puts the child in a state of **disequilibrium**. Disequilibrium occurs if new information does not fit into an existing schema; the individual is then motivated to change the schema or form a new one to fit the information. Once this has been satisfactorily accomplished, a state of **equilibrium** is reached.

Schemas are changed by the use of two processes: **assimilation** and **accommodation**.

Assimilation

Assimilation refers to the process whereby new experiences or information are incorporated into an existing schema without changing any other part of it or requiring a new schema to be formed.

Young babies soon develop a schema for picking things up. If an infant has developed a schema for picking up a rattle, he or she may use the same schema – the same grasp – to pick up other objects such as a toy car, a furry toy, and other small objects. This is the process of *assimilation*.

Accommodation

However, this grasp isn't good enough to pick up very small or very large objects so eventually the schema will change. This brings us onto the second process: *accommodation*.

Accommodation refers to the process whereby new experiences or information cannot be incorporated into an existing schema without either changing the schema in a fundamental way or creating a new schema.

If the infant tries to pick up a very small object using the same grasp schema as he or she used for the rattle, this may not be successful. So the infant changes the schema – perhaps by using finger and thumb instead of the whole hand – in order to grasp this new small object. The grasp schema has been changed by the process of accommodation.

The processes of accommodation and assimilation go on throughout life. They are complementary processes – they are both essential – but it is mainly through the process of accommodation (adjusting your ideas to suit the incoming information) that people adapt to the environment.

ACTIVITY 9.8

A simple way of describing the difference between assimilation and accommodation is that assimilation is changing the incoming information to suit the schema; accommodation is changing the schema to suit the incoming information.

Try to find a way of making this easy to remember, by drawing a diagram or by using a mnemonic.

For example, assimilation uses a <u>si</u>milar schema; accom<u>mod</u>ation <u>mod</u>ifies the schema.

Operations

Operations are the rules by which the child understands the world. Piaget believed that the reason children think in different ways at different stages is because the operations they are capable of performing change as they grow older. Only in the last two stages, the concrete operational and the formal operational stages, are they capable of performing logical operations.

EVALUATION OF PIAGET'S THEORY

✚ Piaget has made an astounding contribution to our understanding of a child's mind. This is the single most comprehensive account of cognitive development during infancy, childhood and adolescence. Piaget's theory has received a great deal of support over the years. His original studies were conducted on a relatively small number of Swiss children. In the 1960s and 1970s the studies were repeated

Diversity

By looking at people from other cultures, it is possible to ascertain the extent to which abilities are innate or dependent on upbringing (including type of education).

using large samples of children from various countries, including America, Africa, Britain, and China. These consistently showed that children do go through the same stages in the order stated by Piaget. Children from non-industrialised countries with little formal education reached the stages later than those from industrialised nations, but all of them reached the concrete operational stage (King, 1985).

Piaget may have underestimated some abilities and overestimated others. Several studies (such as those of Hughes and of McGarrigle & Donaldson – see later) question the findings of Piaget's studies. They indicate that it is possible he underestimated the abilities of young children, especially in terms of egocentrism and conservation of number. Other studies indicate that he may have overestimated some abilities.

Some research shows that many adult people never reach the formal operational stage, especially on scientific reasoning problems (King, 1985). Piaget was aware of this and argued that most people attain some kind of formal operational thinking but can only apply it to certain specialised areas with which they are very familiar. For example, a car mechanic may use formal operations to work out how to repair a car but not in other areas such as discussing philosophical questions.

OCR Studies with different results from Piaget's

There have been many attempts to replicate Piaget's studies and to vary the conditions he and his co-workers used. Some of these studies disagree with Piaget's findings. Two important ones are Hughes' "Policeman doll" study that questioned how egocentric young children are, and McGarrigle and Donaldson's "Naughty Teddy" study that looked at conservation of number.

EGOCENTRISM: THE POLICEMAN DOLL STUDY (HUGHES, 1975)

Hughes wondered if children doing the three mountains task found it particularly difficult because they were not familiar with mountains, and also because they couldn't see the point of trying to tell what another person could see. He was interested in whether the children might understand it better if the task of seeing from another's viewpoint was part of a familiar game, such as hide-and-seek.

Aim: Hughes wanted to see if young children can see things from another's point of view when faced with a familiar task.

Method: Each child in turn sat at a table on which was placed an arrangement of four walls set at right angles to one another to form a cross (see picture). The children were given two dolls, a policeman doll and a boy doll. The researcher explained to the child that the boy doll wanted to hide from the policeman. The policeman doll was put at the end of one wall so it could "see" into the two sections divided by the wall. The child was then asked to put the boy in a place where the policeman couldn't see him.

Results: Hughes found that 90% of children aged $3\frac{1}{2}$ to 5 could cope with this task, whereas not many children under 8 years could cope with the three mountains task. Even when another policeman was added, so that there was only one place for the boy doll to go, a significant number of these young children could succeed at the task.

Critical thinking
Why might the task used by Hughes in the policeman doll study make more sense to the children than the task used in the three mountains study?

Conclusion: Children may not be as egocentric as Piaget imagined. This does not mean that young children are entirely lacking in egocentrism; it simply means that they are not as egocentric as tasks like the three mountains would imply.

Why did the children find this task so much easier than the three mountains task? There are probably two reasons:

1. The task made more sense to the child. Although most children do not go around hiding from policemen, most of them are familiar with "hide-and-seek" and the principles are the same, so they were able to see the purpose of the task and understand what was expected of them.
2. The children played an active part in moving the boy doll around – they did not have to work out which picture represented the policeman's view, as they did in the three mountains task.

CONSERVATION: THE NAUGHTY TEDDY STUDY (MCGARRIGLE & DONALDSON, 1974)

Aim: McGarrigle and Donaldson wanted to test children's ability to conserve using the standard method that Piaget used and a variation on this method,

in which a naughty teddy is introduced and the children are not asked the same question twice.

Method: In this study, 80 children took part; each of them was put into two different conditions.

Condition 1 was the *control condition* in which children were given conservation tasks identical to those used by Piaget and using the same procedure (asking the children if, for example, the two rows of counters were identical, then rearranging them and asking the same question again).

Condition 2 was the *experimental condition* in which the same tasks were used, but this time a glove puppet called Naughty Teddy would appear and make the rearrangement. So, for example, when the two identical rows of counters had been laid out "Naughty Teddy" would appear from under the table and spread out one of the rows.

Results: When the study was carried out in the same way as the original study (with the experimenter rearranging the counters) only 16% of the 6-year-olds showed number conservation. When Naughty Teddy rearranged the row, 62% said that the number of counters was still the same.

It's difficult to pin down why there's such a large difference between these two sets of results. McGarrigle and Donaldson argue that Piaget was mistaken in thinking that most 6-year-olds cannot conserve. They believe that when the children were asked the same question twice (Are there the same number of counters?) they might have thought that the adult *must* have changed the number of counters, or why ask the question again?

However, it is quite possible that Piaget was correct and that children aged 6 years do not actually understand number conservation. Different researchers (Moore & Frye, 1986) also followed the Naughty Teddy routine, but this time the teddy *did* actually remove or add a counter. The children still said the rows were the same. It's possible that the teddy distracted them and they were not really paying attention to what was going on.

So at present we are still unclear as to how much 6-year-olds understand about conservation.

OCR The methodology used by Piaget

Throughout his long career, Piaget used a variety of methods to investigate the way in which children's minds work.

Naturalistic observation

When Piaget was looking at how children in the sensorimotor stage develop, he used naturalistic observation, mainly on his own three children. Naturalistic observation involves looking carefully at behaviour in its natural setting. He watched his children in great detail, but no other researcher checked on his observations.

EVALUATION

⊕ These observations have **ecological validity** because they were done in a natural setting (the children's home) on everyday, naturally occurring behaviour. They therefore tell us something about how children learn and behave in their ordinary everyday lives.

⊖ In writing about the sensorimotor stage, Piaget used a small number of children and his observations were not checked. A problem with this is that he assumed all children behaved in the same way as his children did, and he used these observations as the basis of some of his theory. However, researchers should not make generalisations based on only a few people or when their observations have not been checked by other people.

Clinical interview

A **clinical interview** is an unstructured interview, the purpose of which is to gain insight into the individual's thought processes. Piaget would start with a particular question (such as "Is there the same number of counters in the two rows?"), listen carefully to the child's answer, and then vary the next question according to the answer they gave. Piaget did not want to use a formal, structured interview in which every question is asked in exactly the same way for every child, because he wanted to understand the way the child's mind worked. He had originally worked on IQ testing of children, in which every child is asked the same questions and all that is recorded is "correct" or "incorrect" before you go on to the next question. Piaget soon lost interest in this because he wanted to enquire further when a child made a mistake. In essence, then, the use of the clinical interview was central to Piaget's investigations because he was not so much interested in what a child could or could not do but the *reasoning behind it*. Piaget questioned hundreds of children between the ages of 3 and about 12 in order to discover what they thought about all manner of things.

EVALUATION

⊕ The clinical interview gives rich insight into the working of a child's mind by probing into the reasons behind a child's thinking.

⊖ A problem with a clinical interview is that children may be led by the researchers into certain answers. The researcher may lead the interview in a particular direction by the manner in which the questions are asked. Also, since no two interviews are the same, it is difficult to compare the results from each of the children. (Piaget responded to these criticisms by making his procedures more standardised and objective.)

KEY TERMS

Ecological validity: the degree to which the behaviour observed and recorded in a study reflects behaviour that actually occurs in natural settings.

Clinical interview: an unstructured interview through which a researcher hopes to gain insight into an individual's thought processes.

Methodology

The term "clinical interview" originated in a clinical setting. If you think about what happens when you visit a doctor, there is a focus of interest: "What can I do for you?" (a way of saying "What is the problem?"), and once you describe your symptoms, the interview is guided by what you say and the comments (usually questions) from the doctor. No two "interviews" are ever the same.

The Russian psychologist Lev Semeonovich Vygotsky, 1896–1934

OCR The work of Vygotsky

An alternative approach to children's cognitive development was advanced by a Russian psychologist, Lev Vygotsky. There are some very fundamental similarities between Piaget's approach and Vygotsky's (as we will see when we consider applications to education), but there are some important differences that we will now consider.

The importance of culture

Vygotsky criticised Piaget for not paying sufficient attention to the cultural influences on children's cognitive development. According to him, each culture provides its children with the *tools of intellectual adaptation* that permit them to use their mental functions more adaptively. For example, in Western culture, we teach children to write things down and take notes in order to organise information and help them to remember it. Other cultures teach their children to remember in an entirely different way. For example, in some cultures children accompany the adults as they go about their daily work and are shown how to carry out tasks required for survival. Writing notes is inappropriate in learning to fish, hunt or herd animals. In this sense, Vygotsky proposed that cultures teach people *how* to think as well as *what* to think.

The role of others

A very important difference between Piaget and Vygotsky is the extent to which children's cognitive development is influenced by more skilled people giving advice and guidance. Put simply, Piaget thought that children developed well if they were given appropriate tasks and challenges, but worked alone to discover things for themselves. In contrast, Vygotsky believed that children make better progress if they work with people who are more experienced than they are. Adults play a crucial role in Vygotsky's view of children's cognitive development; indeed, he believed that little progress can be made if the child is left to explore the world alone. A major theme of Vygotsky's theory, then, is that *social interaction plays a fundamental role in the development of understanding of the world.*

The zone of proximal development (ZPD)

One of the reasons why adults (or older children) can help a child to develop is based on the idea of the **zone of proximal development** (although this sounds a bit of a mouthful, it's a fairly straightforward idea). Let's explain it first by example.

Three-year-old Chris is trying to do a jigsaw. His first attempts are not very successful but his mother suggests that it is a good idea to do the outside first. She shows him the type of pieces he needs to look for – those with a straight edge. He sorts them and starts fitting them together. His mother points out that the ones with two straight edges are the ones that need to go into the corner. And so the activity proceeds. Chris does most of the work and his mother helps him occasionally, guiding him when he comes to a standstill. On his own, it is very unlikely the jigsaw would be completed, but with help he can manage it. A more complex jigsaw may be beyond him, however much help he is given.

Vygotsky used the term "zone of proximal development" (ZPD) to describe the difference between what a child can do with assistance from a more knowledgeable person and what she or he can do alone. *The ZPD can therefore*

> **KEY TERM**
>
> **Zone of proximal development**: the skill range between what a child can do without help and what they could not achieve even with help.

be defined as the area between the level of performance a child can achieve when working independently and a higher level of performance that is possible when working under the guidance or direction of more skilled adults or peers (Wertsch & Tulviste, 1992). The fundamental idea is that there is a range of skills that children cannot do alone, but which can be developed with adult guidance or help from more experienced children. Equally, there is a limit to what a child can do, even with adult help. So the ZPD is the skill range between what a child can do without help and what they could not achieve even with help.

Vygotsky distinguishes between a child's *actual* developmental level and his or her *potential* level of development. When children are operating within their ZPD – their potential developmental level – they can work with more advanced ideas and concepts as long as they are working with someone who is more of an expert than they are.

Cognitive development, then, is limited to a certain range at any given age, and full cognitive development requires social interaction. What factors are important in this social interaction? This brings us on to another concept, that of **scaffolding**.

ZPD is the skill range between what a child can do without help, and what they could not achieve even with help

Scaffolding

As we have seen, Vygotsky believed that children will achieve little if left to their own devices, but neither do they learn very effectively if they are constantly told what to do. Adults, especially parents and teachers, provide the "scaffolding" necessary for children to be able to learn for themselves and eventually internalise the concepts. *Scaffolding can be defined as the appropriate support framework for children's learning.*

In the course of everyday life, adults guide children all the time and they quite automatically change this guidance, or help, to suit the particular child according to their age and ability. Psychologists have looked at the interaction between adults and their children when they are doing certain tasks. McNaughton et al. (1990) observed how mothers automatically change the type of help they give when working with their children in completing jigsaws of different levels of difficulty. The researchers noted three types of assistance given.

> **EXAM HINT**
>
> Make sure that you can define the term "zone of proximal development" in the exam. This is quite likely to be asked with reference to Vygotsky.

- *Direction maintenance* refers to remarks that are intended to keep their attention focused ("look at that piece").
- *Feedback* refers to remarks that give no information but praise the child's efforts ("well done").
- *Task completion* comprises remarks that give direct guidance, such as "try this one here".

> **How psychology works**
>
> Notice how psychologists observe everyday behaviour in people and use these observations as the basis of their theories. Vygotsky observed everyday interactions between adults and children, and between older and younger siblings, and built on these to understand how children are guided to learn.

Mothers automatically adjusted the level of detail of instruction, using more of all three types of remarks as the tasks got more difficult, but especially increasing the amount of task completion on the more difficult jigsaws. Scaffolding can also be provided by peers or older children, such as older brothers and sisters, who have developed these skills already.

Children eventually develop the problem-solving techniques that they have used with those of greater experience and then use them on their own. In this way, new cognitive skills are learnt.

> **KEY TERM**
>
> **Scaffolding**: the provision of an appropriate support framework for children's learning that can be provided by a more able peer or by an adult.

OCR Applying Piaget's theory to education

Piaget's ideas have been extensively used as the basis for the conduct of education. The main principles involved in applying Piaget's theory to educational practice can be summarised as follows:

- *Children must discover for themselves*: One of the most important principles that Piaget emphasised was that children are innately curious and are pre-programmed to acquire and organise knowledge. They do not require adult intervention in order to do this. In fact, Piaget believed that attempts to directly teach ideas and concepts could be counter-productive. In his opinion, "Every time we teach a child something, we prevent him from discovering it on his own" (Piaget, 1964). According to Piaget, *growth must come from within*; children must discover for themselves.
- *Children are **active learners***: The role of the teacher should therefore be to encourage the child to be active and to provide opportunities that foster their natural capacity to learn. Asking children questions also encourages them to be active in their own learning. When they give incorrect responses, the teacher should use these to gain insight into their thought processes and stage of development.
- *Children must be cognitively ready*: Learning experiences build on existing schemas and you cannot rush this; you cannot move a child from one stage to another if they are not capable of understanding the necessary concepts. For example, you may be able to get young child to rote learn multiplication tables but that does not mean that they understand the principles involved in multiplication. If they forgot what 6×7 was, they would not be able to calculate it.

  The role of the teacher is to provide materials and activities that make children experience a moderate amount of disequilibrium so that accommodation is encouraged, but not to attempt to make them take too great a cognitive leap. The teacher needs to prepare lessons that encourage curiosity, challenge the child's current understanding and so force them to re-evaluate what they already know. If the concepts are too complicated, students will be unable to assimilate them, so no new learning will occur.
- *Teachers need to take account of individual differences*: Since children mature at different rates, they are better working in small groups on activities specially designed for their state of readiness. Teaching the whole class the same thing is therefore not a good idea because each child is at a different stage of readiness. It is also unhelpful because giving out ready-made information goes against Piaget's ideas on active learning.

In sum, Piaget advised that, in school, children should not have to sit and listen passively. Instead, they should be encouraged to use a variety of resources, such as storybooks, arts and crafts, puzzles and games, which enable them to learn by doing. Piaget emphasised that a teacher's job should not be to transmit facts and concepts but to enable children to develop their innate curiosity and experience satisfaction by discovering things for themselves. He believed strongly that the goal of education was to create adults who were creative and inventive and therefore capable of doing new things.

[OCR] Applying Vygotsky's theory to education

Vygotsky, like Piaget, emphasised that learning is not passive but that children need to be active in order to learn well. However, as we've already mentioned, Vygotsky put more emphasis on the role of the adult than did Piaget. The following ideas on educating children are apparent from Vygotsky's theory:

- *Scaffolding is very important in educating children*: Youngsters do not learn readily when they are constantly told what to do, but neither do they benefit by being left to struggle. The teacher's role is to collaborate with them, allowing them to do more and more of a task as their understanding increases. There is also a role for peer mentoring: for children helping each other. Since children learn at different speeds, it is possible that a child who is helped in one task by a particular child can offer help in another area to that same child. Some of you may also be familiar with older children helping younger ones with reading. This is the basis of scaffolding as discussed earlier.
- The *zone of proximal development* can be used as a guide to providing what the child needs in order to progress and learn at the maximum possible rate.
- When designing educational programmes, this should *take account of the context in which the knowledge is to be applied*. Schools should not be isolated places where children learn concepts that they never apply to real life. Students should be given every opportunity to experience "real-world" situations to which they can apply their knowledge.

Chapter summary

- Piaget states that children's cognitive development occurs in four stages:
  - In the *sensorimotor stage* children learn via senses and actions. They live in the here and now, lack symbolic thought, and have not developed full object permanence.
  - In the *pre-operational stage* children have developed symbolic thought but cannot conserve and are egocentric. Egocentrism is demonstrated by the "three mountains" study.
  - In the *concrete operational stage* children can conserve, are no longer egocentric, and can think logically provided that situations are presented in a "concrete" way using familiar concepts.
  - In the *formal operational stage* people are able to deal with hypothetical concepts and can solve problems in a systematic, logical manner in which all possible combinations of factors are considered.
- Children organise everything they know about a particular object or activity into *schemas*. These schemas are modified throughout life by the processes of assimilation and accommodation. *Assimilation* involves fitting new experiences or information into an existing schema without changing any other part of it or requiring a new schema to be formed. *Accommodation* involves changing a schema in a fundamental way or creating a new schema in order to cope with new incoming information.

- Hughes' policeman doll study indicates that children may not be as egocentric as Piaget believed.
- The "naughty teddy" study by McGarrigle and Donaldson indicates that children may be able to conserve number earlier than Piaget believed, but this is controversial.
- Piaget used *naturalistic observations* and *clinical interviews* to investigate children's behaviour and thinking.
- Vygotsky's theory is an alternative to Piaget's. He emphasised the importance of adults and other skilled people in helping children learn. He talked of the *zone of proximal development (ZPD)*, which is the range of skills that a person can demonstrate if helped but could not manage if they were left to their own devices.
- Piaget's theory has been applied to education. The main principles are that children are active, not passive, learners; that they need to discover for themselves; and that there are certain concepts that are beyond their reach until they have acquired the appropriate schemas to deal with them. Teachers need to recognise this and provide appropriate materials to challenge children.
- Vygotsky's ideas have also been applied to education. He emphasised the usefulness of *scaffolding*, a means by which adults can provide the right framework in order for a child to learn.

OCR Exam-style questions for OCR

1. Piaget believed that young children are egocentric.
   a. Outline what is meant by egocentrism. (2 marks)
   b. Describe **one** study that demonstrates that children are not as egocentric as Piaget believed them to be. (4 marks)

2. Describe **one** criticism of Piaget's theory of cognitive development. (3 marks) [OCR, 2008, Specimen Paper 2]

3. State whether the following statements are true or false: circle the correct answer. (4 marks)
   a. Children in the pre-operational stage are capable of symbolic thought.   TRUE   FALSE
   b. The "naughty teddy" study tested whether children were egocentric.   TRUE   FALSE
   c. Children in the concrete operational stage can deal with abstract concepts.   TRUE   FALSE
   d. Children in the formal operational stage can deal with hypothetical concepts.   TRUE   FALSE

4. Describe and evaluate Piaget's experiment into the conservation of number. (10 marks) [OCR, 2008, Specimen Paper 2]

5. Describe how Vygotsky's theory has been applied to education. (5 marks)

Part 5

Cognitive psychology

Cognitive psychology is a study of how the mind works and how it influences our behaviour and experience. Cognitive psychologists are interested in internal mental (cognitive) processes such as those of perceiving, thinking, talking, and attention.

Simple everyday behaviours involve complex mental processes. For example, a person driving their car to work will have to use their memory to take the correct route, their attention will need to be focused on other traffic, and their perceptual system will be making sense of road signs.

Chapter 10 • Memory

We will consider the stages of memory, how we remember, and why we sometimes forget even important things.

Chapter 11 • Perception

We will look at how our brain makes sense of the visual information it receives, and whether perception is innate or something we learn through experience.

What you need to know OCR

The specification lists the following things that you need to be able to do for the examination:

- Describe information processing as input, encoding, storage, retrieval and output
- Distinguish between accessibility and availability problems in memory
- Distinguish between sensory store (buffer), short-term memory and long-term memory with reference to duration and capacity
- Describe the processes of attention and rehearsal
- Explain how forgetting occurs through decay and displacement
- Consider levels of processing as an alternative theory
- Describe and know the limitations of Terry's (2005) study
- Outline an application of research into memory: Memory aids

What you need to know AQA

The specification lists the following things that you need to be able to do for the examination:

- Describe the processes of encoding, storage and retrieval
- Describe the multistore, reconstructive and levels of processing explanations of memory
- Describe and evaluate studies to investigate explanations of memory
- Describe explanations and studies of forgetting, including interference, context and brain damage
- Describe and evaluate studies of eyewitness testimony, including Loftus and Palmer (1974) and Bruce and Young (1998)
- Outline practical applications of memory: Memory aids

Memory

■ ■ ■ ■ ■ ■ ■ ■ ■

Drug companies are developing a series of potentially memory-enhancing pills that it is claimed could soon be adapted to help people get ahead at work or in exams.

The new medicines are currently aimed at treating Alzheimer's disease but could be licensed for over-the-counter sales in a few years.

One new memory drug is being developed by the British-based multinational Astra-Zeneca in collaboration with Targacept, an American company. Epix Pharmaceuticals, also from the United States, is developing a second. Both have "cognitive-enhancing effects" which are aimed at treating patients with age-related memory loss.

But Steven Ferris, a neurologist and former committee member of the Food and Drug Administration, America's licensing authority, said there was nothing to stop mild versions being cleared later for use as "lifestyle pills" by healthy consumers.

"My view is that one could gain approval, provided you showed the drugs to be effective and safe," said Ferris. "It could be a huge market." There is plentiful anecdotal evidence that mind-improving drugs are being taken in Britain by healthy users. They include Provigil, which was developed for narcolepsy, a condition in which sufferers keep falling asleep unexpectedly. Students also use the drug to stay awake.

People are also using Adderall XR and Ritalin, treatments for attention deficit disorder, to promote concentration, and Inderal, a medicine for high blood pressure that can also calm people down.

Tamryn Shean, 23, an engineering student at Cambridge University, used to take Ritalin to treat attention deficit disorder and said she had noticed her performance decline after she stopped. She plans to start using it again to help with her academic work. "It's not a good idea to take the strong ones without prescription, but come exam time everyone's pumped up with pills," said Shean.

The Department of Health said it was not illegal to buy the medicines over the internet, but it was not recommended.

Barbara Sahakian, professor of clinical neuropsychology at Cambridge, said: "It's hard to quantify the scale of the phenomenon but it's definitely catching on."

"For many, enhancement is a dirty word, but the benefits are clear. The reality is we're not always at our best. After being up at night looking after the kids or travelling, many people would love to have something to sharpen them up. It's not taboo to drink Red Bull [a caffeine-rich energy drink]. The principle with cognition enhancers is not so different."

A spokesman for Shire, the British company that manufactures Adderall XR, acknowledged many of its customers were likely to be healthy.

"The perception is that it's youngish people between 18 and 35 or professionals who use it – people who are starting new jobs and want to perform well," he said. "We get a lot of calls from college campuses asking about it."

"There are risks though. It can raise blood pressure, people shouldn't do it."

"Memory pills to help you get ahead," by Chris Gourlay and Joe Lauria. From *The Sunday Times*, 18 January 2009.

OCR AQA Encoding, storage and retrieval

Encoding (input) means that we create a memory trace when presented with material (this could be visual, sound, smell, etc.). So it is the taking in of information through our senses.

Storage refers to where we keep the information that we have encoded and then processed in some way (e.g. rehearsed the information). So it is keeping information that we can then use again if necessary.

Retrieval (output) involves us finding information that we have *encoded* and then *stored* in the brain. It means getting information from our memory system that we can then use.

OCR Accessibility and availability problems in memory

Accessibility problems linked to memory are all about attempting to find information that has already been processed. A person may think they have forgotten the information completely but the real reason is that they simply cannot access it. Imagine that your memory system is made up of rows of filing cabinets. You process some information and place it into a drawer in one of these cabinets. However, you put it in the wrong drawer, which makes it very difficult to access the information again. As a result you say you have forgotten the information when in fact it is still there, you just cannot access it quickly! Later on in this chapter we will look at **long-term memory (LTM)** and **cue dependency,** which can be used as examples of accessibility problems in memory.

Availability problems linked to memory are all about losing information that may already have been processed in the brain. Therefore it is no longer *available*, as it has disappeared for good. Later on in this chapter we will look at **displacement** and **brain damage,** which can be used as examples of lack of availability of information.

OCR AQA ## Multistore model of memory

Atkinson and Shiffrin (1972) proposed their theory of memory mainly based around how we store information that we have processed (done something with). Below is a diagram of their model.

As can be seen, a lot of information hits our **sensory buffer,** but only a fraction of it can be processed as our brain has a limited processing unit. The sensory buffer picks up information based around our senses. So we can form very brief echoic memories (those based on what we hear) or iconic memories (those based around what we see) for instance. This information is only taken further if we pay *attention* to it.

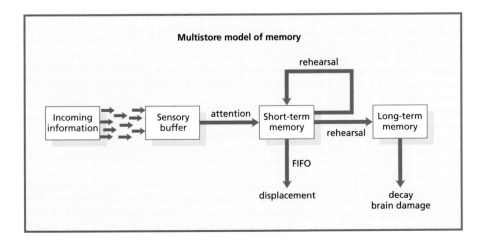

Multistore model of memory

If we do pay attention to the information then it can enter our **short-term memory (STM)**. This has a limited capacity – it is believed that it can hold seven plus or minus two items (maybe depending on the size of the item). An item could be one word, the line from a song or part of a telephone number. It is believed that memories last from 15 to 30 seconds in short-term memory.

However, once the amount of information goes above the maximum that can fit into our short-term memory, something happens called *displacement*. This is based around the idea of *FIFO* (First In First Out) – so the item that was first into your short-term memory will be the first one out!

If we do not fill up our short-term memory and **rehearse**/*repeat* the information then it could go into *long-term memory*. Here it can be stored indefinitely until you need to retrieve the information for use. It is believed that information potentially lasts forever in here. However, two things could happen that could make information disappear from long-term memory, according to Atkinson and Shiffrin: **decay**, where the information simply gets more and more faint (think of what happens to photographs over time – they can fade) or *brain damage*, where the memories that were physically stored in the brain are literally removed when physical damage or deterioration takes place.

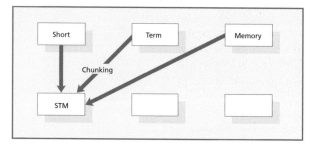

The term "Short-Term Memory" takes up three slots in your short-term memory. However, if you chunk information (i.e. condense it down) you can fit more into your short-term memory. So, if you use the acronym STM it is now taking up just one slot in your short-term memory!

ACTIVITY 10.1

Create a list of 20 words that are all one syllable or all two syllables long. Read them out to three people and then ask them to recall as many as possible. Note down which words they recall. Notice whether they forget many from the middle of the list – if so, then those words have been displaced!

EVALUATION OF THE MULTISTORE MODEL OF MEMORY

➕ There is some supporting evidence for the limited capacity of short-term memory. Glanzer and Cunitz (1966) reported that when people were asked to recall a list of words they had just heard, they performed much worse recalling the end words of the list if they were set a 30-second counting exercise in between. That is, the words had been displaced. A fuller overview of their study follows this evaluation.

➕ Case studies of brain-damaged patients can lend support to there being separate short-term and long-term memory stores. For example, the case of KF (Shallice & Warrington, 1970): after a motorcycle accident that caused some brain damage, KF had very disrupted short-term memory but virtually intact long-term memory.

- Atkinson and Shiffrin may have been incorrect about the potential capacity of short-term memory. Boutla et al. (2004) tested the short-term memory capacity of people who were deaf compared with those who could hear. They were all given the same word list, but the deaf participants *saw* it via sign language whereas the hearing participants *heard* the words. Intriguingly, the deaf participants were only able to recall, on average, four words from the end of the list. Compare this to the hearing participants who could recall around seven, which is predicted by the multistore model. It would appear that visual information may well take up more space in short-term memory compared to acoustic information.

- The multistore model cannot explain how some distinctive information gets into long-term memory without going through the processes highlighted in the model. So, for example, some shocking or surprising news does not need to be rehearsed for it to be stored in long-term memory. All information should be processed in the same way – it hits the sensory buffer, attention is paid to it, it goes into short-term memory where it must be rehearsed a few times before entering long-term memory. It would appear that distinctive information hits the sensory buffer and then goes straight into long-term memory, missing out the rest.

AQA Studies that investigate explanations of memory

A STUDY INTO DISPLACEMENT (GLANZER & CUNITZ, 1966)

Aim: To test out whether short-term memory has a limited capacity.

Method: A total of 46 army-enlisted men took part in Glanzer and Cunitz's experiment. They were shown words projected onto a screen every 3 seconds. The word list consisted of 15 words. Once the participant had seen all 15 words, one of three things happened:

1. The participant was allowed to recall as many words as possible.

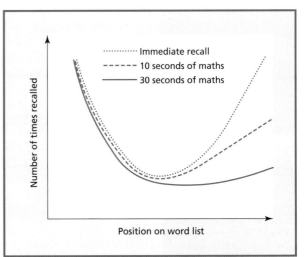

Immediate recall
10 seconds of maths
30 seconds of maths

Number of times recalled

Position on word list

First in, first out!

Methodology

This is a typical laboratory experiment, with all the advantages and disadvantages that entails. It has carefully controlled variables, so we can be fairly confident that the independent variable causes the dependent variable; i.e. that the gap between hearing and recall affected the number of words recalled from the end of the list. However, it's an artificial task that only tests one portion of memory (that of a list of words), so it cannot be applied to every type of everyday memory.

2. The participant had to begin counting for 10 seconds, then was allowed to recall as many words as possible.
3. The participant had to begin counting for 30 seconds, then was allowed to recall as many words as possible.

Results: The results are plotted on the graph on page 219.

As can clearly be seen, the participants' long-term memory was not affected, as they could all recall the first words in the list. However, differences emerged for recall of the words at the end of the list.

Conclusion: It would appear that the results support the idea of short-term memory having a limited capacity. The participants in the third group had undergone displacement via FIFO and all that was left in their STM was numbers, hence they could not recall any of the words from the end of the list.

EXAM HINT

This is a very useful study to use to evaluate (support) the multistore model, but you need only the findings (not the aim or method). Practise summarising these in a couple of sentences, starting "In support of this model, Glanzer et al. demonstrated that…" Always end by stating clearly WHY the findings support the model (i.e. it demonstrates that STM has limited capacity).

ACTIVITY 10.2

Generate a list of 20 words that are quite easy to remember. You will need to find two different groups of participants for this. Read the list of words to the first group and then ask them to recall as many as possible. Read the words to the second group and then get them to start reciting their four-times table for 30 seconds – after that ask them to recall as many words as possible. You should find that the second group cannot recall many words from the end of the list. This is because their STM no longer contains the words – it contains the numbers from the four-times table!

KEY TERM

Structural processing: processing things in relation to the way they look (e.g. the structure of things).

OCR AQA Levels of processing

Craik and Lockhart (1974) proposed a different theory of memory called levels of processing. They stated that memories are a by-product of the way in which we process information. As we complete tasks during the day, the amount of effort assigned to them means that we are more or less likely to remember them. They proposed three different levels of processing:

1. **Structural:** This refers to processing things in relation to the way they look (e.g. the structure of things). This is called "shallow processing" as not much

effort goes into processing the information. As a result, these memories are weak and do not last long.

2. **Phonemic/Phonetic**: This refers to processing things in relation to how they sound.
3. **Semantic**: This refers to processing things in relation to what they mean. This is called "deep processing" as a lot of effort has to go into processing the information. As a result, these memories are strong and last for a long time.

An example to help you

One of the ways in which the levels of processing theory has been tested is by using a series of questions to "force" people to process the information either structurally, phonemically or semantically. The following examples should help you understand the differences between the three levels. A participant is given a question with a word as an answer. The participant has to answer either yes or no. After all questions have been asked, the participant is usually asked to recall as many as possible of the words that were answers:

- *Structural*: Is the following word in UPPER CASE? waffle
- *Phonemic*: Does the following word rhyme with water? daughter
- *Semantic*: Does the following word fit into the sentence "_____ is a type of fruit"? banjo

> **ACTIVITY 10.3**
>
> With the three questions above, work out how much of the word you have to process to be able to answer yes or no. For which one do you not have to process any of the word, and for which do you have to process the entire word?

The more effort that has to go into processing the word, the easier it is to remember that word. This is called depth of processing – the deeper the processing (based on effort), the stronger the memory will be.

OCR AQA A study into levels of processing

CRAIK AND TULVING (1975)

Aim: To test the levels of processing theory of memory proposed by Craik and Lockhart. They were interested in whether there would be a difference in the recall of words that were structurally, phonemically or semantically processed.

Procedure: Craik and Tulving ran a series of 10 experiments (we are going to look at Experiment 2). A series of questions were posed to the participants (as highlighted below) – 20 for each level of processing, with 10 *yes* answers and 10 *no* answers. After each question the participant looked into a

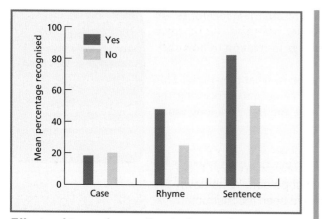

Effects of type of encoding task on subsequent word recognition. Based on Craik and Tulving (1975)

Everyday life

Although this study may not immediately appear to relate to ordinary everyday memory, it does in fact have important applications as it shows how significant it is to understand the *meaning* of information in order to remember it. Just bear that in mind when revising your psychology notes!

tachistoscope where a word was presented for 200 ms. They then responded with either yes or no.

After this particular task, the 24 participants were given a typed list of 180 words (60 they had seen and 120 distractors). They had to choose which ones they recognised from the tachistoscope. All words were five-letter common concrete nouns.

Examples of questions were:

1. Is the following word in capital letters? table
2. Does the following word rhyme with shower? grass
3. Does the following word fit into the sentence "_____ is a type of fruit"? apple

Findings: Above is a bar chart showing the percentage of words recognised.

Conclusion: The findings do support levels of processing. The words that were semantically processed were recognised more often than the phonemically processed and structurally processed words. This is because the semantic words produced deeper processing.

AQA Reconstructive memories

This particular approach to memory tries to explain what happens when information is stored and then we want to retrieve it. As the name of the approach suggests, we may reconstruct what we *think* we saw or processed to help us to retrieve it.

Bartlett (1932) proposed this idea of reconstruction. When we retrieve stored information, it is influenced by the attitudes and feelings we had at the time we processed it. Therefore, we actively reconstruct our memories from a range of information. Bartlett tested this out by getting participants to read a passage of information and then pass that information on to the next person, who passed it on to the next person and so on (it sounds very similar to a game called Chinese Whispers).

He used a Native American story called "War of the Ghosts" because it would have been unfamiliar to the participants. After the story had been passed on through six people it had changed in many ways. It was much shorter (usually less than half the original length). Also, the details that were left out were about Native American culture, so the story sounded more like an English one. Therefore, the participants were reconstructing the memory from a range of information including the story itself but *changing* it to fit in with their own attitudes and feelings. The reason this could happen is because of schemas (pockets of memory that hold information about a particular thing – for example we can all visualise a cat or a tree and we are activating our schemas of those when we think). Therefore when we are reconstructing we activate these schemas and make use of them.

> ### ACTIVITY 10.4
>
> Write out a story (about 15 sentences), then get someone to read it and pass the information on to the next person. Do this with five people and see what story is recalled by the last person. Write down which bits of the story are correct and which have been reconstructed in a different way.

Another example comes from Allport and Postman (1947). Participants were shown a picture of a scruffy white man arguing with a black man in a suit. The white man was holding a razor to the black man. Participants had to recall the picture to describe to the next participant and so on. By the end the descriptions had changed so much that it was claimed that the black man was holding the razor! The participants had reconstructed their memories using incorrect information.

AQA Interference and forgetting

There are two types of interference that can cause forgetting: **proactive interference** and **retroactive interference**.

- *Proactive interference*: This is when information that you have already processed interferes with new information you are trying to process, with the end result that you forget the new information.
- *Retroactive interference*: This is when new learning interferes with material that you have previously processed and stored.

For a study showing that proactive interference affects people's ability to recall television advertisements, see Terry (2005) on page 226. Participants could recall advertisements from the beginning of a commercial break but not from the end.

Critical thinking

Think about how this can explain why you would be much slower sending a text message on a different model of phone than your own. What type of interference is this?

When you change phones, you soon get used to the new one and, after a couple of weeks, would make a lot of mistakes if you went back to using your old one. What type of interference is this?

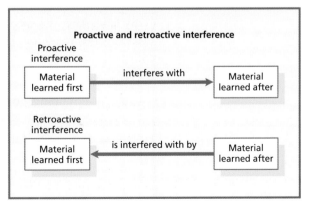

Proactive and retroactive interference

KEY TERMS

Context dependent: cues that are external to us, i.e. the environment in which the information is encoded into memory.

State dependent: cues that are internal to us, i.e. our emotional "state" when information is encoded into memory.

AQA Context and forgetting

ACTIVITY 10.5

Before reading on, what do you think is meant by cue-dependent forgetting? What does the "cue" bit refer to?

Cue dependency attempts to explain forgetting in long-term memory. This theory proposes that we forget information because there is a *mismatch* between cues at encoding and cues at retrieval. There are two types of cue dependency:

1. **Context dependent:** This refers to cues that are external to us. An example might be where you sit in the classroom. If you sit in the same place every lesson and the displays do not change too much, then your surroundings are context cues.
2. **State dependent:** This refers to cues that are internal to us. An example of this is emotions (being happy, sad, fearful, etc.). Encoding information while being very happy is a state cue.

AQA A study into cue dependency

GODDEN AND BADDELEY (1975)

Aim: Godden and Baddeley wanted to test out whether we need cues to help us recall information.

Method: A total of 18 participants (13 male and 5 female) from a diving club were tested. Participants were asked to attempt to remember a word list consisting of 36, unrelated, different words. The participants were split into four different conditions, as shown in the table below.

"Wet" means the divers participating were underwater when they learned (encoded) or remembered (retrieved) the word list. "Dry" means they were on dry land. After the encoding phase, a 4-minute delay occurred so that, in the underwater condition, the divers could reach the surface and begin writing

Encoding condition	Retrieval condition
Dry	Dry
Dry	Wet
Wet	Dry
Wet	Wet

down the words they could remember. To ensure fairness, the participants encoding on dry land also waited for 4 minutes until they were allowed to recall. All participants were given 2 minutes to recall as many of the 36 words as possible.

Results: The results are shown in the bar chart on the right.

Conclusion: As can clearly be seen, the participants who had a mismatch between cues at encoding and cues at retrieval were more likely to forget words from the list. This supports the idea of cue dependency.

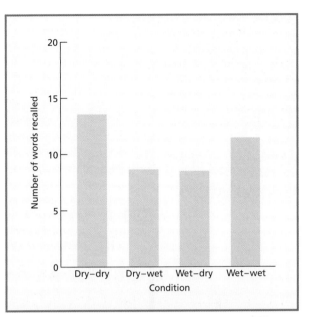

AQA Brain damage and forgetting

For this section we will examine two case studies that can show how brain damage affects memory and forgetting. They are the case of HM and the case of Clive Wearing.

The case of HM

HM was a patient who suffered from severe epilepsy. When he was 27 years old he underwent surgery to relieve the epilepsy. During the procedure large parts of his temporal lobes were removed. This had a very large effect on his memory systems. After the operation HM was unable to form new memories for facts or events. However, he showed only mild difficulty in recalling events from around 11 or so years before the operation, and could remember virtually everything from 16 or more years before the operation. Even though he had severe difficulty transferring information to his long-term memory, his short-term memory was virtually normal. This meant he could handle the seven items of information in his short-term memory but could not then get the information into his rehearsal loop to transfer it to long-term memory. Therefore his long-term memory was damaged but not his short-term memory.

The case of Clive Wearing

In 1985, Clive wearing contracted a virus that normally causes cold sores (a type of herpes virus). However, instead of it forming a cold sore it attacked his brain (around the temporal lobes and in particular a region called the hippocampus) causing damage. Since then he has not been able to form new memories (psychologists call this **anterograde amnesia**). The area of the brain that had been damaged meant he could not transfer information to long-term memory.

Why psychology matters

Cue-dependency theory has been used by the police to improve the memory of witnesses. If you take people back to the scene of the crime, do a reconstruction, or ask people to imagine the situation they were in when a crime or accident occurred, they are likely to recall things they might otherwise have forgotten. This method, and other similar techniques such as imagining yourself back in the situation, have been crucial in gathering as much evidence as possible from witnesses.

Methodology

Case studies of unusual people (including those who have amazing memories as well as those who are brain damaged) are fascinating, and give us insight into how the brain works. Nevertheless, we must be cautious about generalising the findings to the ordinary population.

KEY TERM

Anterograde amnesia: a complete inability to recall memories from LTM, or to form new memories.

As a result of this, it has been argued that in effect he restarts his memory system every 18 seconds (the length of time his short-term memory lasts for). He only remembers fragments of his life prior to 1985 – he knows he has children from a previous marriage but cannot name them. He shows no loss of affection for his wife though, and he greets her joyously every time he sees her as if he hasn't seen her in years. One thing that is amazing about Clive is that prior to the virus he was a well-known pianist and conductor. He still has both of those skills because the part of his brain responsible for that type of memory (the cerebellum) was not damaged. So he cannot remember anything about being educated on the piano or learning to become a conductor, but he can still perform those tasks well.

OCR A study into serial position effects in recall of TV commercials

OCR CORE STUDY: TERRY (2005)

Aim: Terry asked the question "… *does the position of a television commercial in a block of commercials determine how well it will be recalled?*" (p. 151). This was done using three different experiments.

Method: *Experiment 1*: A sample of 39 undergraduates (22 women and 17 men) took part in this experiment. There were four lists of 15 advertisements, which gave a total of 60 advertisements used in the study. There were some local and some national brands. Half of the advertisements lasted 15 seconds and the other half lasted 30 seconds. All advertisements were for different products and companies. Also, product categories were not repeated in any list (e.g. two car brands never appeared together in one of the lists).

The participants were told that they would have to recall the advertisements, and that they should try to remember brand names if possible. Participants were tested on recall three times – immediately after being presented with the advertisements, after completing a 3-minute verbal assessment test, and then after they had completed their research participation form.

Results: The results from Experiment 1 are shown in the graph.

As can be seen from the graph, when the participants were tested immediately they recalled more from the beginning and the end of the list (called the *primacy–recency* effect). As soon as the participants had to complete any task (the verbal task and the form filling) the advertisements at the end of the list were not remembered very well. There was no difference in whether the advertisements were 15 seconds or 30 seconds long.

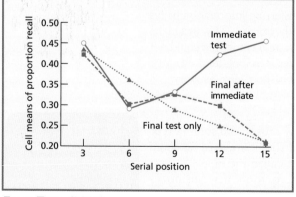

From Terry (2005)

Method: *Experiment 2*: Terry wanted to increase the ecological validity of the study. He stated that immediate recall might not be good because advertisements usually separate the two halves of a television programme. Therefore recall was tested differently.

A total of 27 new participants took part in Experiment 2. The lists still contained 15 advertisements, but each one lasted 30 seconds. There were three lists of advertisements – labelled A, B and C. The participants were asked to watch a comedy show and the programme was stopped at 4, 8 and 15 minutes when the advertisements were presented. The programme was then stopped at 18 minutes and the participants were asked to recall as many of the advertisements as possible. Each time the programme stopped for advertisements a different list was presented to that group of participants. So, for example, the first group could have been given A then B then C; the second group B then C then A, and so on.

Experiment 3: Experiment 2 was repeated with a separate sample of 23 students, but instead of a recall task at 18 minutes, they were given a recognition task. That is, they were presented with brands that had or had not been part of any advertisement list and they had to state whether they had seen them advertised or not.

Results: The results for Experiments 2 and 3 are shown in the graph below.

As can be seen with the recall task, participants were good at recalling advertisements that happened at the beginning of the list. For the recognition task there was little effect of position in the advertisement list, although the early advertisements were recognised at a higher rate than those in the middle or at the end of the list.

Conclusions: Advertisements that appeared in the first three or four positions in a list of 15 were better recalled. Therefore, advertisers should want their products to be advertised then, and television companies could charge more for these "prime" positions in a commercial break.

Limitations: Some psychologists may criticise the small sample sizes used by Terry in the studies. Taking this further, there was usually a slight gender imbalance in each experiment. This could affect the results, as he did not test whether females were more likely to have better recall for products aimed at females, and males the reverse. Also, the initial experiment was nothing like the way we view advertisements when we watch our favourite television shows (i.e. just watching

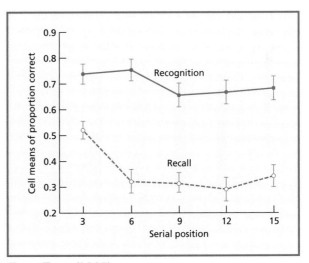

From Terry (2005)

advertisements and nothing else). However, he did attempt to change this in Experiments 2 and 3 to make the advertisements appear during a television show.

AQA Studies of eyewitness testimony

STUDY ONE: LOFTUS AND PALMER (1974)

Aim: Loftus and Palmer wanted to investigate whether language could affect memory of a car crash. They conducted two experiments to test this out.

Method: *Experiment 1*: A total of 45 students participated in the study. They watched seven films depicting traffic accidents, then had to try to recall what they had just seen. However, there was one question asking the participants to estimate how fast the cars were going when the accident happened. The crucial difference was the wording of the question. The first group of nine participants were given the question "*About how fast were the cars going when they* hit *each other?*" The remainder of participants were split equally into four other groups and the word "hit" was replaced by either *smashed, collided, bumped* or *contacted*.

Results: *Experiment 1*: The bar chart below shows the average estimate of speed by the five different groups.

Conclusion: *Experiment 1*: It would appear that the verbs used in questions may affect people's perceptions of a car accident. Those who had the verb "smashed" in their question perceived the cars as going much faster than those who had the verb "contacted". As we know, all participants watched the same film.

Method: *Experiment 2*: This time, 150 students watched a film showing a multiple car accident. The film lasted for less than 1 minute, with the accident lasting just 4 seconds. After watching the film the participants were asked to write down all they could remember from what they had seen. The participants were actually split into three groups. One group were asked the same question as those in Experiment 1: "*About how fast were the cars going when they* hit

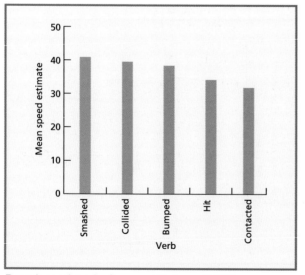

Data based on Loftus and Palmer (1974)

each other?" The second group had "hit" replaced with "smashed". The final group were not asked about the speed of the cars (a control group).

One week later the participants returned and were asked more questions about the film (they were not shown the film again). A critical question was placed into the questionnaire. It was *"Did you see any broken glass?"*, with a simple yes/no response next to it. In reality there was no broken glass in the film.

Results: *Experiment 2*: The table below shows the number of participants per group who answered yes or no to the glass question.

Distribution of "Yes" and "No" responses to the question "Did you see any broken glass?"			
	Verb condition		
Response	Smashed	Hit	Control
Yes	16	7	6
No	34	43	44

Conclusion: *Experiment 2*: It would appear that the wording of questions again can cause participants to report things that they didn't see. The use of the verb *smashed* had more of an effect, as it would be expected that cars smashing would have broken glass somewhere (especially as use of this verb led to the highest speed estimates in Experiment 1). And as we know, there was no broken glass in the film.

EVALUATION

- The Loftus and Palmer study may lack ecological validity in two ways. The first is that the study is a well-controlled laboratory experiment. In a real-life crime scene there is no high level of control, so how do we know if what Loftus and Palmer reported happens in real-life eyewitness accounts? Also, the task was to watch a film of an accident. Again this is not what happens in real-life crimes, so validity is low.

- As the study is well controlled, Loftus and Palmer can be confident that it was the independent variables in both studies that were affecting eyewitness recall.

➕ One of the studies had a large sample size, meaning that it is *more likely* to have a range of people in it, and so making it easier to generalise to the target population.

➖ However, both studies used students who may have a superior memory system to other types of people because they are at university. This means that it may be difficult to know whether the the same processes would happen in real eyewitness testimonies.

STUDY TWO: BRUCE AND YOUNG (1998)

Please note that Bruce and Young is a book about face perception. Within there is one study by Burton, Wilson, Cowan and Bruce (1999).

Aim: To examine the ability of participants to identify faces from video security devices. Burton et al. conducted a range of studies. We will look at one of these.

Method: Sixty participants were recruited for the study. They were tested individually in an experimental room, where they watched 10 video clips of people entering buildings (the people were university staff). The participants watched each clip twice. After this they were shown high-quality pictures of people's faces. They had to rate each image using the following rating scale: 1 = that person definitely did not appear in the video, to 7 = they were sure that the person appeared in the video. They were shown faces of people who had appeared, but also faces of people who had not (seen and unseen).
The 60 participants were from three different populations:

1. Twenty students who had been taught by the people on the videos.
2. Twenty students from other departments in the university, not taught by the people in the videos.
3. Twenty police officers.

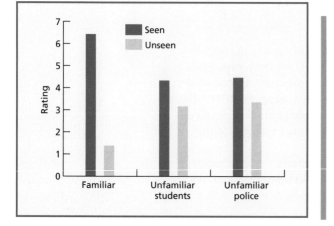

Results: The results are shown in the bar chart.
The students who knew the people on the video were very good at identifying them from the high-quality pictures. However, the other two groups found it difficult to distinguish between people they had seen or not seen on the video clips.

Conclusion: Familiarity with the target on the video clip had a large effect on identification. This needs to be looked at when evidence from devices such as CCTV cameras is used in courts.

EVALUATION

➕ As the study is well controlled, Burton et al. can be confident that it was familiarity that affected the ratings given for each picture.

➖ A small sample size could make it difficult to generalise beyond the sample used, as there were only 20 participants in each group. Additionally, as it was an independent groups design there could have been participant variables within each group that were affecting the ratings, rather than familiarity.

➖ The rating system is subjective, so a rating of 5 from one participant may not be the same as a rating of 5 from another.

KEY TERMS

Hierarchies: a method of outlining information in a structured way, beginning with general information and ending with specific information.

Mind maps: free-ranging diagrams that use organisation and imagery to encode information so that it can be retrieved more easily.

OCR AQA Practical applications of research into memory: Memory aids

There are two techniques that we will examine in this section: **hierarchies** and **mind maps**.

Hierarchies

With this technique, material that you wish to learn is placed into a hierarchy. The hierarchy begins with something general and the further down the hierarchy we go, the more specific the information is. An example of a hierarchy that you could use for the section on Moral development is shown below.

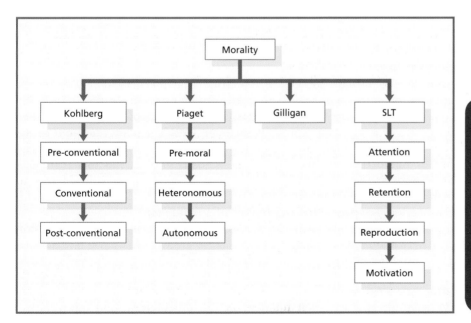

EXAM HINT

After reading about organisation and imagery, why not put them into practice for your mock exams? See if you show an improved score compared to other tests you may have done, and find the technique that suits you best. Use this when you come to revise for the final exams.

So, a hierarchy is a form of outlining the information in a structured way. Information we learn is not always simple and cannot always form a hierarchy, but the basics can easily be placed into some form of structure.

> ### ACTIVITY 10.6
>
> Take another topic area from GCSE Psychology and produce a hierarchy of knowledge similar to the one on Moral development on page 231.

Evidence

Bower, Clark, Lesgold and Winzenz (1969) asked people to learn words that had been placed into a hierarchy diagram, like the one for Moral Development. One group were given a diagram presented in a logical, organised manner. The second group's hierarchy diagram had the words randomly placed in the diagram (e.g. in our Moral development diagram Retention would have been where the word Morality is). For the organised group, the average recall was 73 words. For the random group, the recall averaged only 21 words. Other studies such as that of Wittrock (1974) showed similar results, even when the words had been randomly chosen from a dictionary.

> ### ACTIVITY 10.7
>
> Create a hierarchy for anything you want (e.g. animals) and then draw another version of the same diagram but with the words randomised. Give people the same amount of time to look at one or other diagram and then ask them to recall as many words as possible. What differences do you find?

Everyday life

Mind maps are obviously good tools for revision, as mentioned in Chapter 1 as well as here.

KEY TERMS

Organisation: a memory technique that encodes information in a specific way (e.g. always using a yellow sticker on cognitive psychology notes).

Imagery: a memory technique that encodes information as pictures (e.g. illustrations of memory models).

Mind maps

According to Buzan (2005, p. 6) "a Mind Map is the easiest way to put information into your brain and take information out of the brain". He compares mind maps to the map of a city. The centre of a mind map is like the centre of a city, as it represents the main idea. The main roads out of the city represent the main areas of information we are wishing to learn. The further out of the city we go, the more roads appear, and this represents more information and thoughts. We are very good at using landmarks to highlight interesting things around a city, and we can do exactly the same with information. See page 9 for an example of a mind map.

So, an effective mind map uses *colours* to help the brain process information creatively and *images* to help you to visualise the *key words* you have chosen as the essential information you wish to learn.

Imagery and memory

We have already seen that mind maps use **organisation** and **imagery**, but are there other techniques that use imagery? Imagery refers to "…mental representations of objects or actions that are not physically present" (Matlin, 1989, p. 127).

One way that we can use *imagery* to help us to recall information is to visualise images of the material. This has been shown to be successful by Bower and Winzenz (1970). Participants were given word pairs to learn. Group 1 were simply told to repeat the pairs several times. Group 2 were asked to construct a mental picture of the two words interacting. The latter group recalled over twice as many word pairs as the first group.

Taking this a step further, Wollen, Weber and Lowry (1972) wanted to see if bizarreness in imagery helped us to recall word pairs. Participants were split into four groups:

KEY TERM

Method of loci: a memory technique of associating items to be learned with physical locations (e.g. remembering a shopping list by linking items to where they are in the supermarket).

1. images interacting and bizarre
2. images interacting but not bizarre
3. images not interacting but bizarre
4. images not interacting and not bizarre.

Interestingly, if the images were interacting, recall improved. Bizarreness did not improve recall any further.

Method of loci

With the **method of loci** technique, people learn to associate items to be remembered with *physical* locations. Bower (1970) highlighted the steps that should be used in this technique:

Recall is not improved further if the image is bizarre.

1. Memorise a list of locations that are already arranged in a logical order. A good example could be your route to school, college or workplace.
2. Create an image for each item of information that you wish to remember.
3. Take these items in the order that you feel they need to be learned and associate them in turn with locations you have chosen.

A good example of how method of loci (pronounced low-sigh) can be used in an everyday context is a shopping list. Many people can visualise their way around a supermarket and hence always remember their shopping "list" as the items are linked to their position in the supermarket. However, if a supermarket rearranges its locations for items, then that person will forget items as they are not where they used to be!

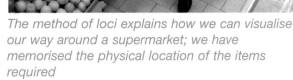

The method of loci explains how we can visualise our way around a supermarket; we have memorised the physical location of the items required

Evidence

Groninger (1971) tested out the method of loci with a list of 25 words. Group 1 participants were asked to use a familiar route and place the 25 words along it.

Group 2 were simply asked to try to remember the 25 words in any way they liked. Before leaving they were told *not* to rehearse any of the information. The participants had to return 1 week and 5 weeks after the initial task. At both time points the method of loci group performed much better, especially at 5 weeks when they recalled about twice as many words as the other group.

ACTIVITY 10.8

Generate a list of 12 items that could feature on a shopping list. Use the method of loci to try to remember the items by using a familiar route and attaching each item to a location. So, for example, you may wish to choose your route to school or college, or use *any* route that you are familiar with. See how many of the items you can recall after you have created your own method of loci.

Chapter summary

- There are three processes involved in memory – encoding (taking it in), storage (placing it somewhere) and retrieval (getting it back).
- You can have accessibility and availability problems with memory. Accessibility is about trying to locate information that might have been stored somewhere incorrectly. Availability is when information could well be lost forever through things like decay and brain damage.
- The multistore model explains memory in the following way. Information hits the sensory buffer and the bits we pay attention to go into short-term memory. However, as short-term memory has limited capacity, information may be displaced. If information is rehearsed enough it makes its way to long-term memory where it could well be stored forever.
- Levels of processing is another explanation for memory. It all depends on the depth to which you process the information. You can do this structurally (what things look like), phonemically (what things sound like) or semantically (what things mean). Structural processing produces weak memories, but semantic produces strong memories.
- There is also reconstructive memory. This particular approach to memory tries to explain what happens when information is stored and then we want to retrieve it. As the name of the approach suggests, we may reconstruct what we *think* we saw or processed in order to help us retrieve it.
- We could forget through interference. *Proactive interference* is when information that you have already processed interferes with new information you are trying to process, with the end result that you forget the new information. *Retroactive interference* is when new learning interferes with material that you have previously processed and stored.

- We may also forget as a result of a mismatch in the cues we had when encoding compared to the cues at retrieval. State cues relate to internal things like emotion. Context cues relate to external stimuli like our surroundings.
- We can experience brain damage that makes us forget. Case studies into HM and Clive Wearing have shown us this.
- A core study by Terry looked at the recall of TV advertisements. Participants were better at recalling advertisements that appeared at the start of a break. Recognition of an advertisement was not affected by its position in the advert break.
- Loftus investigated eyewitness testimony. She found that the way in which an accident was described affected the speed at which the participants perceived the cars to be going.
- A study from Bruce and Young's book investigated our ability to recognise faces from CCTV images. If the participants knew the person they saw on CCTV, then identification was excellent. However, if they did not know the person, identification was poor.
- Memory can be applied to the real world by looking at how to improve it. Techniques such as hierarchies, mind maps and imagery could all help to improve memory.

OCR Exam-style questions for OCR

1. Define the term storage using an example. (2 marks)

2. State **two** differences between long-term and short-term memory based on capacity and duration. (4 marks)

3. Describe levels of processing as a theory of memory. (3 marks)

4. Describe **two** things about the procedure used in the Terry (2005) study. (2 marks)

5. Describe **one** weakness of the Terry (2005) study. (2 marks)

EXAM HINT

Question 2 may sound complicated, but it's really very simple and straightforward. Capacity is how much the memory holds; duration is how long it lasts. So it's a dead easy 4 marks!

AQA Exam-style questions for AQA

1. Define the term storage using an example. (2 marks)

2. Describe the reconstructive theory of memory. (3 marks)

3. Outline the difference between proactive and retroactive interference. (2 marks)

4. Describe the study by Loftus and Palmer (1974). You must outline the purpose of the study, what participants had to do, what the results were, and a conclusion. (6 marks)

5. Outline **one** way in which we can improve memory. (4 marks)

What you need to know OCR

The specification lists the following things that you need to be able to do for the examination:

■ Describe the difference between sensation and perception using shape constancy, colour constancy and visual illusions

■ Explain depth cues including linear perspective, height in plane, relative size, superimposition and texture gradient

■ Outline the role of experience in perception

■ Explain the concept of top-down processing

■ Explain the concept of perceptual set

■ Explain the criticisms of the constructivist theory of perception

■ Consider the nativist theory as an alternative theory, with specific reference to bottom-up processing in perception

■ Describe and outline limitations of the Haber and Levin (2001) study

■ Outline an application of research into perception: Advertising

Perception

The traditional subject of the tug of war over language and perception is color. Because languages divide the spectrum differently, researchers have asked whether language affected how people see color. English, for example, distinguishes blue from green. Most other languages do not make that distinction. Is it possible that only English speakers really see those colors as different?

Last year, Lera Boroditsky and colleagues published a study in *The Proceedings of the National Academy of Sciences* showing that language could significantly affect how quickly perceptions of color are categorized. Russian and English speakers were asked to look at three blocks of color and say which two were the same.

Russian speakers must distinguish between lighter blues, or goluboy, and darker blues, siniy, while English speakers do not have to, using only "blue" for any shade. If the Russians were shown three blue squares with two goluboy and one siniy, or the other way around, they picked the two matching colors faster than if all three squares were shades from one blue group. English makes no fundamental distinction between shades of blue, and English speakers fared the same no matter the mix of shades.

In two different tests, subjects were asked to perform a nonverbal task at the same time as the color-matching task. When the Russians simultaneously carried out a nonverbal task, they kept their color-matching advantage. But when they had to perform a verbal task at the same time as color-matching, their advantage began to disappear. The slowdown suggested that the speed of their reactions did not result just from a learned difference but that language was actively involved in identifying colors as the test was happening. Two other recent studies also demonstrated an effect of language on color perception and provided a clue as to why previous experimental results have been inconclusive. In *The Proceedings of the National Academy of Sciences*, Dr. Paul Kay of the International Computer Science Institute at Berkeley and colleagues hypothesized that if language is dominant on the left side of the brain, it should affect color perception in the right visual field. (The right visual field is connected to the left side of the brain, and vice versa.)

English-speaking subjects were shown a ring of 12 small squares that were all the same color except an odd one on the left or the right. If the odd square was shown to the right visual field and it was from a completely different color category in English, like a green square compared to the ring of blue squares, then subjects were quick to identify it as different. If the odd square shown to the right visual field was the same basic color as the ring of squares, perhaps just being a different shade of blue, subjects were not as fast to recognize the difference. If the odd square was shown to the left visual field, it didn't matter if it was a different color or only a different shade.

Abridged extract from "When Language Can Hold the Answer" by Christine Kenneally in the *New York Times*. Published 22 April 2008.

EXAM HINT

Notice what the "What you need to know" section says – the *difference* between sensation and perception. Make sure you know what this is!

OCR Differences between sensation and perception

Sensation refers to when we are sensing the environment around us using touch, taste, smell, sight and sound (the senses). The information we pick up is stored in our brain for further use and this is where perception comes in. **Perception** is about making sense of and using the information we have stored via our senses. It is about how we interpret this information to make sense of the world.

KEY TERMS

Sensation: our interpretation of the environment around us using touch, taste, smell, sight and sound (the senses).

Perception: making sense of and using the information we have stored via our senses. It is about how we interpret this information to make sense of the world.

Retinal image: the image that your eye processes.

Perceptual system: carries sensory information from the environment to the brain, allowing perception to occur.

OCR Shape constancy, colour constancy and visual illusions

Shape
Shape constancy refers to our ability to understand that objects remain the same basic shape even when viewed from a variety of angles. The information hitting your retina (the **retinal image**) does change, yet with shape constancy your **perceptual system** helps you to understand that what you are seeing is the same object.

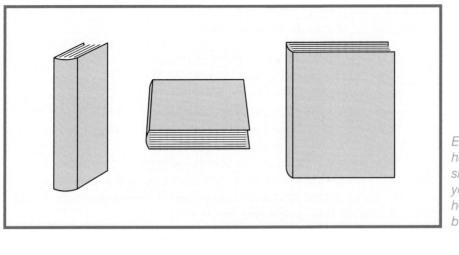

Even though the book has many different shapes in this picture, your perceptual system helps you to label it a book in every picture

Daffodils in daylight, dusk, and artificial light. Despite differing light levels we still perceive the daffodils as being yellow

Colour

Colour constancy refers to our ability to understand that objects remain the same colour even when viewed in differing levels of light.

Illusions

Visual illusions can tell us a great deal about how our perceptual system attempts to make sense of the world around us. You may have your own favourite illusion but we will look at two very simple ones as they are easily explained. They are the Müller-Lyer illusion and the Ponzo illusion.

The Müller-Lyer illusion

Look at the two lines in the diagram on the right. Which one is longer? Of course, the answer is that they are the same length (you can check with a ruler)! So why are we "tricked" into believing that the one on the *right* is longer? Before reading on, try to work it out.

The Ponzo illusion

Now look at the diagram overleaf on the left. Which is longer, A or B? Of course, the two rectangles are the same length! So, why are we tricked here?

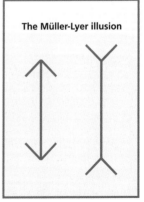

The Müller-Lyer illusion

Which line is longer, the one on the left or the one on the right?

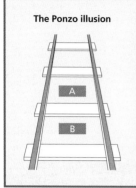

The Ponzo illusion

Which of the two rectangles is longer, A or B?

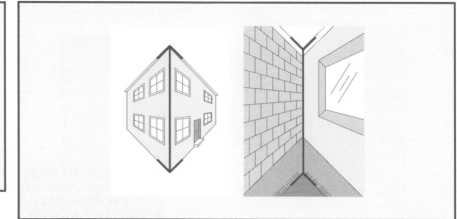

The left one is the outside of a building going away hence gives the perception of being smaller as it is "going away from our eyes". The right one is the corner of an inside room so the perception is that it is coming towards you and getting larger. Hence the right-hand one is perceived to be larger

It's all about our perception of distance and depth. The two lines either side of A and B are converging into the distance, hence we perceive that the picture is going further away. Of course, our perceptual system knows that things get *smaller* the further away they are, so because the gap between A and B and the converging lines gets smaller, we perceive A to be longer. If it were *really* the same size as B it would be much smaller on the picture!

ACTIVITY 11.1

Try out the Müller-Lyer and Ponzo illusions on your friends. Do they get tricked by them? If so, tell them why they have been tricked!

KEY TERMS

Depth cues: a variety of cues in the environment that help us to understand depth. These are linear perspective, texture gradient, superimposition, height in plane and relative size.

Linear perspective: parallel lines such as train tracks appear to get closer together as they recede into the distance.

Texture gradient: fineness in detail decreases the further away the object is from the eye. So sections of an object or setting become less clear the further away they are.

Superimposition: if one object hides part of another object, then the object that is "complete" is perceived to be closer.

OCR Depth cues

There are a variety of cues in the environment that help us to understand depth. These **depth cues** are **linear perspective**, **texture gradient**, **superimposition**, **height in plane** and **relative size**. We will look at each of these in turn.

Linear perspective

Think about looking at a railway track. The tracks run in parallel in reality, yet when we look at a train track going off into the distance, the tracks seem to get closer and closer the further away they are from our eyes. This is called convergence. It allows us to perceive distance and depth in a two-dimensional picture.

Texture gradient

This is also a **two-dimensional cue** that allows us to perceive distance and depth. Fineness in detail decreases the further away the object is from the eye. So sections of an object or setting become less clear the further away they are.

Superimposition

This is another two-dimensional cue that allows us to perceive distance and depth. If one object hides part of another object, then the object that is still "complete" is perceived to be closer.

Height in plane

Another two-dimensional cue that allows us to perceive distance and depth. It follows the "rule" that the closer an object is to the horizon, the further away it is compared to other objects seen in the same picture or scene.

Relative size

This is the final two-dimensional cue that allows us to perceive distance and depth, in which an object's smaller size on your retina means it is further away from you. Also, larger objects are seen as being closer.

Linear perspective: As the tracks disappear into the distance they converge, so we know that the track is getting further away

Texture gradient: We still perceive the whole picture to be a field of sunflowers disappearing into the distance even though the level of detail gets poorer the further away we look

This is because the participants *adapted* to life wearing the inverting goggles and so could *learn* to cope with the changes. If it was all down to nature, then no one would have been able to perform tasks while wearing the goggles.

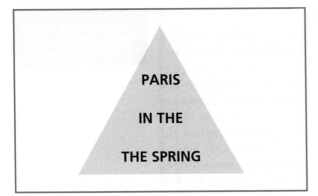

You probably read the message in the triangle as "Paris in the spring". Look again, and you will see that the word "the" is repeated. Your expectation that it is a well-known phrase (i.e. top-down processing) overrides the information available in the stimulus

OCR Top-down processing

Top-down processing of information, your past experiences, your thoughts and expectations, affects your perception. This could affect you consciously or unconsciously. You are expecting to come across various patterns, and therefore you focus your attention on finding that pattern, so you do not just process information *automatically*. See the figure on the left for an example of top-down processing.

OCR Perceptual set

Leading on from top-down processing is the idea of perceptual set. Perceptual set refers to a readiness or a predisposition to perceive things in a specific way. This is affected by previous experiences and expectations of what can be perceived. Perceptual sets can be affected by immediate prior experience. With the rat–man picture on the left, if you had been looking at pictures of rats beforehand it is predicted that you are much more likely to see the rat. Try it out on your friends!

If you were shown a series of animal pictures followed by this ambiguous drawing, you would be likely to see a rat, whereas if shown an ambiguous drawing you would be more likely to see a man's face

OCR Criticisms of the constructivist theory of perception

The constructivist theory of perception encompasses all the ideas from the previous sections that state that we develop our perceptual systems over time based on our experience and expectations. We can criticise the whole idea of the constructivist theory by simply stating that it ignores the role of our inborn abilities. We can still try to perceive objects, pictures and so on that we have never come across before in order to make sense of the world. The constructivist theory would predict that we could never make sense of anything novel as we have no prior experience to draw on. As we know, this is not true!

The next section on *nativist theory* and *bottom-up processing* can be used as evidence against the constructivist approach.

OCR Nativist theory and bottom-up processing

The nativist theory of perception predicts that we are born with many perceptual capabilities. We simply use them when we need them, even if we have to wait until adulthood. Therefore, perception is encoded in our genetic make-up.

Bottom-up processing refers to the idea that when information arrives from our senses it sets a pattern recognition process into motion. The combination of these simple data allows us then to perceive more complex patterns. Therefore, perception is solely influenced by our sensory input and nothing else (remember that top-down processing is based on past knowledge and experience).

OCR Studies into nature and perceptual abilities

STUDY ONE (INFANT STUDY): GIBSON AND WALK (1960)

Infant studies are useful in the nature–nurture debate. They allow us to see if newborns and infants have things like depth perception. If they do, then psychologists believe that it is through nature, as the infants have not had time to learn those skills. The infant study we will examine in depth is Gibson and Walk (1960).

Aim: To test out whether infants have depth perception.

Method: Gibson and Walk created a visual cliff. As can be seen in the figure below, all of the apparatus is covered in thick glass. Half of it has the patterned material just below the glass surface (shallow side). The other half has the same patterned material but 1 foot (30 cm) below the glass surface (cliff side). There were 36 infants used in the study ranging from 6 months to 14 months old. Each infant was tested individually. They were placed on the glass near the centre of the apparatus and their behaviour was recorded. Additionally, each infant was then placed on the shallow side and the

Gibson and Walk's visual cliff

KEY TERM

Infant studies: research using infants as participants. In perception research, they allow us to see if newborns and infants have things like depth perception.

EXAM HINT

Never confuse nature with nurture. You may score no marks at all if the question asks you about nature (innate) and you write about nurture (what we learn). It is crucial that you know which studies support each side of the argument.

Ethical issues

Some psychologists would disagree with any research that is likely to make infants cry. Others argue that little harm is done and what is found out is important. Most ethical issues are concerned with trying to balance the "costs" with the benefits gained from what is discovered.

mother stood at the end of the cliff side to see if the infants would "risk" crawling towards her from the shallow side to the cliff side.

Results: Of the infants who moved once placed on the visual cliff, 27 crawled towards the shallow side. Only three crawled over the cliff side. The remainder did not move at all. The majority of infants crawled away from their mother when she called them from the cliff side, while others cried because they could not reach her without crossing the apparent large drop on the cliff side.

Conclusion: Some psychologists believe this shows that depth perception already exists in human infants because the majority of infants instantly crawled onto the shallow side (the idea is that they may have sensed danger on the cliff side and thus avoided it). Therefore, it supports the idea of nature and perception. However, some psychologists would argue that because the infants were aged between 6 and 14 months, not newborn, it may not all be nature as they could have *experienced* some depth perception before being placed on the visual cliff.

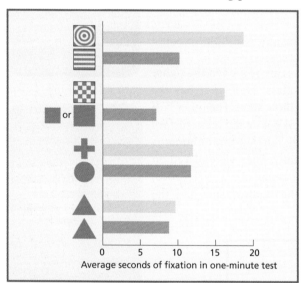

The results of Fantz's (1961) experiments

Another infant study was conducted by Fantz (1961). In a series of experiments he showed infants aged between 1 week and 15 weeks a range of visual stimuli as shown in the figure on the left. The more complex of a pair of stimuli was fixated on (looked at) for longer. So with the chequer board and black square pair, all infants focused more on the chequer board. This has been used as evidence that an infant is born with a perceptual system that is drawn towards processing complex shapes and patterns.

STUDY TWO (DEPRIVATION STUDY): GREGORY AND WALLACE (1963)

KEY TERM

Deprivation studies: in this topic, research using participants who have been deprived of visual input. If their sight is later surgically restored, the impact of their "new" vision on their perception can be examined.

Deprivation studies are also useful in the nature–nurture debate. If we examine humans who have been deprived of visual input (e.g. people who have been blind since infancy who later have their sight restored) and they can correctly perceive the world around them, then it is clear that we are "set up" with a perceptual system. Hence, it is nature and not nurture. The deprivation study we will examine in depth is the case of SB (Gregory & Wallace, 1963).

Aim: Gregory and Wallace wanted to investigate the perceptual abilities of a man who had been blind for 50 years but then had his sight restored.

Method: SB was born in 1906 and became blind at the age of 10 months. At the age of about 50 years he received a corneal graft, which restored his sight. So after 50 years he could see again. About 48 days after his final operation, the first tests and observations began.

Results: SB was initially questioned about whether he had any visual memories before becoming blind. He could only remember what the colours red, white and black looked like. He could actually name those colours immediately after the operation and tended to confuse other colours.

When Gregory first observed SB walking down a corridor, SB did it with "ease", even guiding himself through a doorway without the use of touch. It was difficult to spot that he had only just had his sight restored after 50 years!

However, there were some differences compared to a normal sighted person. SB would never look around the room and would only focus on objects when specifically asked to do so. But when he was asked to name the object he rarely got anything wrong. He could also tell the time with great accuracy. He even read out the name of a magazine that Gregory had (called *Everybody's*) – but what was more intriguing was when he was asked how he knew the word SB stated he recognised the letters EV and thought that it then had to be the word *Everybody's*! He also stated that he'd learnt capital letters by touch and had transferred this to lower-case letters as they were not taught in his school for blind people.

His estimates of lots of things were quite accurate. For example, he was surprised by the height of a bus but not by its length. Presumably he had "felt" the length of the bus while blind but obviously never the height.

On his first trip to London, SB thought the buildings were dull but appreciated more anything that moved, especially the pigeons in Trafalgar Square. He stated that when blind he felt isolated, so went to places that had lots of activity and movement. He found traffic very frightening and would not cross a road without assistance, even though when blind he was very confident with this behaviour.

SB did get better at perceiving depth and distance over time, up until his death in 1960. But he appeared to be a different person post-operation, with his energy and enthusiasm for life somewhat reduced.

Conclusion: Some psychologists believe this study shows that our perceptual system is with us from birth, and that even if "dormant" through blindness it can still be used when sight is recovered. Although not perfect, the case of SB does highlight how he could use his post-operation perceptual system quite adequately. He could not "learn" the visual world while blind, so he learnt it through touch instead. However, some psychologists point out that it was 48 days before he was tested, so SB may have had a chance to "learn" things before the test. We cannot know what was already there (nature) and what he learned (nurture).

Another study that examined the role of early experiences (and deprivation) used kittens (Blakemore & Cooper, 1970). For the first 5 months of their lives, the kittens were placed in a large cylinder with only vertical or horizontal

Methodology

Remember that this is a case study involving one unusual individual. You could not generalise the findings to support a universal theory of perception. Nevertheless, the evidence "mounts up", so it is useful if combined with other research findings.

Critical thinking

This is yet another example of how very difficult it is to separate out the effects of nature and nurture. This is not to suggest that we should not try, but humans are very complex, with a host of different life experiences, so it is never going to be an easy task. It will, however, always be fascinating!

Methodology

There are occasions when psychologists use animals in their research because it would be totally unacceptable to use humans. However, many species are very different from humans, both in terms of their brain structure and the types of activities for which their perceptual systems have evolved. This means there is a limit to how much we can learn about the human perceptual system by investigating other species.

one three-thousandth of a second during a film called *Picnic*. The claimant, James Vicary, reported that sales of the products increased quite dramatically as the people had "seen" the word Coca-Cola and/or popcorn without having "actually seen it". This is called *subliminal perception*, whereby we process information that we are not consciously aware of. It was later revealed that Vicary was lying, and a replication of his idea showed no such increase in sales. However, his legacy could still be useful for advertisers!

Karremans (2006) tested out whether subliminally projecting a branded drink to a group of participants would subsequently affect their choice of drink. Half of the participants had the words "Lipton Ice" projected for 24 ms onto a computer screen during a task. The other half had no such subliminal message. Those who were subliminally primed did choose Lipton Ice more often. The control group showed no preference. Therefore, advertisers could use this with an audience to "promote" their product without the viewers actually knowing.

Key (1973) showed the phrase "U Buy" embedded backwards (so at some point the word "Yubu" appeared) in a presentation advertisement for alcohol. Prior to the study itself, all participants were asked to identify any hidden message in the advertisement. None did. However, 80% of participants chose the U Buy rum after they had watched the advertisement. In addition, Byrne (1959) highlighted that it is probably only single words or two-word phrases that can be perceived subliminally and then affect behaviour. He projected the word "beef" for 5 ms quite often throughout a movie to half the participants, while the other half of the participants did not get such subliminal messages. However, even though there was no difference in food preference between the two groups later (measured by choice of sandwich that included beef), the experimental group did report higher levels of hunger.

Williams et al. (2005) tested out whether we could pick up on emotions subliminally, which may be useful for advertisers. Participants were shown faces representing fear either subliminally (16.7 ms) or *supraliminally* (500 ms so you would actually see the face – this is the term psychologists use for this type of processing). Participants had their brain scanned via neuroimagery while looking at the pictures. Different parts of the brain were used when processing subliminally and supraliminally, but there was much more processing happening in the latter group. This indicates that showing the emotion so the participant could actually see it produced more brain activity and processing than showing it subliminally. This could be useful for advertisers.

Finally, Moore (2006) reviewed the field of subliminal perception linked to advertising, self-help tapes that you listen to when in bed, and in psychotherapy, and found no real evidence for its effectiveness, especially with regard to changing/manipulating complex behaviours.

ACTIVITY 11.2

You have been asked by an advertising agency to promote a new type of fizzy drink. In groups, plan out a campaign that uses a subliminal message. Then, plan out a campaign that doesn't. Assess your efforts or get the rest of the class to!

Chapter summary

- Sensation refers to when we are sensing the environment around us using touch, taste, smell, sight and sound (the senses). Perception is about making sense of and using the information we have stored via our senses.
- There are many visual constancies that form our perceptual system – these include shape constancy and colour constancy. Each one allows us to make sense of the world on a daily basis.
- Visual illusions can tell us a lot about our perceptual system by telling us why we misperceive pictures and objects that we see. Two of these are the Müller-Lyer and Ponzo illusions. The former can be explained using our perception of buildings, and the latter by our perception of convergence.
- There are many depth cues in two-dimensional pictures that aid our perceptual system – these include linear perspective, texture gradients, superimposition, height in plane and relative size.
- Experience may play a role in perceptual abilities (nurture). There are psychologists who believe that our perceptual system is built through experiences we have throughout life. Hudson reported that many of his participants found the perception of a man–antelope–elephant picture to be a struggle as they had never experienced 2D pictures before. Also, Kohler reported on a few case studies where people wore inverting goggles, so they saw the world upside down or inverted from left to right. They quickly adapted to this new environment and one participant could even ride a motorcycle while wearing inverting goggles!
- These experiences form part of top-down processing. You are expecting to come across various patterns, and therefore you focus your attention on finding that pattern, so you do not just process information *automatically*.
- Perceptual set refers to a readiness or a predisposition to perceive things in a specific way. This is affected by previous experiences and expectations of what can be perceived.
- There are psychologists who believe that we are born with a fully functional perceptual system. There is some research evidence for this idea. For example, Gibson and Walk showed that infants would not crawl over the deep side of their visual cliff apparatus towards their mother. Also, the case of SB who was blind from the age of 10 months to 50 years showed that he still had perceptual abilities even though he had been blind for so long, hence he could not have learnt them.
- This is a bottom-up approach to perception, which suggests perception is solely influenced by our sensory input and nothing else.
- Haber and Levin (2001) wanted to investigate whether size perception and distance perception are separate parts of our perceptual system. Participants had to estimate size of objects from different viewpoints. They concluded that because the participants were quite accurate under all conditions, distance and size perception are skills that

operate independently in humans. That is, participants could accurately estimate object size irrespective of distance, and they could also accurately estimate distance irrespective of size of object.

- One application of perception is advertising. There is a debate as to whether subliminal perception should be used in advertising. This involves flashing imagery of a product at an audience for such a brief period of time that we detect but do not directly see it. There is conflicting evidence as to whether it really does make people go out and buy that product.

OCR Exam-style questions for OCR

1. What is the difference between sensation and perception? (2 marks)

2. Describe the following terms linked to perception:

    (a) superimposition

    (b) height in plane. (4 marks)

3. What do psychologists mean by top-down processing? (2 marks)

4. Outline **one** criticism of the constructivist theory of perception. (2 marks)

5. Describe the procedure used in the Haber and Levin (2001) study into perception. (4 marks)

6. Assess **one** application of research into perception. Be sure to include research evidence in your answer. (6 marks)

Part 6

Individual differences

Most of psychology is concerned with looking for laws of behaviour that are applicable to everyone. However, there is a huge diversity of human behaviour, and in fact people (individuals) can differ from each other in terms of their attitudes, reasoning, and behaviour.

The environment around you may cause you to behave in certain ways and change your behaviour to adapt to it. This could then affect your personality or your sense of self, potentially affecting your self-esteem. Other things may happen within the environment that cause you to become scared of various things – for example you may witness someone being very scared of a spider so you may then become fearful of spiders too!

Chapter 12 • Learning and atypical behaviour

We will consider different ways in which we learn (e.g. do we learn by consequences, association or through watching others?). To put these into context we will consider if they can explain things like phobias.

Chapter 13 • Development of personality

We will look at what personality is and whether we are born with a temperament. We will examine a theory and studies that have tested out personality and also look at antisocial personality disorder.

Chapter 14 • The self

We will investigate whether people and their experiences really are unique. In addition we will examine how effective counselling is for people.

What you need to know OCR

The specification lists the following things that you need to be able to do for the examination:

- Distinguish between typical and atypical fear
- Outline common types of phobia: agoraphobia, social phobia, school phobia, acrophobia and arachnophobia
- Distinguish between an unconditioned stimulus, a neutral stimulus and a conditioned stimulus; and between an unconditioned response and a conditioned response
- Use the process of classical conditioning to explain the onset of phobias
- Explain the criticisms of the behaviourist theory of atypical behaviour
- Consider evolutionary theory as an alternative theory with specific reference to preparedness
- Describe and outline the limitations of the Watson and Rayner (1920) study
- Apply research into atypical behaviour: behaviour therapy

What you need to know AQA

The specification lists the following things that you need to be able to do for the examination:

- Describe the principles of classical conditioning: unconditioned stimulus; unconditioned response; conditioned stimulus; conditioned response; extinction; spontaneous recovery; generalisation; discrimination; the contributions of Pavlov
- Describe the principles of operant conditioning: Thorndike's Law of Effect and the contributions of Skinner; behaviour shaping; the distinction between positive reinforcement, negative reinforcement and punishment
- Describe and evaluate attempts to apply conditioning procedures to the treatment of phobias (flooding and systematic desensitisation) and to change unwanted behaviour (aversion therapy and token economy), and the ethical implications of such attempts

Learning and atypical behaviour

12

■ ■ ■ ■ ■ ■ ■ ■ ■

Amanda is scared of lifts. It's not that she can't take them at all, but she doesn't like to. Unfortunately, her office is on the 10th floor. "I get a bit panicky in lifts," she explains. "I start to feel dizzy and have to take long, deep breaths to calm myself down. My colleagues and my boss don't know about it, so when I'm with them, or when I'm late or just don't have the energy to use the stairs, I take the lift and suffer it."

Amanda considers her problem to be "silly" and refuses to admit it to her boss. But her phobia has clear implications for her career. She keeps an eye out for opportunities for advancement, but won't consider another job above the fourth floor. In the meantime, she has learnt to live with the fleeting moments of fear, and to combine meetings out of the office and with colleagues on other floors so that several can be accomplished in one trip.

According to experts, more and more of us are suffering from phobias and irrational fears, a situation that has been made worse by the real or imagined terrorist threat. Unfortunately, many of the most common phobias are ones that we are likely to encounter at work, like fear of driving, public speaking, socialising and enclosed spaces. Unsurprisingly, fears of elevators, heights and flying have increased since the attacks on the Twin Towers. In fact, according to the National Phobics Society, one in four people in the UK are suffering from an anxiety disorder at any given time.

"People are more likely to experience high-anxiety states or panic attacks when their general stress levels are higher," says therapist Roger Elliott, managing director of self-help company Uncommon Knowledge. Unfortunately, stress levels in British offices have never been higher. "Phobias at their worst (that is when they are being triggered regularly) are crippling. Fear will pretty much take over your volition as you are 'hardwired' to avoid fearful situations. Public speaking phobia can dominate someone's life if there is even a possibility that they will be required to do some at work. Social phobia as well is a terrible condition and can quickly lead to depression as the person restricts their life experiences."

Specific phobias, like the fear of lifts or heights, can be a nuisance. Social phobias can be devastating, especially for someone trying to forge a successful career. According to the American Psychiatric Association, the most common social phobia is the fear of speaking in public. Many people have a generalised form of social phobia, in which they fear and avoid interpersonal interactions. This makes it difficult for them to go to work at all.

OCR Typical and atypical behaviour in relation to fear

We all have fears about things, but some can be described as *typical* and some as *atypical*. Typical fears are ones that make evolutionary sense as they represent a dangerous situation (e.g. feeling fear on top of a high building with no railings around the edge: this is obviously dangerous). However, atypical fears are ones that do not make sense at all. Does being fearful of baked beans or cotton wool make sense? Are they dangerous? No! So these are examples of atypical fear.

OCR Common types of phobia

We may all fear something in our lives, but what turns this into a **phobia**? Psychologists are interested in what causes people to develop phobias, and the rest of this chapter will look at some competing ideas.

A phobia is defined as an irrational fear of something, someone or some object. By irrational we mean silly, unreasonable and illogical. There may be no reason why we fear the object or situation.

Common types of phobia include the following:

What might make an individual develop a phobia of spiders?

- **Agoraphobia:** This is the intense fear of open spaces and/or public areas. For example, a person may fear leaving the house.
- **Social phobia:** This is the intense fear of being in social situations, so people actively avoid them. People with this phobia may also feel that

other people are judging them. Also, people with this phobia dislike social interactions.

- **School phobia:** This is an intense fear of going to school. Some psychologists believe this is a type of separation anxiety (being separated from parents causes distress).
- **Acrophobia:** This is an intense fear of heights.
- **Arachnophobia:** This is an intense fear of spiders.

Classical conditioning

Classical conditioning is all about learning through **association**. It is a form of conditioning where the organism (be it human or animal) associates an **unconditioned stimulus** with a **neutral stimulus**. After repeated associations, the organism then responds to the neutral stimulus (now called a **conditioned stimulus**) without having the unconditioned stimulus present anymore. The diagram below shows what happens in classical conditioning.

KEY TERMS

Classical conditioning: when an organism "learns" through establishing associations between different events and stimuli.

Association: forming a learned connection between a stimulus and a response, or between one stimulus and another.

Unconditioned stimulus: a stimulus that elicits an involuntary bodily response all on its own, such as dogs dribbling at the sight of food.

Neutral stimulus: any stimulus that causes no response from the organism being conditioned.

Conditioned stimulus: the name given to the neutral stimulus after the association with the unconditioned stimulus has been conditioned.

EXAM HINT

If you are studying the OCR syllabus, you need to be able to name some common phobias.

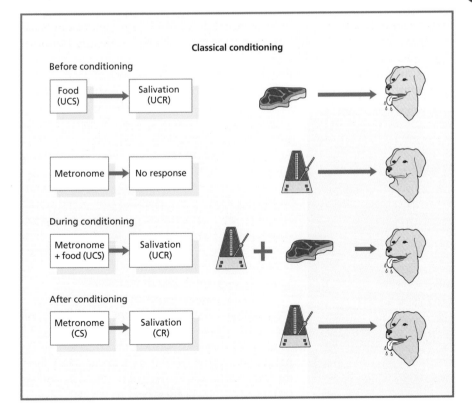

Classical conditioning

Before conditioning

Food (UCS) → Salivation (UCR)

Metronome → No response

During conditioning

Metronome + food (UCS) → Salivation (UCR)

After conditioning

Metronome (CS) → Salivation (CR)

"Well, I simply trained them to give me fish by pressing this over and over again."

Ivan Pavlov (1927) brought us the idea of classical conditioning. However, his research was not on humans – he used dogs in his experiments. He was researching digestion in dogs and noticed how some of them reacted to seeing and hearing the people who fed them (e.g. by barking) before they were given food or just as the person happened to be walking by. He believed that the dogs had made a connection between the person and the food. This is known as association. Pavlov created a simple experiment to show that his ideas were correct.

Pavlov already knew that dogs salivate when they smell meat powder. Every time the powder was given to the dogs he sounded a metronome (a device that clicks at set intervals). He repeated this a few times. Then he sounded the metronome *without* the meat powder and noticed that each dog still salivated. He had successfully classically conditioned the dogs.

AQA Other important terms linked to classical conditioning

Generalisation occurs when we produce a **conditioned response** to a stimulus that is *similar* to but not the same as the conditioned stimulus. For example, we may produce a fear response to wasps. We could *generalise* this fear to other flying insects like bees and hornets.

Extinction occurs when the conditioned stimulus no longer produces the conditioned response. This could be because the conditioned stimulus has no longer been paired with the unconditioned stimulus. So, for example, with the person above who fears wasps, over time the conditioned response of fear disappears in the presence of the conditioned stimulus of the wasp.

Spontaneous recovery occurs after extinction. Suddenly, in the presence of the conditioned stimulus the conditioned response reappears. Again, using the person who fears wasps, there could have been many months since extinction happened but one day they see a wasp and suddenly they show lots of fear again.

Discrimination occurs when we produce a conditioned response to only *one* specific stimulus even if there are similar ones in the environment. That is, we may only show a fear response to the particular buzzing sound of a hornet, but show no fear response to similar buzzing noises produced by bluebottles, bees or wasps.

KEY TERMS

Generalisation: the production of a conditioned response to a stimulus that is *similar* to but not the same as the conditioned stimulus.

Conditioned response: the name given to a response to a stimulus that has already been learned.

Extinction: when the conditioned stimulus no longer produces the conditioned response. This could be because the conditioned stimulus has no longer been paired with the unconditioned stimulus.

Spontaneous recovery: after extinction, in the presence of the conditioned stimulus, the conditioned response suddenly reappears.

Discrimination: when we produce a conditioned response to only *one* specific stimulus even if there are similar ones in the environment.

OCR The case of Little Albert

OCR CORE STUDY: WATSON AND RAYNER (1920)

This classic study in psychology conducted by Watson and Rayner (1920) shows how classical conditioning may explain how we develop phobias. Watson and Rayner had two aims. The following is taken directly from the paper they wrote about their case study of Little Albert:

1. Can we condition fear of an animal, e.g. a white rat, by visually presenting it and simultaneously striking a steel bar?
2. If such a conditioned emotional response can be established, will there be a transfer to other animals or other objects?

At approximately 9 months of age, Little Albert was presented with a range of stimuli (e.g. a white rat, a rabbit, a dog, a monkey, etc.). Albert showed no fear towards any of the objects.

When Albert reached 11 months and 3 days, the experimental procedure began to test out the first aim. Albert was presented with a white rat again and, as before, he showed no fear. However, as Albert reached out to touch the rat, Watson struck an iron bar immediately behind Albert's head. Of course, Albert "jumped violently and fell forward, burying his face in the mattress" (p. 4). Albert tried to approach the rat again but as soon as he got close the iron bar was struck. After the two associations of the rat and loud noise, the rat was taken away.

Seven days later, Watson and Rayner wanted to see if the experience that Albert had had with the loud noise had made him fearful of white rats. He was very wary around the rat and did not really want to play with it or touch it. When he did reach out, the loud noise was made, the same as the previous week. This was done five times during the session. So, in total, Albert experienced the loud noise and the white rat occurring together on seven occasions. Finally, the rat was presented by itself. Albert began to cry and crawled away rapidly. This was the first time he had cried during the study in response to the rat.

Over the next month Albert's reactions to a range of objects were observed. He was still fearful of the white rat. He showed negative reactions to a rabbit being placed in front of him and a fur coat (made from seal-skin). He did not really like cotton wool but the shock was not the same as it was with the rabbit or the fur coat. He even began to fear a Santa Claus mask! Albert's experiences can be explained via the mechanisms of classical conditioning that you were introduced to on page 259. The diagram above highlights this. So, as can be seen, classical conditioning may be able to explain why some phobias are formed.

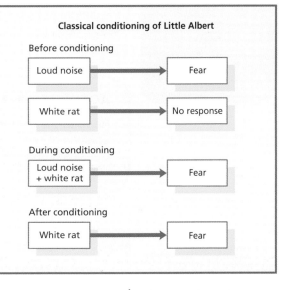

Classical conditioning of Little Albert

Before conditioning

Loud noise → Fear

White rat → No response

During conditioning

Loud noise + white rat → Fear

After conditioning

White rat → Fear

> **Methodology**
>
> A case study is usually a detailed description of a single individual. This is rather an unusual case study as it is not an in-depth look at Little Albert. In a sense it is an experiment done on a single individual. Try not to confuse it with the usual meaning of a case study.

> **EXAM HINT**
>
> When trying to work out what the UCS, UCR, NS, CS and CR are for a study (e.g. Little Albert) draw out the stages and work *backwards*. So you begin with the CS–CR link (what was the final outcome of the study; i.e. Rat–Fear). The CS was the NS, and the UCR and CR are *always* the same thing. That means whatever is left over is the UCS. Easy!

Limitations of the study

The study was essentially a case study, therefore it could be difficult to generalise to a wider population. That is, the procedure used to create the phobia in Little Albert may only apply to him. Also, as the procedure was highly controlled in nature, it may *not* explain how we acquire phobias in everyday life where controls are not high. Therefore, the study lacks ecological validity. Finally, the study has been deemed unethical as Albert was not *deconditioned* – that is, they did not get rid of Albert's phobia at the end of the study, so he did not leave the study in the same psychological state as when he began.

ACTIVITY 12.1

Using the classical conditioning boxes on page 261, create your own example of how someone has become fearful of a spider.

ACTIVITY 12.2

Re-read the account of Little Albert and his phobia of white rats. In addition re-read the section on page 260 about other terms linked to classical conditioning. Which of these happened in the Little Albert study?

OCR Criticisms of the behaviourist theory of atypical behaviour

KEY TERMS

Social learning: an organism "learns" through observation and imitation of the actions of others.

Attention: the necessity for a learner to notice and be interested in an observed behaviour.

Retention: the necessity for a learner to memorise the observed behaviour.

Reproduction: the ability of the learner to produce the observed behaviour.

Motivation: the learner's desire to repeat the observed behaviour. For example, if the behaviour results in a reward and the learner is able to reproduce it, they will be more strongly motivated to repeat it.

To criticise the behaviourist approach, we can look at alternatives to see if they are more plausible in the explanation for phobias. We can do this because this approach shows that not all phobias can be accounted for via behaviourist theory (in this case, classical conditioning).

Social learning

In the chapter on Aggression (Chapter 4), you were introduced to the idea of **social learning** theory. This theory could also explain how we develop phobias. If we use the four principles of **Attention**, **Retention**, **Reproduction** and **Motivation** we will see how social learning theory can also explain the development of phobias.

If we use the example in the activity above, we will see how social learning theory can explain why the child also developed a phobia of spiders:

- *Attention* – Mummy draws attention to herself by screaming loudly and running around. The child sees this and is immediately paying attention to the actions of Mummy. The child may also see Mummy getting a cuddle (probably from Daddy) after the spider has disappeared.
- *Retention* – Especially if Mummy is rarely seen running around and screaming loudly, the child will retain this event in their memory.
- *Reproduction* – Remember how a person has to be *capable* of reproducing the behaviour for it to be truly socially learnt. Well, the child can also run around and scream loudly.
- *Motivation* – The child must be motivated to reproduce the behaviour. Well, Mummy is a **role model** so will motivate the child to reproduce her behaviour. Also, the child saw the consequence of Mummy's actions: the spider is disposed of and she gets a cuddle! This should clearly motivate the child to want to reproduce the behaviour.

However, social learning is not very good at explaining why we become scared of objects or things that we have never encountered, or objects and things that we have never seen anyone being frightened of. The following theory might help us to explain these phobias.

OCR Evolutionary explanation of phobias

Preparedness

Could it be that we are pre-programmed to fear certain objects that may be potentially harmful? That is, there are certain objects or things that we are *expected* to be frightened of so we are *biologically prepared* to fear them. This theory of **preparedness** could help us to explain fears that are not totally irrational (e.g. snakes – they can be dangerous!). Seligman (1971) proposed the idea that we evolved to be frightened of fear-relevant stimuli. So we fear objects and things that might be of a survival threat in evolutionary terms (Mineka & Öhman, 2002). We have fear-relevant

Are we frightened of snakes because we are biologically prepared to fear them?

KEY TERMS

Role model: any person whose actions are imitated by the learner; this may be peers, family members, or even celebrities.

Preparedness: the idea that organisms have evolved to be frightened of fear-relevant stimuli – those objects or situations that may have been historically life threatening (e.g. rats, spiders, snakes, etc.).

Everyday life

If social learning theory can account for how phobias are learnt, it is possible that it could be used to treat phobias by showing a person calmly dealing with the feared object or situation.

Methodology

This is a carefully controlled experiment in which each group is treated in exactly the same way, except on one critical factor – in this case, the object that the monkey on the film is shown as being afraid of.

stimuli such as snakes that we may be "prepared" to fear. We also have fear-irrelevant stimuli such as flowers that we are *not* "prepared" to fear.

One classic study into this used rhesus monkeys as the participants rather than humans. Cook and Mineka (1989) wanted to see if the monkeys could become phobic of objects such as a crocodile, a flower, a snake or a rabbit even though they had never seen them before. The set-up was as follows: some rhesus monkeys were the participants. They were split into four separate groups so they only saw one of the objects. Cook and Mineka controlled what the monkeys saw as they watched a video. Using the technique of splicing the video, each monkey saw the same rhesus monkey being scared of the object that their group had been assigned. So, for example, one monkey saw another monkey on the video being scared of the crocodile. The next monkey saw the same monkey on the video but this time being scared by the flower. And so on.

Monkeys are prepared to fear dangerous objects, but not neutral objects

Each monkey was then tested on their fear towards the object. The monkeys in the crocodile and snake groups showed fear towards a toy crocodile and a toy snake. However, when the other two groups were shown their "feared object" (i.e. the flower or the rabbit), they did *not* show any fear. Cook and Mineka took this as showing that the monkeys were already *prepared* to fear the dangerous objects but not the neutral objects.

Some psychologists question whether research on rhesus monkeys can be *generalised* to humans as we are different species. They would state that we do not know if humans are *prepared* to be fearful of dangerous objects or not. However, there may be some basic brain functions that we do share that could be involved in fear reactions, so some psychologists think we can generalise to humans from monkeys.

KEY TERM

Genetics: the idea that our genetic make-up (DNA) can explain particular phenomena, such as phobias.

Genetics

Could it be that we are born fearful of certain objects? This takes the idea of *preparedness* further by saying that certain phobias are encoded into our **genetic** make-up (DNA) and passed down through generations.

Ost et al. (1991) examined people who were needle phobic within the same family. This study reported that 64% of patients with a blood and/or injection phobia had at least one first-degree relative (immediate family) with the same phobia. In the general population, 3–4% are phobic of blood and/or needles.

Fredrikson, Annas and Wik (1997) examined 158 phobic females who were scared of snakes or spiders. The participants had to report on the family history of their phobia. Fredrikson discovered that 37% of mothers and 7% of fathers also had the same phobia. This looked as if it supported the idea that the phobic women had *inherited* their phobia.

However, Fredrikson asked the participants another question: whether direct exposure to the phobic stimulus (i.e. being frightened by the phobic object directly) or indirect exposure to the phobic stimulus (i.e. seeing someone else being phobic towards the object) had happened. Indirect exposure was more common for snakes (45%) than for spiders (27%). So, even though it looked as if the phobia was caused by genetics, nearly half of the snake-phobic participants could have their phobia explained via social learning.

AQA Operant conditioning

Operant conditioning is all about learning through consequences. It is a form of conditioning in which an organism's behaviour (be it human or animal) is moulded by the use of **reinforcement** (reward) or **punishment**.

Edward Thorndike was one of the first scientists to look into learning by consequences. He had noticed how quickly cats could learn by this technique. He placed a hungry cat in a "puzzle box" with food outside. The box was set up so that if the cat pulled on a piece of string inside the box, a catch would be released and the door would open (via a lever-press mechanism), so the cat could get out and eat the food.

On the first trial, the cat took a long time to escape. It moved around the box and *by chance* tugged on the piece of string and released the catch on the door. Each time the cat was placed back in the box, it escaped more and more quickly. Thorndike believed that the cat had learnt through **trial and error**. From his study he created the **Law of Effect**, which states that if behaviour is followed by a pleasurable experience, the organism will be more likely to repeat that behaviour. However, if behaviour is followed by something not pleasurable, then the organism will be less likely to repeat that behaviour.

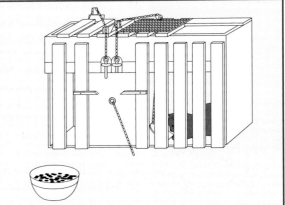

Burrhus F. Skinner took Thorndike's ideas to a wider audience by introducing a series of terms in **behaviour shaping** that are still used to explain how operant conditioning works. They are as follows:

- **Positive reinforcement:** The addition of something nice (e.g. reward) that *increases* the probability of that behaviour being repeated.
- **Negative reinforcement:** The removal of something aversive that *increases* the probability of that behaviour being repeated.
- **Positive punishment:** The addition of something aversive that *decreases* the probability of that behaviour being repeated.
- **Negative punishment:** The removal of something nice that *decreases* the probability of that behaviour being repeated.

KEY TERMS

Behaviour shaping: the distinction between positive reinforcement, negative reinforcement, and punishment.

Positive reinforcement: the addition of something nice (e.g. reward) that increases the probability of that behaviour being repeated.

Negative reinforcement: the removal of something aversive (unpleasant) that increases the probability of that behaviour being repeated.

Positive punishment: the addition of something aversive that decreases the probability of that behaviour being repeated.

Negative punishment: the removal of something nice that decreases the probability of that behaviour being repeated.

EXAM HINT

Try not to get reinforcement and punishment, muddled up! Remember that to *reinforce* a building you are *strengthening* it. So it is the same idea with behaviour: reinforcement is *strengthening* that behaviour.

EXAM HINT

With the positive and negative elements of operant conditioning, remember that the symbol for positive is "+", which also means *addition*, so it is *adding* something to the situation. The symbol for negative is "–", which also means *subtraction*, so it is *taking something away* from the situation.

ACTIVITY 12.4

Read the four scenarios below and decide which is an example of positive reinforcement, which is an example of negative reinforcement, which is an example of positive punishment, and which is an example of negative punishment.

1. You have toothache. After a few days of pain you decide you have to see a dentist even though you hate it! During your appointment the dentist states that you need a filling, and fills your tooth. A few hours later the pain has gone and you agree that next time you have toothache you will go to the dentist straight away.
2. You are told by your parent/guardian that you must be back in at 10 pm. You get back home at 11 pm and you are then grounded for 1 week. You are annoyed and chat with your friends on the telephone but agree with your friends that you are less likely to be late in next time you go out with them.
3. Your little sister gets carried away while painting and paint goes all over the living room wall. Mum gets annoyed as she has to clean the wall thoroughly to get the paint off. Your sister loves her night-time story but Mum says that she will not have one for a week because of her painting on the walls. Your little sister says that she will not paint the walls next time.
4. You tidy your room after Mum has nagged you about it for a week. You do a really good job of it and are allowed to choose a new computer game from the shop. Next time Mum asks you to tidy your room, you do it straight away!

ACTIVITY 12.5

Watch an episode of the television programme *Supernanny*. Look at the techniques she uses and try to identify if she uses reinforcement and/or punishment.

ACTIVITY 12.6

Find out the real phobia names for five other phobias – find some that are common and some that are strange or interesting!

OCR AQA ## Behaviour therapy

We have examined the role of classical conditioning in the formation of phobias. Therefore, if it can explain *how* this happens then surely we can *reverse* the process so then we can help to *cure* the phobia. There are two main techniques that in theory can do this: **systematic desensitisation** and **flooding**.

Systematic desensitisation

If we look at the case of Little Albert again (see page 261), it can clearly be seen that the conditioned stimulus of the white rat elicited the conditioned response of fear. The phobia had been *learnt*. Systematic desensitisation works on the idea that the phobia can then be *unlearnt*. The end point should recondition the patient so that the conditioned stimulus (which is the phobic stimulus) produces a conditioned response of relaxation rather than fear.

The principles

First, the phobic patient is taught relaxation skills so that they understand what it feels like to have relaxed muscles. This should enable them to recreate this feeling in a variety of situations, including when confronted with their phobic stimulus.

Second, the patient produces an anxiety or fear hierarchy to work through with the therapist. A simple one would be as follows (the person is fearful of snakes):

1. Least anxious situation – looking at a cartoon snake in a children's book.
2. Looking at a real snake in a book.
3. Watching a snake on a wildlife programme.
4. Seeing a snake in the same room but in a cage.
5. Seeing a snake in the same room out of the cage.
6. Being within 3 feet of the snake.
7. Touching the snake.
8. Most anxious situation – letting the snake go around their neck.

You can only move up the hierarchy of fear once each stage has been successfully completed. This means the patient shows signs of relaxation in

KEY TERMS

Systematic desensitisation: a method of treating phobias, whereby relaxation skills are associated with increasingly phobia-associated stimuli. It works on the principle that relaxation and fear cannot be experienced at the same time.

Flooding: a method of treating phobias whereby the patient is exposed to direct contact with the feared stimulus. As the body cannot sustain high levels of arousal for long, fear quickly subsides and the stimulus–fear association is broken.

Why psychology matters

Although many people with phobias are able to function in the everyday world without too much trouble, there are a significant minority of sufferers whose lives are seriously blighted by a phobia. Some may even be "prisoners" in their own homes for fear of leaving it. For these people, treatment can improve their life beyond measure.

the specific situation on the hierarchy (e.g. looking at a book, touching the snake, etc.).

Below is a diagram of the principles of classical conditioning linked to systematic desensitisation. You can see from the diagram that in the conditioning phase there are competing responses of fear and relaxation. This is called *reciprocal inhibition,* which means it is impossible to experience both emotions at the same time. The idea is to promote the relaxation response more than the fear response. If the patient is feeling more fear than relaxation, then that stage of the hierarchy is stopped until the patient feels relaxed again and is willing to have another go.

ACTIVITY 12.7

Think of one of your main phobias. You must now construct a hierarchy of eight situations from the least fearful to the most fearful, like the snake example on page 267. Can it be done?

Evaluation

There have been many studies that support the use of systematic desensitisation to treat phobias and fears. For example, Capafons, Sosa and Avero (1998) reported on 20 patients with a fear of flying. These patients had several sessions working up through their anxiety hierarchy, and became much less fearful of flying after the study ended. However, like most studies in this area, there was no follow-up to see if the fear reduction lasted.

Another study is that by Zettle (2003), who showed that systematic desensitisation can be applied to people who fear maths. Twenty-four college students underwent treatment for 6 weeks (split between systematic desensitisation and a different therapy) and had to rate their anxieties towards maths before, during and after the treatment. Anxiety decreased markedly for those who completed the systematic desensitisation process, even though their maths ability never changed!

Finally, Ventis, Higbee and Murdock (2001) found that both relaxation techniques and simply laughing at the phobic stimulus were effective in reducing the fear in arachnophobics. All participants had been matched on fear: some worked up through their hierarchy using relaxation, and others by laughing. However, neither Zettle nor Ventis conducted follow-ups.

Some psychologists believe that even though you work slowly up a hierarchy of fear, you are still being unethical by making people confront their

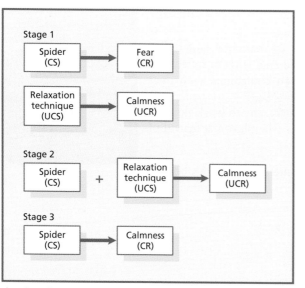

As the diagram demonstrates, you cannot be fearful and calm at the same time, so the UCS–UCR association takes over

phobias. Also, many researchers do not conduct follow-up studies (as noted above) to see if the therapy works in the long term. However, it is seen as being much more ethical than the following technique: flooding.

> ### ACTIVITY 12.8
>
> Using the internet, find some more studies that have tested out systematic desensitisation. Is it always effective? Try to find a range of fears that have been treated using the technique.

KEY TERM

Aversion therapy: a method of decreasing unwanted behaviours using the principle of associating a noxious stimulus with an already conditioned stimulus to produce a desired conditioned response.

Flooding

This is another way to treat phobias using the idea behind classical conditioning. However, it doesn't take the "gentle" approach of systematic desensitisation. The patient is exposed to the largest anxiety-provoking stimuli straight away (usually direct contact with the stimuli: this is called *in vivo*). Obviously, the patient is going to feel extreme levels of fear and anxiety when confronted with the phobic stimulus. However, this dies off quite rapidly as the body cannot sustain such a high level of arousal for a long time. Therefore, the fear and anxiety will diminish. As a result of the phobic stimulus *not* causing any more fear or anxiety, the patient quickly learns that there is now nothing to be fearful of. The association between the phobic stimulus and fear has been broken, to form a new relationship of the phobic stimulus producing calm.

Evaluation

Many psychologists believe that this therapy is *unethical* as it causes distress, both physiologically and psychologically, to the patient. Causing high levels of anxiety, stress and fear is not protecting the patient in any way! However, other psychologists would argue that the end outcome of curing the phobic fear is enough to justify the high level of distress caused in the short term. Finally, even though this technique is used by psychologists, there have been hardly any studies testing its effectiveness, so we are still unsure about the long-term effectiveness of such a technique.

Another therapy based on classical conditioning: Aversion therapy

Aversion therapy is a technique based on the idea of trying to break a different type of conditioned stimulus–conditioned response association. It follows the principle of associating a noxious stimulus (something horrid) with an already conditioned stimulus to produce a different conditioned response. This is called higher order conditioning as it uses an already conditioned stimulus and not a neutral stimulus. It is used

In flooding, the patient is exposed to the anxiety-provoking stimulus straight away; usually this means direct contact with the feared object

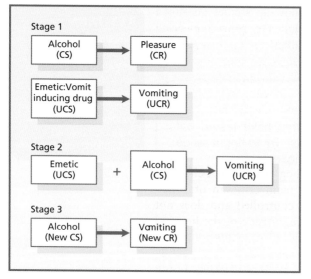

Stage 1

| Alcohol (CS) | → | Pleasure (CR) |

| Emetic:Vomit inducing drug (UCS) | → | Vomiting (UCR) |

Stage 2

| Emetic (UCS) | + | Alcohol (CS) | → | Vomiting (UCR) |

Stage 3

| Alcohol (New CS) | → | Vomiting (New CR) |

As the diagram demonstrates, the alcoholic no longer has the desire to drink, as alcohol has become associated with vomiting

ACTIVITY 12.9

How do you think aversion therapy could be used to treat a paedophile or other sex offender? Draw out the chart as above.

Ethical issues

Nowadays it is virtually unheard of for people to be forced into treatment such as flooding or aversion therapy.

KEY TERM

Token Economy: a method of behaviour shaping that rewards appropriate (desired) behaviours with secondary reinforcers (tokens) that can be collected and exchanged for primary reinforcers (something that is wanted).

to decrease unwanted behaviours (see the figure on the left). Therefore, after repeated "new" associations, the unwanted behaviour (conditioned stimulus) decreases as it is now associated with something noxious.

Aversion therapy has been used to "cure" people of homosexuality, or to treat sex offenders such as paedophiles.

Evaluation

A great number of psychologists believe that aversion therapy for homosexuals is highly unethical. Who has the right to change someone else's behaviour just because they consider it to be "abnormal" or "atypical"? If the aversion therapy is combined with some social skills training alongside it, it has been shown repeatedly to be effective for paedophiles and transvestism (Davison & Neale, 1998). Even though the behaviour that needs to be changed is not totally eliminated, the technique provides the patient with a greater control over that behaviour (Monaghy, 1994). Finally, Cautela (1966) reported that *covert sensitisation* as a form of aversion therapy is effective. The patient has to simply imagine unpleasant circumstances (e.g. a cocaine addict visualises a scene in which they are just beginning to snort, and then straight away they see themselves being violently ill). This could reduce the ethical dilemma posed when an actual emetic is used to cause physical vomiting.

Operant conditioning and therapy: Token Economy

Finally we will examine the role of operant conditioning in changing unwanted behaviour via **Token Economy**. As highlighted on page 265, reinforcement of any kind should increase the probability of a behaviour being repeated. This technique is based on that idea.

In an institution like a prison or a school, a Token Economy can be set up. People are rewarded for appropriate behaviour with tokens that can be exchanged for privileges and other rewards. The tokens themselves are worthless (called a secondary reinforcer) but they can be exchanged for something that is needed, such as food (called a primary reinforcer) or access to activities they would not normally have. The institution sets a "price" on each primary reinforcer or activity so that each person has to earn them (e.g. in a prison, a prisoner may have to earn five tokens to watch some TV). People exchange their tokens at the rates set by the institution (in a similar way to when we buy products). The overall theme of the Token Economy is to promote good and appropriate behaviour while ignoring bad or inappropriate behaviour.

Evaluation

Again, you have the ethical dilemma of deliberately changing a person's behaviour without consent. There could be problems of people in authority abusing the system and making prisoners, for instance, do more and more for one token, changing the boundaries unfairly just because they can. There is some evidence for its effectiveness however. In a classic early study, Ayllon and Azrin (1968) set up a Token Economy in a mental hospital. The 45 female patients were given rewards for carrying out tasks like making their bed or combing their hair. They could then exchange these for privileges such as listening to records, going to the movies or visiting the canteen more often. The system was highly effective at controlling unwanted behaviour and encouraging wanted behaviour. However, one main criticism of Token Economy regimes is that the outside world is not controlled and does not give out tokens for appropriate behaviour. Therefore, outside of the hospital or prison, the unwanted behaviour could quickly reappear as appropriate behaviour is no longer rewarded. Other studies have shown that Token Economy procedures can be effective in increasing appropriate behaviour in emotionally disturbed youths (Hogan & Johnson, 1985), reducing impulsive behaviour in academically handicapped children (Errickson, Wyne & Routh, 1973), and reducing swearing in institutionalised adolescents (Feindler & Elder, 1977). For some, combining a Token Economy with a "Response–Cost" regime, where tokens are taken away for inappropriate behaviour, is effective (e.g. Errickson, Wyne & Routh, 1973), but this is not always the case (e.g. Feindler & Elder, 1977).

Chapter summary

- Typical fears are ones that make evolutionary sense as they represent a dangerous situation (e.g. feeling fear on top of a high building with no railings around the edge: this is obviously dangerous). However, atypical fears are ones that do not make sense at all. Is being fearful of baked beans or cotton wool dangerous? No! So these are examples of atypical fear.
- There are many types of phobias. Common ones include agoraphobia, school phobia, social phobia, acrophobia, arachnophobia.
- Classical conditioning is learning by association. It was discovered by Pavlov. He got dogs to salivate to the sound of a bell and a metronome. Terms linked to this type of conditioning include unconditioned stimulus, neutral stimulus, conditioned stimulus, conditioned response. Further terms include generalisation, extinction, spontaneous recovery and discrimination.
- Classical conditioning and the development of phobias was shown in the Little Albert study (Watson & Rayner). A small child was made to fear a white rat because every time he reached for the rat a loud noise

happened behind him. He associated the loud noise with the rat to produce a fear response.

- Operant conditioning is learning through consequences of behaviour. It was created by Thorndike and developed further by Skinner. The technique is based around the idea of reinforcement and punishment. Each of these can be positive (addition of) or negative (removal of).
- Alternative explanations include the theory that we socially learn phobias (e.g. observe and imitate a role model); that we are prepared to fear certain things from our evolutionary past (e.g. snakes); or genetics, whereby we are born with a fear of an object or situation as it is in our DNA.
- Learning theory can be applied to a range of behavioural therapies that try to cure a range of atypical behaviours. These include systematic desensitisation to remove phobias; flooding to remove phobias; aversion therapy to reduce alcohol consumption; Token Economy to promote positive behaviour.

OCR Exam-style questions for OCR

1. Define atypical fear. (2 marks)

2. What is acrophobia? (1 mark)

3. How can classical conditioning explain how we acquire phobias? (3 marks)

4. Describe an alternative way in which we could acquire phobias? (3 marks)

5. Describe the procedure of the Watson and Rayner (1920) study of Little Albert. (3 marks)

6. Outline **one** limitation of the Watson and Rayner (1920) study of Little Albert. (2 marks)

7. Describe and evaluate **one** application of research into atypical behaviour. (6 marks)

AQA Exam-style questions for AQA

1. Define the term conditioned response. (2 marks)

2. With reference to classical conditioning, what is meant by the term extinction? (2 marks)

3. What is the difference between positive and negative reinforcement? In your answer use an example. (3 marks)

4. Describe and evaluate **one** way in which we can treat a phobia. (6 marks)

5. Discuss the ethics of treating phobias and/or changing unwanted behaviours in humans. (6 marks)

What you need to know [AQA]

The specification lists the following things that you will need to be able to do for the examination:

- Define personality, including temperament
- Describe and evaluate studies of temperament including
  - Thomas (1977)
  - Buss and Plomin (1984)
  - Kagan (1991)
- Describe Eysenck's Type Theory of personality: extraversion, introversion, neuroticism
  - Describe personality scales, including the EPI and the EPQ
- Evaluate Eysenck's Type Theory
- With respect to antisocial personality disorder (APD):
  - Outline the characteristics of APD
  - Describe and evaluate causes of APD:
    - Biological: including the work of Raine (1997)
    - Situational: including the work of Farrington (1995) and Elander (2000)
- Describe and evaluate studies of the causes of APD
- Consider implications of research into APD

Development of personality

13

■ ■ ■ ■ ■ ■ ■ ■ ■

John has just finished a 4-year prison sentence for fraud, bigamy (being married to more than person) and false pretenses. John's conviction for fraud and false pretenses was the result of him passing himself off as an executive of a major charity and doing a television appearance to appeal for funds. His charm, intelligence and apparent knowledge of the work of the charity persuaded the television company to give him airtime and the appeal was successful. John had planned the money-raising carefully and opened bank accounts in a name very similar to that of the charity, and had forged documents at the bank in order to enable him to do this. Again his charm, combined with an ease of manner, smart appearance and financial acumen, had enabled him to open these accounts. After the viewers had watched his heart-wrenching appeal, the funds rolled in. However, one of the real executives of the charity saw the programme and John was arrested and eventually convicted. Very little of the money was recovered – he had covered his tracks well.

During his trial John appeared remorseful and expressed regret over his wrong-doing, throwing himself on the mercy of the judge. Once imprisoned, however, it was a different story: he boasted about his activities and showed no regret or guilt over his actions. He said that most donations to charity were given by those who felt guilty about something and who therefore deserved to be cheated.

John was the third of four children, born to intelligent, middle-class parents. His sister and brothers all led normal, productive lives. His father spent a great deal of time with his business. His mother was a gentle timid woman who tried to appease everyone.

John was a wilful and difficult child. If he didn't get his own way he would turn on the charm. This usually worked, but if not, he would throw a tantrum. From a young age, he would lie, cheat, steal and bully younger children.

As he grew older, John became more and more interested in sex, gambling and alcohol. When he was 14 he made crude sexual advances towards a younger girl and when she threatened to tell her parents he locked her in a shed and left her. It was 16 hours before she was found. He denied any wrong-doing, saying the girl had made advances to him and the shed door must have locked itself. His parents managed to prevent charges being brought against him and he was sent away to a boarding school.

In adult life, John married several times bigamously to women with considerable money. He would spend a great deal of this and then leave. He sees nothing wrong with his behaviour. He has no guilt over the distress he causes others. His needs are satisfied with no concern whatever for the feelings and welfare of others. He has no conscience.

This case study is an example of an extreme pattern of **personality**, known as **antisocial personality disorder**. We will consider this in some detail in the second part of this chapter. Before that we will look at the development of more usual personality.

AQA Definition of personality and temperament

Personality refers to a relatively stable set of behaviours, thoughts and feelings that a person shows to others. It could also be a distinctive set of traits and characteristics that a person has. So it is a combination of the physical, emotional and mental characteristics of a person.

ACTIVITY 13.1

How would you describe your personality to someone you had never met? Construct a letter to a new pen friend and describe yourself in terms of your personality.

Temperament refers to your *natural* disposition in terms of personality traits. That is, it refers to the personality you are apparently born with. It is the genetic component of your personality. It helps to mould your personality as you get older, depending on your experiences. Therefore, personality traits that are observed in childhood still remain in adulthood.

AQA Description and evaluation of studies into temperament

Are people born with a certain personality or is it shaped by their environment, by the way their parents treat them and their experiences with other people? This is another aspect of the nature–nurture debate that we have considered

several times during this course. The following studies look at how children's temperament develops and attempt to try to answer this question.

The work of Thomas, Chess and Birch

Thomas and colleagues were interested in whether children had a consistent temperament throughout their lives, and they conducted longitudinal studies to investigate this. Thomas and Chess (1977) reviewed a lot of studies of temperament, including a classic by Thomas, Chess and Birch (1968).

THOMAS ET AL. (1968): CHILDREN'S TEMPERAMENTS – EASY, DIFFICULT AND SLOW TO WARM UP

Methodology

Longitudinal studies involve studying the same people over a long period of time, often years. This is an excellent design as it allows us to see how individuals develop, and the extent to which they change or remain the same. However, it obviously takes a long time!

Aim: Thomas et al. wanted to investigate whether people respond to the environment in a similar way throughout life, that is, to see whether temperament is consistent throughout life and shapes personality.

Method: A total of 85 families were included in this study. All of them were from New York. At the testing point (in 1968), there was a total of 136 children aged between 4 and 10 years; 69 were boys, 67 were girls.

During the study, the researchers collected data about each child. These included:

- An interview with the parents in which they were asked about their children's personality and behaviour, including how the children reacted to change and what their routines were. These interviews took place at regular intervals over each child's life starting at 2–3 months of age.
- Observations made by independent trained observers to see if the parents' reports were reliable.
- Teacher interviews.

Results: After analysing all of the data, the children appeared to be consistent in their temperament over time and to fall into three distinct groups: difficult, easy and slow to warm up.

- Children labelled "easy" tended to be happier, adapted to situations much faster and were regular in their behaviour compared to the other two groups.
- Children labelled "difficult" tended to be much more demanding in their behaviour, were less flexible with their behaviours and tended to cry more.
- Children labelled "slow to warm up" initially did not react well to changes in their environment or to new environments. However, once they had got used to these environments they tended to be happy.

Conclusion: As these characteristics remained stable over time, Thomas et al. concluded that people are born with a predetermined temperament (which is innate) and that their personality is shaped by the constant interplay of temperament and environment.

EVALUATION

➕ The study used several measures of the child's temperament. Trained observers checked on the reports from parents. This means that it was possible to check how reliable (consistent) the measures of the child's temperament were.

➕ The study was done over a long period of time in order to study whether behaviour was consistent. It did not rely on retrospective data (on asking people how the children used to be).

➖ The measures might not be entirely accurate. Once a child behaves in a certain way, other people may expect them to carry on behaving like this and may not really notice any changes.

➖ Even if the child's temperament is consistent over time, this does not necessarily mean it is innate. If they are brought up in a stable environment (in terms of such things as family and school) then it could be this that is making them behave the way they do.

ACTIVITY 13.2

Think about whether people you have known for many years have always been the same. Did any of them change when they experienced a significant change in their environment, such as moving from primary to secondary school? How about people who came to your school from another one? Did they change as they got to know people and settled down?

Do you think that the categories of easy, difficult and slow to warm up apply to people you know?

BUSS AND PLOMIN (1984): A STUDY OF TWINS' TEMPERAMENTS

Aim: To examine the similarity between MZ (monozygotic, or identical twins, formed from the same zygote) and DZ (dizygotic, or non-identical/fraternal twins, from two separate zygotes) twins in terms of temperament.

Method: Buss and Plomin used 228 pairs of MZ twins and 172 pairs of DZ twins in this study. Their average age was 5 years 1 month. They were assessed on three measures of personality:

- emotional
- active
- sociable

(see box opposite for more information on these characteristics).

EXAM HINT

In an exam, use the initials MZ and DZ because they are a convenient shorthand. However, the first time you mention them, explain in brackets what they mean; i.e. identical and non-identical, or monozygotic and dizygotic if you can remember those terms.

Results: The correlations for both types of twins were positive, and the correlation coefficients for MZ twins were consistently considerably higher than for the DZ twins. This implies that genetics was an important contributor to the temperament of the children.

Conclusion: Buss and Plomin conclude that temperament is largely innate. They do acknowledge that it can be modified by experience, but they believe that the most important influence on temperament is our genetic make-up.

> **Methodology**
> See the Research methods chapter (Chapter 15) in order to understand what a positive correlation is.

Buss and Plomin used three personality traits to compare twins: emotionality, activity and sociability. The scale they used is known as the EAS Scale (from the initials of these characteristics) and consists of 20 items. Each of the characteristics was measured on a scale from high to low, so the low scores give the opposite characteristic. Here are some of the types of questions that they wanted answered:

* *Emotionality–impassiveness*: How emotional and excitable were the babies? How often were they given to emotional outbursts of distress, fear and anger?
* *Activity–lethargy*: How vigorous, how active, how energetic were the babies? Were they always on the move or quite still?
* *Sociability–detachment*: How much did the babies enjoy or avoid contact and interaction with other people?

Temperament and other characteristics

If our temperament is shaped by our biology, is it possible that it may be related to certain physical characteristics we have? The next study looks at whether people with a certain type of temperament are more prone to certain medical conditions such as asthma and eczema.

KAGAN ET AL. (1991): TEMPERAMENT AND ALLERGIC SYMPTOMS

Aim: To test the idea that temperament is linked to allergies.

Method: Kagan et al. looked at a sample of 89 children (using 528 of their relatives). The children had been part of a previous study into temperament in which they been tested at 21 months, 31 months and 7.5 years of age. Their temperament had remained virtually the same across the three time points.

On the basis of this they were split between being either uninhibited (e.g. sociable) or inhibited (e.g. shy). There were 48 inhibited children and 41 uninhibited children.

The relatives took part in a telephone interview in which they were asked about a series of 63 medical symptoms alongside at least five

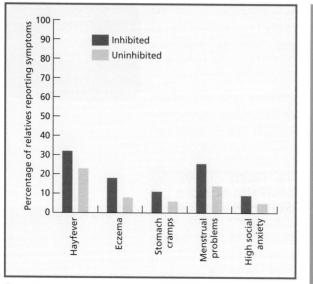

Data based on Kagan et al. (1991)

psychological symptoms. The participant simply had to answer whether the child had ever had any of the conditions on the list. The answer, "yes" or "no", was then recorded for each symptom.

There are a couple of important methodological points:

1. All the conditions were described in the same way to each participant.
2. A doctor's formal diagnosis was not needed, for example if they reported sneezing when exposed to pollen or fur, they were recorded as having hayfever even if their doctor had not diagnosed it.

Results: For the vast majority of symptoms there were no differences between the groups. However, for five symptoms there were statistically significant differences – as shown in the bar chart above.

Therefore, for these symptoms there appears to be a link between temperament and medical/psychological symptoms. More relatives of inhibited children reported the five symptoms.

Conclusion: You may be asking yourself why Kagan et al. would want to examine a link between temperament and allergies, and why a link was predicted. Kagan et al. did explain it for the most common of the symptoms: hayfever. It would appear that the same chemicals in our body that control hayfever symptoms also affect emotional mood. This could well be genetic; hence temperament is linked to these symptoms.

EVALUATION

➕ Kagan et al. used a fairly large sample of children, so their results can be generalised to other groups.

➕ The study interviewed a very large number of relatives, so the information provided on the children was supplied by several people. This means that the results are likely to be reliable.

➖ There was no diagnosis from a doctor. The relative simply answered yes/no to a series of questions asking whether the children showed symptoms. There was no opportunity to answer "sometimes", so we have no record of how often the children experienced the symptoms.

AQA Eysenck's Type Theory

There have been many theories that have attempted to *categorise* people into different types of personality. One that has stood the test of time is Eysenck's Type (or Trait) Theory.

ACTIVITY 13.3

The main personality types highlighted by Eysenck are extraversion, introversion, neuroticism and psychoticism. Before reading on, what do you think each of these personality types is about? Use examples to help define your answers. Then, read the definitions below and see if you were right.

EXAM HINT

Psychoticism is included here to give you the complete picture of the theory, but you do not need to be able to describe this trait in the exam. You do, however, need to be able to explain the characteristics of extraversion, introversion and neuroticism.

Eysenck created the Eysenck Personality Inventory (**EPI**) and Eysenck Personality Questionnaire (**EPQ**) to measure personality types of people with some yes/no questions. We will examine these measures further on page 282.

Once completed, a score can be given to show the level of Eysenck's personality factors, which are:

- **Extraversion** (E score): People scoring high on this scale tend to be more sociable and impulsive compared to low scorers (labelled **introverts**) who tend to be more cautious and not as social.
- **Neuroticism** (N score): People scoring high on this scale tend to be more anxious, depressed and tense compared to low scorers who tend to be more relaxed.
- **Psychoticism** (P score): People who score high on this scale tend to be more aggressive, egocentric and cold compared to low scorers who tend to be warm, more aware of others and not aggressive.

Some psychologists believe that it appears quite restricting to have three dimensions that all personalities can be measured on. However, as Eysenck (2002) points out, the personality type "optimism" does not exist on the EPQ, but people who have higher E scores and lower N scores tend to be optimistic. Therefore, there is no need for an optimism score. Hence, all personality traits could be a combination of E, N and P.

Finally for this section, Eysenck was a firm believer in personality being genetic (he claimed up to two-thirds of it could be), therefore some of

---

KEY TERMS

EPI: a personality questionnaire that measures Extraversion and Neuroticism. There are two forms, simply called EPI-A and EPI-B, which can be used to correlate people's scores to see if they score high or low on both questionnaires.

EPQ: a personality questionnaire developed to add the third dimension of Psychoticism. Therefore participants completing this questionnaire can be scored for Extraversion, Neuroticism and Psychoticism.

Extraversion: a personality trait that is characterised by more sociable and impulsive behaviours than those shown by introverts.

Introversion: a personality trait that is characterised by less sociable and more cautious behaviours than those shown by extroverts.

Neuroticism: a personality trait that is characterised by anxious, depressed and tense behaviours.

Psychoticism: a personality trait that is characterised by aggressive, egocentric and cold behaviours.

these types are fixed. He also believed that some of the personality types were physiological and were caused by the way the brain processes and handles information. Introverts have higher levels of brain activity compared to extraverts. Therefore extravert's brains are *stimulus hungry* as their brains need to be stimulated more than introverts. Hence they are more likely to be sociable and impulsive to stimulate the brain more.

Personality scales

Eysenck created two difference questionnaires to test out his ideas about personality: the Eysenck Personality Inventory (1965) and the Eysenck Personality Questionnaire (1975).

The Eysenck Personality Inventory asks questions that measure Extraversion and Neuroticism. There are two forms, simply called EPI-A and EPI-B, that can be used to correlate scores of people to see if they score high or low on both questionnaires.

Examples of the types of questions asked in Eysenck's Personality Inventory		
Do you quite enjoy taking risks?	YES ☐	NO ☐
Are you fairly talkative when you are with a group of people?	YES ☐	NO ☐
Do you enjoy telling jokes?	YES ☐	NO ☐
Do you occasionally tell lies?	YES ☐	NO ☐
Would you say that you dwell on the past?	YES ☐	NO ☐
Would you say that you are sometimes moody?	YES ☐	NO ☐
Can you usually let yourself go and have a good time at a party?	YES ☐	NO ☐
When the odds are against you, do you still feel it is worth taking a chance?	YES ☐	NO ☐
Do you rely on friends to cheer you up?	YES ☐	NO ☐
Do you sometimes speak before you think?	YES ☐	NO ☐

The traits associated with the three temperaments in Eysenck's model of personality		
Psychoticism	**Extraversion**	**Neuroticism**
Aggressive	Sociable	Anxious
Assertive	Irresponsible	Depressed
Egocentric	Dominant	Guilt feelings
Unsympathetic	Lack of reflection	Low self-esteem
Manipulative	Sensation-seeking	Tense
Achievement-oriented	Impulsive	Moody
Dogmatic	Risk-taking	Hypochondriac
Masculine	Expressive	Lack of autonomy
Tough-minded	Active	Obsessive

EXAM HINT

In the exam make sure you can describe the EPI and the EPQ. In addition, you may be given a few items and be asked to say which characteristic (of extraversion or neuroticism) they are exploring.

The Eysenck Personality Questionnaire was developed to add the third dimension of Psychoticism. Therefore participants completing this questionnaire can be scored for Extraversion, Neuroticism and Psychoticism.

Methodology

The problem with questionnaires that only offer alternatives of "yes" or "no" as answers is that there is no opportunity to say "sometimes". In some of the example items, are there any to which you would want to give the response "sometimes", or "it all depends on…"?

AQA Evaluation of Eysenck's Type Theory

There are a number of competing theories that explain personality in a different way. For example, Rogers and Maslow, who are humanistic psychologists, see humans as being unique individuals. They have to self-actualise (reach their full potential) and decide on their own destiny and personality via free will. This is the term used to describe how we all make conscious choices about the way we live and the pathway we wish to take. Therefore, it is incorrect to categorise people via E, N and P as this is too constraining and misses out the richness of individual differences we observe in personality.

Fahrenberg (1992) reviewed the field of personality to see if there was any evidence for a physiological basis for personality as highlighted by Eysenck. He concluded that over many decades there had been a great deal of research into this but none of it had really shown any link between physiology and personality.

However, research examining the genetic basis of personality has produced more positive findings. In twin studies, where psychologists can examine similarities between two people with the same genetics, neuroticism has been shown to be 80% inherited (Eysenck & Prell, 1951) and extraversion has been shown to be 62% inherited (Eysenck, 1956). More recent research is producing

Critical thinking

Think about the extent to which you believe people are free to make choices in life, and the extent to which their lives are "determined" by their biology, their upbringing, their culture, their friends, and so on.

Twin study research has shown high levels of genetically inherited personality traits

positive results that are not as strong as Eysenck's earlier work but are still showing high levels of inherited personality. For example, Zuckerman (1989) reviewed four studies and concluded that both extraversion and neuroticism were 40–50% inherited. One final study that used the EPI was conducted by Pedersen et al. (1988). A large sample of over 650 pairs of twins (identical and non-identical) showed that neuroticism is 31% inherited and extraversion is 41% inherited. Therefore there appears to be some limited support for the genetic basis of Eysenck's personality types.

Finally, there are competing type theories that some psychologists believe are more comprehensive and useful than Eysenck's.

The *Five Factor Model* based on the work of Norman (1963) states that there are obviously five main personality factors: extraversion, agreeableness (e.g. being cooperative), conscientiousness (e.g. being responsible), emotional stability (e.g. being calm in situations) and culture (e.g. being imaginative). Psychologists argue that this gives a better picture of an individual as there are more factors to discuss. This could also be true for Cattell's approach, which states that there are 16 main personality traits.

AQA Antisocial personality disorder (APD)

So far in this chapter we have considered the types of personality that exist in "normal" individuals, people who are not unusual. However, there are a small number of people who are considered to suffer from a condition known as a personality disorder, in which their personality is a cause of serious concern, because it is damaging to them or to others, or both. There are about 10 different types of personality disorder, all very different – we are going to look at one called *antisocial personality disorder*.

Characteristics of APD

People with APD are typically liars, cheats and bullies, often involved in crime, with a very irresponsible approach to life. Most of all, they simply don't care if they hurt other people and never show any true remorse (regret) for what they have done. So what exactly is APD?

Antisocial personality disorder involves a disregard for the rights of others that has been going on since the person was 15 years of age or younger. Only people over the age of 18 can be diagnosed with this disorder.

The types of symptoms that a person with APD may show are:

1. Taking no notice of rules and breaking the law.
2. Telling lies and being deceitful. This may include using aliases (false names) and conning people in order to get money out of them.
3. Acting on impulse rather than planning ahead.
4. Being aggressive, getting into fights and attacking others.

5. Doing things that may be very dangerous, either for themselves or for other people.
6. Being irresponsible in some way, for example, not holding down a job for very long, not paying bills, getting into a lot of debt without any care for the consequences.
7. Not being in the least sorry if they hurt other people, steal from them or mistreat them in some other way.

One of the key factors that might account for the symptoms above is that people with APD may have a *lack of emotion*, both positive and negative. Think for a minute about how emotions make you feel – happy, sad, disappointed, loving, angry, sympathetic, scared. If you lack these emotions, then you are never really frightened, so you don't learn from your mistakes; you never feel shame, so you don't care if you cause hurt; you never really feel excitement, so you try to get some in your life; you never really love anyone, so you are utterly selfish.

The character of Dr Hannibal Lecter in The Silence of the Lambs *displayed many of the characteristics of APD, especially a total disregard for others. His high intelligence made him extremely dangerous*

DSM-IV criteria for APD

Below are the definition and symptoms of APD as they appear in a classification system called DSM-IV. DSM is one of two major classification systems that list every single type of mental disorder and their symptoms. DSM stands for *Diagnostic and Statistical Manual of Mental Disorders*. Because it has been revised several times over the years, it is now called DSM-IV, because this is the 4th edition. The 5th one is due to be published in 2012.

The DSM-IV diagnostic criteria for antisocial personality disorder include:

A. A pervasive pattern of disregard for and violation of the rights of others occurring since the age of 15 years, as indicated by at least three of:
  1. failure to conform to social norms with respect to lawful behaviours, as indicated by repeatedly performing acts that are grounds for arrest
  2. deceitfulness, as indicated by repeated lying, use of aliases, or conning others for personal profit or pleasure
  3. impulsivity or failure to plan ahead
  4. irritability and aggressiveness, as indicated by repeated physical fights or assaults
  5. reckless disregard for safety of self or others
  6. consistent irresponsibility, as indicated by repeated failure to sustain consistent work behaviour or to honour financial obligations

EXAM HINT

You will not have time (nor will it be necessary) to write a great many symptoms in the exam, so learn three well. However, it is useful to be aware of the others. This means that, if you are given a description of an individual with APD, you can say which aspects of their behaviour/personality would lead to a diagnosis of APD (see exam question 4 at the end of this chapter).

How psychology works

The classification systems of mental disorders are essential in order to diagnose and treat these disorders. You can think of them in comparison to a diagnosis system of biological disorders, such as mumps and measles. However, they are more controversial as there is not always agreement about what should constitute a mental disorder.

7. lack of remorse, as indicated by being indifferent to or rationalising having hurt, mistreated, or stolen from another.
B. The individual is at least 18 years of age.
C. There is evidence of conduct disorder with onset before the age of 15 years.
D. The occurrence of antisocial behaviour is not exclusively during the course of schizophrenia or a manic episode.

Causes of APD

So what might be responsible for the fact that some people have this type of personality disorder? We will consider several possible explanations.

Biological causes
Brain dysfunction

One of the reasons why people may have APD concerns the functioning of their brain, in particular a part of the brain known as the amygdala. The following study provides some evidence for this theory.

RAINE ET AL. (1997)

Aim: To use a brain scan (called PET) to see if there are any differences in the brains of murderers and a matched group of non-murderers.

Method: Raine et al. compared the brains of two groups of people:

- A group of 41 murderers who had pleaded not guilty by reason of insanity. There were 39 men and 2 women; 6 of them were diagnosed as schizophrenic.
- A group of 41 people who had not committed murder and were matched on a one-to-one basis with the murder group in terms of age and sex, so there were 39 men and 2 women; 6 of these were diagnosed as schizophrenic.

The murderers had been referred for a brain scan in order to obtain information relating to their plea of not guilty by reason of insanity. Their brains were examined using a PET scan. This type of scan allows researchers to see which parts of the brain are being used during any particular activity. The participants were asked to do various tasks for 30 minutes while the scan took place.

Results: The important findings were:

- The murderers had less activity than the controls in the prefrontal cortex, an area linked to self-control.
- In the amygdala, there was less activity in the left side than the right side of the brain in the murderers than in the controls. The amygdala is one of

the structures in the brain that helps control violent behaviour, so if it is not functioning very well the person may be violent. They may also be rather fearless and not learn from any negative effects that their violence may have.

Conclusions: The results do indicate that there may be a link between brain dysfunction and a *predisposition* towards violence in this specific group.

EVALUATION

➕ Raine et al. used a fairly large sample of murderers, who were compared with a matched group of controls.

➖ There was no control over the level of violence used in the murders and some were not very violent (some people in the sample were accused of manslaughter).

➖ Brain scans are not always easy to interpret.

For these reasons, it is necessary to be careful in interpreting the results of this study. The researchers believe that brain dysfunction alone cannot cause a person to become a murderer. Other factors, such as the home and the community, contribute to whether or not an individual will become violent.

In addition, it's not clear if the brain dysfunction was there before the murders took place. It's possible that the violent behaviour caused changes to the brain.

Why psychology matters

It is important to recognise that behaviour can affect the brain as well as the brain affecting behaviour. Rats brought up in cages that contain lots of toys have more "grey matter" in their brains than rats reared in empty cages.

Genetics

Research seems to indicate that genetics could be a factor in causing APD. Several studies show that the fathers of people with APD tend to show antisocial behaviour. Of course, this could be a result of the way the children are treated by their parents but adoption studies also show that adopted children who have a biological parent with APD are more likely, as adults, to have APD than other adults (Ge et al., 1996).

Situational factors
The role of the family

In Chapter 8 we looked at the work of Bowlby on attachment. He believed that if young children did not have a continuous positive relationship with one main carer (usually their mother) during the first 3 years of their life, then this could, in certain cases, result in a lack of affection and love

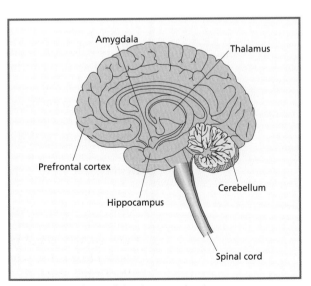

A cross-section of the human brain

for others that lasted into adult life. Such a personality pattern is known as affectionless personality and could result in APD.

McCord and McCord (1964) looked at many studies of people with APD and concluded that these people had been severely neglected by their parents and had had very little if any affection during their childhood years.

Other studies provide a similar story. In many cases the parents are inconsistent in their discipline. For example, the father is a strict disciplinarian and the mother compensates by being very lenient, giving the child frequent but secret rewards such as sweets or money and giving in to the child's demands. In other cases neither parent disciplines the child or teaches them responsibility towards others. In many cases the fathers are themselves antisocial.

However, we need to be careful not to jump to the conclusion that the way the parents treat the children is the only cause of their behaviour. It is possible that the children have been very difficult from the start and the parents' irregular discipline is a way of trying to cope with a very disruptive child. In addition – and this is an important point – many children brought up by parents whose discipline is poor never show signs of antisocial behaviour or a lack of concern for other people, so there are probably other factors involved.

We will now look in more detail at a study that followed many youngsters over a large number of years in order to see which factors predicted later delinquent behaviour.

FARRINGTON (1995)

Aim: To investigate the progress of a group of boys in order to see if certain behaviour in early childhood could predict behaviour in later life.

Method: In Farrington's study, 411 males from South London were followed up from age 8 to age 32. The researchers were interested in many aspects of the individuals and their families including:

- IQ (intelligence quotient)
- school attainment (how well they achieved at school)
- antisocial behaviour
- history of criminality in the family
- the financial circumstances of the family
- how parents treated their children.

Results: The main characteristics that predicted whether the child grew up to be an adult with APD were:

- antisocial behaviour
- low IQ and school attainment
- poor child-rearing by the parents
- the family is involved in crime
- impulsive behaviour.

Conclusion: In order to reduce the rates of APD in adults, it is necessary to tackle childhood problem behaviour. This can be done by developing special programmes to reduce delinquency, help children achieve more at school, tackle poor parenting and reduce poverty. This leads us on to the implications of research into APD.

AQA Implications of research into APD

Earlier we mentioned that APD is only diagnosed over the age of 18, but that there has been a history of conduct disorder from at least the age of 15 (often from a far younger age than that). Conduct disorders are behaviours such as disobedience to parents, breaking rules at school, being aggressive, bullying, mistreating animals, stealing and generally being out of control. Several studies have shown that APD is preceded by such conduct disorders.

Elander et al. (2000) studied 13 criminals whose first conviction was after the age of 22 years. All except one had shown minor juvenile delinquency, while four had a major mental illness that had started before they had been convicted. The researchers concluded that criminality had not suddenly appeared after an uneventful childhood, but had been indicated by antisocial behaviour and/or major mental illness.

So what can be done to try to prevent APD? Hagell (2003) has produced a policy document to address this issue and makes several recommendations. She points out that youth offending is not only undesirable because of the damage it does but because, in the long term, it costs a huge amount of money.

> **ACTIVITY 13.4**
>
> Think of at least four ways in which youth offenders cost taxpayers money.

There are many recommendations so we cannot consider them all, but one important one is that it is necessary to spot the antecedents of serious antisocial behaviour, that is, the factors in a child's early life that are associated with later APD. These factors include:

- Children who are difficult to manage from a very early age.
- Children born to teenage parents.
- Children in families already known to the police.
- Parents who are inconsistent, harsh and very brutal in the punishment they use.
- Families with a history of abuse and neglect.
- Families in which there is so little money that children are not cared for well.
- People who have very few opportunities to feel worthwhile or needed by anyone.

If children and families with a lot of these risk factors are identified and helped when the children are quite young, then it is possible that the rates of APD in later life could be reduced.

Chapter summary

- Personality refers to a relatively stable set of behaviours, thoughts and feelings that a person shows to others. Temperament refers to your *natural* disposition in terms of personality traits. It is the genetic component of your personality.

- Thomas et al. (1968) found that children are consistent in their temperament and that it can be classified into three types: difficult, easy, slow to warm up. The researchers believed that people are born with a predetermined temperament but that personality is also affected by the environment.

- Buss and Plomin (1984) examined the difference in temperament between MZ (identical) and DZ (non-identical) twins. They found that the correlation between MZ twins was higher than that of DZ twins and concluded from this that temperament is largely innate.

- Kagan et al. (1991) looked at the relationship between temperament and allergies. They compared children considered to be uninhibited with children considered to be inhibited on various medical symptoms. Although there was no difference on most symptoms, there was a difference on five (including hayfever), with the inhibited children more likely to show them. Kagan et al. point out that the chemicals which control hayfever also control emotional mood, indicating that both hayfever and temperament are genetic.

- Eysenck has developed a type theory of personality which states that individuals vary on three personality dimensions: extraversion; neuroticism; psychoticism. Eysenck believed these characteristics to be genetically determined: extraverts are believed to have far less brain stimulation than introverts, hence they seek stimulation while introverts avoid it. This is a genetic difference.

- Eysenck created two questionnaires to measure personality: the EPI (Eysenck Personality Inventory) and EPQ (Eysenck Personality Questionnaire)

- Eysenck's theory can be evaluated as follows:
  - On the positive side:
    - Research shows high levels of similarity between twins on neuroticism and extraversion, indicating high levels of inheritance.
  - On the negative side:
    - It underestimates the richness of individual differences by reducing personality to only three dimensions.
    - There is little if any physiological evidence that extraverts are less stimulated than introverts (Fahrenberg 1992).
    - Other models of personality, including The Five Factor Model, offer a more comprehensive and insightful view of personality than does Eysenck's theory.

- Antisocial Personality Disorder (APD) is a personality type that involves a disregard for the rights of others that has been going on since the person was 15 years of age or younger.

- Some psychologists argue that there is a biological explanation for this disorder. They explain it in terms of brain dysfunction as supported by the study by Raine et al. (1997) who found differences in the brains of murderers compared with non-murderers.
- Another biological explanation is that the condition is genetic. Ge et al. (1996) found that adopted children who have a biological parent with APD are more likely, as adults, to have APD than other adults.
- Others argue that environmental factors, including upbringing, can affect the degree to which children grow up to have APD. Farrington (1995) suggested that the main factors that predicted whether children became adults with APD included poor school attainment, poor parenting and a family involved in crime. However, this does not mean that these factors caused the condition.

AQA Exam-style questions for AQA

1. Look at the following items that appeared in a personality scale to measure both extraversion and neuroticism. Say whether each item is designed to measure extraversion (E) or neuroticism (N) by putting the appropriate letter next to each one. (4 marks)

   (a) Do you like plenty of bustle and excitement around you?

   (b) Are you touchy about some things?

   (c) Would you rather plan things than do things?

   (d) Do you get very bad headaches?

2. Describe Eysenck's Type Theory of personality. (4 marks)

3. Describe and evaluate **one** study in which temperament was investigated. Include in your answer the method used in the study, the results obtained, the conclusion drawn and an evaluation of the study described (use continuous prose). (6 marks) [AQA, 2009, Specimen Paper]

4. Explain what is meant by antisocial personality disorder, referring to the article below in your answer. (5 marks)

   Johnny is a charming, good-looking boy who, on the surface, appears to be popular in his school but the truth is that most people in his class try to avoid falling out with him, fearing that he might bully them. He rarely does his homework but usually persuades one of the hard-working students to give him a copy of theirs to give in. Recently he has been caught buying alcohol for younger children, charging them for doing this. Police investigations have uncovered the fact that he had been involved in a lot of illegal activities (including underage sex and drug taking). He says he is really sorry and won't do it again but the psychologist believes that he has no real remorse and that he shows characteristics of antisocial personality disorder.

EXAM HINT

If a question requires continuous prose, it is really important that you answer in sentences and paragraphs. Do not write in note form or use bullet points. See the introductory chapter for more advice on this.

What you need to know OCR

The specification lists the following things that you will need to be able to do for the examination:

- Understand the idea that individuals are unique
- Explain the concept of free will
- Distinguish between self-concept and ideal self in relation to self-esteem
- Explain the idea of unconditional positive regard
- Explain the idea of self-actualisation
- Explain the criticisms of humanism as an explanation of the self
- Consider trait theory as an alternative theory, with specific reference to extraversion and neuroticism
- Describe and outline the limitations of the van Houtte and Jarvis (1995) study
- Outline an application of research into the self: Counselling

The self

It can only be disturbing that the number of students arriving at university with pre-existing and often complex mental health problems is growing each year.

The reassuring thing is that their problems are arguably less severe than those among 18 to 25 year olds in society in general, with the bonus that the universities have dedicated counselling services that are, mostly, more efficient than those offered by the NHS.

Universities are also geared up to deal with the pressures of student life, with exam and modular testing timetables, with the pressures of separation from families and friends and with financial crises. They have a humanitarian as well as a business interest in happy students.

Ann Conlon, the head of student services at King's College, University of London, and a founder of the Heads of University Counselling Services, agrees . . . "I would say the problems have become more serious. We do see a whole range of students, from those who have developmental problems related to their age and being away from home to those with borderline personality disorder problems," she explains.

"Increasingly, there are more students coming with a pre-existing situation. The manifestation can be depression, suicidal tendencies, self-harm. The eating disorders have always been with us. Some people are more psychotic. But I do think one has to be aware that because of the nature of their age, students are very impulsive. They do not always stop and reflect. They feel things very intensely. They feel terrible one day and wonderful the next."

Conlon is careful to point out that students with a serious problem remain a minority. In an institution such as hers, with 17,000 students, there are perhaps half a dozen a year who have severe problems.

It is also important, she said, to create links with the NHS, with local doctors and with hospital accident and emergency services, so that they will refer students taken to hospital with such problems as overdoses back to the university.

However, the figure she gives, she says, covers the whole spectrum of mental ill-health, which can "be anything from the occasional bad day, to intermittent depression, to depression that continues throughout university, to the extremes of suicidal tendencies and serious personality breakdown."

Students' problems can vary, depending on their age, their home background and whether they are living at home or away. Those in halls are often best catered for, since they are integrated into the university welfare organisations. Often, postgraduate students get cheap living accommodation to be a watching but discreet presence. One of the difficulties is that the mentally ill will be reluctant to seek help.

The most important consideration is for those with problems to get appropriate help as fast as possible

Abridged extract from "Students' welfare takes centre stage", by Anne McHardy from www.guardian.co.uk/education/2003/aug/17/studenthealth.students#history-byline#history-byline
Reproduced by permission of the author

OCR Individuals are unique

The humanist movement in psychology has the idea that individuals are unique, moulded by the experiences that they have. As we all have different experiences, we are all unique. Everyone has their own potential to fulfil their capabilities, and this needs nurturing by ourselves and by others. As a result, no two individuals are the same. This is one of the main reasons why humanism emerged as both the behaviourists (conditioning theory) and psychodynamic psychologists (unconscious and early experiences) were reducing humans down to a few general laws that applied to everyone. The main humanistic psychologists are Carl Rogers and Abraham Maslow.

Critical thinking

Of course, to some extent all approaches recognise that humans are unique, but they do not all emphasise to the same extent the universal laws that govern everyone. While learning theory emphasises the importance of theories of learning, and the psychodynamic theorists emphasise the factors that control the unconscious, humanists place less importance on the similarity between individuals and more on their individuality.

KEY TERM

Free will: the conscious choices we make about the way we live and the pathways we wish to take.

OCR Free will

One of the key ideas of humanism is that we all have **free will**. This term refers to us all making conscious choices about the way we live and the pathways we wish to take. Therefore, we are in control of our own destiny. This is the complete opposite of determinism, which states that external forces make us behave in certain ways (e.g. gaining a reward for completing a particular task or behaviour is genetically encoded).

> **ACTIVITY 14.1**
>
> Why are you wearing the clothes you are wearing today? Try to list as many reasons why. Then, try to work out whether they are free will choices or affected by other people/rewards, etc. Which one wins – free will or determinism?

OCR Self-concept, ideal self and self-esteem

These three terms are crucial to understanding humanism.

- **Self-concept** refers to the mental image that we have of ourselves. This features physical attributes like hair colour and dress sense, and psychological attributes like our predominant emotions or our favourite food. This can be made up of our current self (how we are now) but we could add elements from our ideal self.
- **Ideal self** refers to our mental representation of who we ideally would like to be. This features physical attributes and psychological attributes that we want to have.
- **Self-esteem** refers to how we *feel* about our current self. If we do not like much about our self-concept, then we will have low self-esteem. If we quite like our self-concept and can see positive aspects, then we will have high self-esteem. Some psychologists believe that the gap between our current self and our ideal self dictates our level of self-esteem. If the gap is large then we experience low self-esteem, but if the gap is small we should experience high self-esteem.

It might be interesting to note that some psychologists refer to an **ought self**. Remember that the ideal self refers to what *we* would like to be. The ought self is our understanding of what others want us to be (what we ought to be in the eyes of others). This then becomes part of our self-concept.

OCR Unconditional positive regard

This is a concept that is at the heart of humanism. **Unconditional positive regard** is when a person is completely accepting of another no matter what.

KEY TERMS

Self-concept: the mental image that we have of ourselves.

Ideal self: our mental representation of who we ideally would like to be.

Self-esteem: how we *feel* about our current self.

Ought self: our understanding of what others want us to be (what we ought to be in the eyes of others).

Unconditional positive regard: when a person is completely accepting of another no matter what.

Why psychology matters

Some psychologists believe that we do not pay enough attention to the importance of self-esteem in producing happiness. Self-esteem does not depend on how clever or good-looking you are, it depends on the gap between your self-concept and your ideal self. If parents are very critical, children develop low self-esteem whatever their capabilities are.

EXAM HINT

Notice that you are expected to be able to distinguish between self-concept and ideal self in relation to self-esteem. Your self-concept is your belief about yourself; your self-esteem is how much you *value* yourself. Two people can have the same self-concept (I'm average at maths) but very different self-esteem (they can think they are good or poor at maths). This depends on their ideal self.

Unconditional positive regard is when a person is totally accepting of another and displays this attitude towards that person

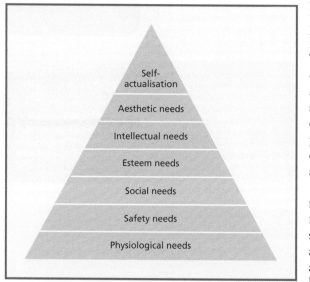

Maslow's hierarchy of needs

Self-
actualisation

Aesthetic needs

Intellectual needs

Esteem needs

Social needs

Safety needs

Physiological needs

You are completely accepting of that person in terms of things you like, and ignore the bad side. It is unconditional because you expect nothing in return, and it is positive regard because it focuses on the good things about that person. In other words, we find the good in all. We do not just simply hold it as an attitude – we must display this behaviour towards the person (e.g. hugging them or telling them how great they are).

OCR Self-actualisation

Self-actualisation refers to us reaching and fulfilling our own potential. As Jarvis (2000) puts it "like a flower that will grow to its full potential if the conditions are right...so people will flourish and reach their potential if the environment is good enough." (p. 62). Therefore, as Rogers pointed out, the potential of every human is unique so we will all self-actualise differently. Maslow took this further by stating that self-actualisation is at the pinnacle of our hierarchy of needs and that we need to progress with other things in our lives first. The diagram on the left shows our hierarchy of needs according to Maslow.

Therefore we need to fulfil our physiological needs first in life. Once this is fulfilled/being fulfilled we can then move up the hierarchy to safety needs and so on. Once we have conquered aesthetic needs, then we can move on to self-actualisation and be a complete and whole human being.

KEY TERM

Self-actualisation: the reaching and fulfilling of our own potential.

Self-concept

Self-actualisation

Ideal self

ACTIVITY 14.2

For each of the stages in Maslow's hierarchy of needs, state two things you would like to fulfil in each. Compare them to a friend in your class. Are they the same or are they unique?

OCR Criticisms of humanism

One of the main criticisms of humanism is that there are other plausible explanations for personality. The next section on trait theory is one of these, so the humanistic approach cannot be the complete answer to personality and the self (see also Chapter 13 on personality).

Other psychologists have criticised Rogers and Maslow on the same grounds – they focus on the individual striving to fulfil their own potential. This could well be culture-bound as other cultures place much more emphasis on group work in fulfilling themselves rather than on the North American ideal of individualism. Some Eastern cultures place worth on collectivism, where people work as a group for the good of that group and the individuals within it. This cannot be explained by self-actualisation and free will.

Also, the concept of free will can be questioned by its opposite: determinism. In Chapter 13, there is evidence to suggest that some aspects of self are determined at birth (temperament) and therefore cannot be changed via unconditional positive regard or self-actualisation.

The ideas of self-actualisation, unconditional positive regard and free will are very subjective and based on opinions. This makes it very difficult to test out these ideas scientifically to establish cause and effect. How can we know that self-actualisation is all we strive for if it is difficult to test it out?

EXAM HINT

If asked to criticise humanism, you will need to give a brief account of the alternative theories. Make sure you can summarise them in a few sentences.

Diversity

It is important to recognise that different cultures have different value systems, and that not all of them value self-fulfilment.

OCR Trait theory: Eysenck's approach to personality

An alternative to the humanistic approach, where the emphasis is on free will and uniqueness, is the trait approach to personality. There have been many theories that have attempted to *categorise* people into different types of personality. One that has stood the test of time is Eysenck's Trait (or Type) Theory.

ACTIVITY 14.3

The main personality types highlighted by Eysenck are extraversion, introversion, neuroticism and psychoticism. Before reading on, what do you think each of these personality types is about? Use examples to help define your answers, then read the definitions below and see if you were right!

Methodology

The problem with questionnaires that only offer alternatives of "yes" or "no" as answers is that there is no opportunity to say "sometimes". In some of the example items, are there any to which you would want to give the response "sometimes", or "it all depends on..."?

Eysenck created the Eysenck Personality Questionnaire (EPQ) to measure personality types of people with some yes/no questions (to read more about this method see the AQA chapter on personality, especially pages 281–283).

Once completed, a score can be given to show the level of his personality factors, which are:

* *Extraversion (E score)*: People scoring high on this scale tend to be more sociable and impulsive compared to low scorers (labelled introverts) who tend to be more cautious and not as social.
* *Neuroticism (N score)*: People scoring high on this scale tend to be more anxious, depressed and tense compared to low scorers who tend to be more relaxed.
* *Psychoticism (P score)*: People who score high on this scale tend to be more aggressive, egocentric and cold compared to low scorers who tend to be warm, more aware of others and not aggressive.

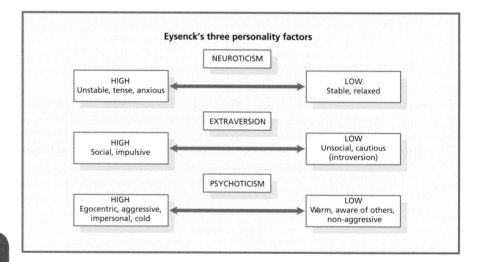

Eysenck's three personality factors

Critical thinking

Do you think that people can be summed up by these three traits alone? Think of your very close family, or anyone else you know really well, and consider whether you believe these three traits can adequately describe them. Does such a description take account of what was mentioned earlier – self-esteem?

Some psychologists believe that it appears quite restricting to have three dimensions that all personalities can be measured on. However, as Eysenck (2002) points out, the trait "optimism" does not exist on the EPQ but people who have higher E scores and lower N scores tend to be optimistic. Therefore, there is no need for an optimism score. Hence, all personality traits could be a combination of E, N and P.

Finally for this section, Eysenck was a firm believer in personality being genetic (he claimed up to two-thirds of it could be), therefore some of these traits are fixed. This goes entirely against the claims of the humanists that we are all unique and develop through differing life pathways.

OCR CORE STUDY: VAN HOUTTE AND JARVIS (1995)

Aim: Van Houtte and Jarvis wanted to examine the role of pets in pre-adolescent (8 to 12 years of age) psychosocial development.

Procedure: A sample of 130 pre-adolescents aged 8 to 12 years of age completed a range of questionnaires. There were 26 third graders (8/9-year-olds), 36 fourth graders (9/10-year-olds), 34 fifth graders (10/11-year-olds) and 34 sixth graders (11/12-year-olds). These included measures of **autonomy** (level of personal independence and less reliance on parents), *self-concept* (how you see yourself in terms of positive traits like "I am happy") and *self-esteem* (how you feel about yourself). Additionally, all participants completed a measure on their attachment to animals. There were two groups of participants: a pet-owning group and a non-pet-owning group. However, for each pet-owning participant, a non-pet-owning participant was *matched* for parental marital status, socioeconomic status and number of siblings. Therefore, for each "pair of participants" the only real thing that differed was whether they owned a pet. Van Houtte and Jarvis felt that these were important variables to control for as they could affect autonomy, self-concept and self-esteem. Therefore it was a *matched pairs design*. Permission for the children to participate in the study was gained via their parents.

Results: Some clear differences emerged between the two groups.

- *Autonomy*: Higher levels of autonomy were reported in pet-owners across all participants irrespective of age. Therefore, pet-owners at this age have more personal independence compared to non-pet-owners.
- *Self-concept*: The only time when the pet-owners significantly differed from non-pet-owners was in sixth graders. Their self-concept was significantly higher.
- *Self-esteem*: There were significant differences in self-esteem between the two groups in fifth and sixth graders. Those who owned a pet reported significantly higher self-esteem compared to the non-pet-owning group.
- *Attachment to animals in general*: There was no difference between the two groups of participants.

Conclusion: Van Houtte and Jarvis stated that *"the significant differences between the groups for both fifth and sixth graders suggest that pets may have their greatest impact on children's lives as they enter into adolescence."* (p. 463). They also concluded that pets could be used to enhance self-concept and increase self-esteem for pre-adolescents with low levels of both.

Limitations: There were small sample sizes in each of the age groups. This means that it may be difficult to generalise to that age group on a wider scale as the group may not have been representative of the target population. Also, the participants completed questionnaires, which could lead to two problems: (1) there is no way of knowing if the participants were telling the truth about their views on animals or their self-esteem, for instance; and (2) there could have been some demand characteristics happening with the questionnaires, with the participants working out the

Person-centred therapy focuses on the present and future, and how things can change there, rather than on the past

aim of the study and potentially giving socially desirable answers. Finally, as the work was not truly experimental there could have been other factors common to the pet-owning group that affected the measures other than simply owning a pet (e.g. had more friends or had experienced fewer life traumas).

OCR Counselling

This section examines the theory behind **person-centred therapy** based on ideas by Carl Rogers. This is a therapy based on the principles of humanism that you have read about in this chapter.

Most people automatically think that people in therapy are patients and they are helped via therapists. Humanists would still call themselves therapists but the patient is called a client. This is because the therapist and the client are on equal terms (so there is no hierarchy based on expertise). A humanistic counsellor would help explore ideas that could be frustrating the client and making them unhappy. Also, there is very little focus on past happenings. The focus is on the present and future and how things can change there. Therefore, one of the main focuses is on personal growth, with the therapist facilitating self-actualisation.

In Rogerian counselling there is an emphasis on three main things:

1. **Empathy**: This is the therapist's ability to understand how the client is feeling about life experiences. They must clearly communicate this to the client.
2. **Congruence**: sometimes called *genuineness*. This refers to the therapist allowing the client to experience them for who they are (other therapists, such as psychodynamic counsellors, reveal little about themselves during sessions; Rogerian counsellors reveal much more about themselves and their feelings).
3. *Unconditional positive regard*: This refers to maintaining a positive attitude towards the client no matter what. Even if a humanistic counsellor does not agree with the actions or pathway of the client deep-down, they remain positive in the counselling sessions.

...warmth, acceptance and empathy on the part of the therapist.

Therefore, a client is treated as being unique. They are nurtured to help them grow to their own full potential with the main goal being to self-actualise, which should then increase self-esteem and self-worth. Any problems should then disappear and the client should feel more confident to tackle other issues that may arise in the future.

KEY TERMS

Person-centred therapy: a type of therapy whereby a therapist uses the principles of unconditional positive regard, empathy, and congruence as a means of helping a client reach self-actualisation.

Empathy: this is the therapist's ability to understand how the client is feeling about life experiences. They must clearly communicate this to the client.

Congruence: sometimes called *genuineness*. This refers to the therapist allowing the client to experience them for who they are.

ACTIVITY 14.4

Find out about psychodynamic counselling as an alternative to this type of counselling. Write down a description of what happens in psychodynamic counselling. Then draw up a table to show similarities and differences between the two types.

Chapter summary

- Humanists believe that people are unique. The main psychologists to believe this are Rogers and Maslow.
- Free will refers to us all making conscious choices about the way we live and the pathways we wish to take.
- Self-concept refers to the mental image that we have of ourselves. Ideal self refers to our mental representation of who we ideally would like to be. Self-esteem refers to how we *feel* about our current self. These are some of the main terms used by humanists.
- Other main terms include unconditional positive regard, which is when a person is completely accepting of another no matter what; and self-actualisation, which refers to us reaching and fulfilling our own potential.
- An alternative idea to the self is trait theory. This refers to groups of characteristics that people may share. For example, people may be extraverted and show similar traits of being outgoing and full of life. These characteristics can be measured by people completing questionnaires about themselves.
- Van Houtte and Jarvis (1995) examined the role pets have in the development of our self during adolescence. Pet-owners tended to show more autonomy (independence) and some even had higher self-esteem.
- Humanistic counselling involves empathy, congruence and unconditional positive regard. An alternative is psychodynamic counselling.

OCR Exam-style questions for OCR

1. Define the term free will. (2 marks)

2. Define the term self-actualisation using an example. (2 marks)

3. An alternative to humanism is trait theory. Outline **one** trait theory you have studied. (4 marks)

4. Describe **two** results from the van Houtte and Jarvis (1995) study. (2 marks)

5. Outline **one** limitation of the van Houtte and Jarvis (1995) study. (2 marks)

6. Outline **one** way in which humanism can be applied to the real world (e.g. counselling). (5 marks)

Part 7

Research in psychology

The difference between our "common sense" ideas about how we behave and theories in psychology is that psychological theories are tested to see whether they are true or false.

Psychology is therefore a "scientific study" of human behaviour. Deciding whether to conduct an experiment or to observe or interview participants is an important part of the research process. Understanding the advantages and disadvantages of each research method allows us to make judgements about the value of a research study.

Chapter 15 • Research methods

We describe and evaluate the different methods that psychologists use to gather information and carry out research. We then consider the steps necessary to plan a research study and to ensure that it is ethical as well as conducted in a reliable manner.

What you need to know OCR AQA

The whole content of this chapter is relevant to you whether you are studying the AQA or the OCR specification. However, for your convenience, both specifications are listed together, at the end of the chapter, since they put the contents of the research methods section in a different order. Please turn to page 338 for the full list.

Research methods

15

■ ■ ■ ■ ■ ■ ■ ■ ■

As you know, psychologists study behaviour and attempt to work out the reasons behind it. As you have seen from all the topic areas you have studied so far, human behaviour is so complex and varied that no single method is ever going to be sufficient to find out what we want to know. Sometimes it's enough to simply observe a particular type of behaviour and make a note of how often it occurs and in what circumstances. At other times, psychologists may want to manipulate one or more variables to see the effect of changing them. In other cases still, they may want to investigate attitudes, so they write a **questionnaire**. What we are saying is that psychologists use a variety of methods depending on the type of behaviour they are investigating. Be careful not to fall into the trap of believing that one method is better than another; they all have their drawbacks and their advantages, and it very much depends on the topic area being studied. In this chapter, we will look at a variety of these methods and consider their disadvantages and advantages.

OCR AQA Experiments

People often use the term **experiment** quite loosely in order to refer to any research in psychology, but you must avoid doing this because an experiment is a very precise method different from all others. Before reading on, do the following activity.

ACTIVITY 15.1

Think what is involved in an experiment as opposed to any other research method (such as an observation or a questionnaire). If it helps, think of what you actually do when you conduct an experiment in a physics or chemistry lesson.

Description

An experiment involves the deliberate manipulation of one variable to measure its effect on another variable while keeping all other variables constant (as far as possible).

Let's use an example to see how this operates. Suppose you believe that loud rock music helps you to revise better, but your friend thinks that it's

KEY TERMS

Questionnaire: a set of questions dealing with any topic. Questions can limit responses (e.g. Are you male or female?) or be open-ended (e.g. Describe your childhood).

Experiment: the deliberate manipulation of one variable to measure its effect on another variable, while trying to keep all other variables constant. This is the only method that allows us to draw conclusions about cause and effect.

better to work in silence. You want to test this with a number of people. What you are trying to find out is whether music has an effect on memory. In psychological experiments (like experiments in other fields) we try to keep all aspects of the situation constant except one – the one we are looking at. So in this case we use two similar groups of people all revising the same piece of work in two identical rooms at the same time of day. Everything is the same except for the variable whose effect we want to measure, so one group works in silence, while the other works with loud rock music playing. They all work for the same amount of time and are then given an identical test.

The independent variable and the dependent variable

The variable that we deliberately manipulate is called the **independent variable (IV)**. In this case, it is the presence of loud rock music or silence. We call the factor that we then measure (in our example, the scores on the memory test) the **dependent variable (DV)**. It is so called because, if our ideas are correct, it is suggested that it *depends* on the independent variable. In our example, we believe it is possible that the amount of noise has an effect on the amount people can remember:

A convenient way of deciding which variable is which, is to remember:

- The IV is the one the experimenter manipulates.
- The DV is the one that is measured.

ACTIVITY 15.2

Identify the IV and DV in imaginary experiments to see whether:

(a) bulls react faster to a red rag than to a blue rag;
(b) men drive faster than women;
(c) people who are stressed produce less work than people who are not stressed;
(d) people in cities are less aggressive than people who live in rural areas;
(e) playing violent video games increases the level of adrenalin in the blood;
(f) men who have beards are perceived as older than men who don't have beards.

Extraneous (confounding) variables

In order to see whether the IV does affect the DV, and that it is not some other factor that is having the effect, we need to keep all other variables constant. Any variables that might affect the results and therefore give us a false set of data are called **extraneous (confounding) variables**. Controlling these variables is largely a matter of common sense. If the "music" group worked at a different time of day from the "silence" group, then it could be the time of day, not the music that had the effect. For the same reason we need to use the same room and the same piece of work, give each group identical instructions as to what to do, get them all to do the task in the same way, and so on. The main things that need to be considered are:

- **Situational variables**: All aspects of the situation have to be kept the same – the room, the time of day, any other noise (such as noise from outside), the lighting, and so on.
- **Participant variables**: If we are using two groups of participants, we need to make sure they are as similar as possible, especially in factors that may affect the DV (in our example, factors that might affect how much they can remember). Other factors that might be important are age, sex, and ability.
- **Standardised procedures**: The experimenter should work out a procedure that is followed in the same way for each group of participants, so that they all get identical experiences.
- **Standardised instructions**: The experimenter should also work out what he or she is going to say to the participants. This must be the same for every participant in any one condition. The instructions are decided beforehand, and given to the participants or read out to them.

> ### KEY TERMS
>
> **Extraneous/confounding variables**: any uncontrolled variable that might affect the results, therefore giving false information.
>
> **Situational variables**: any aspects of the situation that might affect the findings, such as the room, the time of day, the lighting, etc. These must be kept the same for all participants.
>
> **Participant variables**: possible confounding variables if participants are not as similar as possible, e.g. in age, sex, or IQ.
>
> **Standardised procedures**: the same procedures are used on every trial of an experiment to ensure that no confounding variables affect the dependent variable.
>
> **Standardised instructions**: the experimenter must give the same instructions to every participant in any one condition.
>
> **Laboratory experiment**: an experiment carried out in very tightly controlled surroundings, often with special equipment available.

Types of experiments

Not all experiments are carried out by people in white coats in laboratories. Some experiments are like this but many are conducted in more natural settings. There are three main types of experiments and they differ in the amount of control over the variables. No single type of experiment is better than another and the choice largely depends on what type of behaviour you are interested in.

The laboratory experiment

A **laboratory experiment** is carried out in very tightly controlled surroundings (but not necessarily a laboratory), often with special equipment available. For some aspects of psychology – for example investigations of the brain, of sleep patterns, of some aspects of perception – it would be difficult, if not impossible, to conduct such studies without the specialised equipment available in the laboratory setting.

A patient asleep in a sleep research laboratory. Electrodes are attached to his head to measure brainwaves, eye, and facial movements. Heart rate and blood hormone levels can also be monitored. What variables could now be investigated?

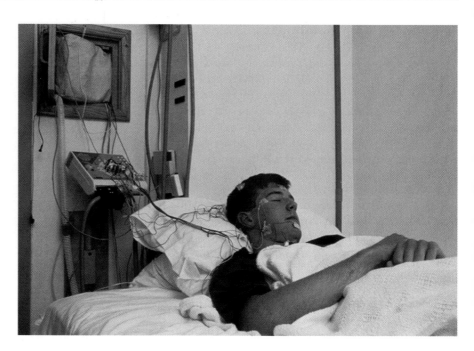

An example of a laboratory study is Sherif's (1935) study on the autokinetic effect (see Chapter 2).

EVALUATION

⊕ These are the only experiments that allow confident conclusions about cause and effect, because of the fact that the confounding variables can be controlled.

⊖ People may well behave very differently in artificial laboratory conditions than they would outside, especially if they feel nervous and intimidated by the situation. The study may therefore lack **ecological validity** because it does not reflect ordinary behaviour.

ACTIVITY 15.3

Design a laboratory experiment to test the idea that people remember things better when they are asked to recall them in circumstances similar to those in which they learned them (this is based on the theory of cue-dependent forgetting in Chapter 10 on memory – you may want to revise that first). The particular circumstances you choose are up to you.

• Think about how you can arrange the IV – there are lots of ways to do this and you can decide which you would like to use.

KEY TERM

Ecological validity: the degree to which the behaviours observed and recorded in a study reflect behaviours that actually occur in natural settings.

- Think about how to measure memory.
- Think about all the situational variables you need to control.
- What would your standardised instructions be?
- What gap would you leave between learning and testing of memory?
- Who would your participants be and how would you obtain them?

The field experiment
Sometimes it is possible to carry out experiments in a more natural setting, that is, "in the field". A famous example of a **field experiment** is the series of studies carried out by Piliavin et al. (1969) in which they arranged for a person (an actor) to collapse on an underground train and waited to see how long it was before the person was helped. One of the independent variables they used was the appearance of the "victim": whether he was carrying a walking stick or appeared to be drunk.

EVALUATION
➕ Behaviour in a field experiment is far more natural than in a laboratory setting, so this has greater ecological validity – it tells us more about ordinary everyday behaviour.

➖ It is not possible to have such tight control over variables in the field, so we cannot be so confident of cause and effect; other factors could influence the DV.

Natural experiments
In some circumstances, psychologists can take advantage of a natural situation in order to carry out an investigation in circumstances that they cannot themselves manipulate. Unlike a laboratory or field experiment, the psychologists do not manipulate the IV, it occurs in real life.

A **natural experiment** is not a true experiment because the psychologist is unable to manipulate or control variables. For this reason this type of study is sometimes referred to as a **quasi-experiment**.

EVALUATION
➕ A natural experiment has very high ecological validity because it is looking at completely natural behaviour. The findings can therefore be generalised to everyday life.

➖ We cannot draw any definite conclusions about cause and effect because there are far too many uncontrolled variables.

KEY TERMS

Field experiment: an experiment where participants are (unknowingly in some cases) observed in natural settings. The researchers can still manipulate variables and observe how people react to these manipulations.

Natural experiment: an experiment where researchers can take advantage of a natural situation in order to carry out an investigation in circumstances that they cannot themselves manipulate.

Quasi-experiment: any experiment in which the researcher is unable to manipulate or control variables, therefore not considered to be a "true" experiment.

OCR AQA # Design of experiments (participant designs)

Independent groups design

Sometimes in experiments researchers use two (or more) groups of people and compare them. In the example used before, one group is subjected to loud music while the other experiences silence. When two (or more) separate groups of people are used, this is known as an **independent groups design**. Sometimes the two groups experience different levels or types of the IV, such as being tested at different times of day or in different rooms. In other experiments, one group experience the IV (such as watching an aggressive model in Bandura's Bobo doll study – see Chapter 4): they are the **experimental group**. The other group does not experience it (some children watched a non-aggressive model): they are the **control group**.

When using an independent groups design it is important that the two groups of participants are not too different to start with, or any difference in their results may be because of this rather than because of the IV. The differences between participants are known as participant variables. There are two ways we can minimise these effects: we can use a large number of people and allocate them randomly to the two groups or we can *match* the groups on important characteristics. When deciding on the characteristics on which to match the groups, you need to consider what might affect the study. For example, if you are interested in the effect of noise on performance, you would need to match the groups on their ability to hear.

Repeated measures design

Sometimes, instead of using separate groups of participants, we are able to test the same group in different conditions. We could, for example, test the same people on how well they remembered something with loud music playing and then test them in silence. This is called a **repeated measures design** and is often more accurate than the independent measures design because we do not have to worry about individual differences between participants. In our example, we would not have to worry about whether one group happened to learn more easily than the other group regardless of the noise level.

However, this design introduces other confounding variables that we must be careful to control; namely **practice effects** and **fatigue** and/or **boredom,** together known as **order effects.** If all the participants did the test under silent conditions followed by noisy ones, they may do better in the second condition because they are familiar with what they need to do, in other words they have had practice. On the other hand, they may do worse the second time because they are tired or bored. The way to control for this is to **counterbalance** the conditions. The group is split randomly in two and one half are in the noisy condition first then the silent one, while the other half do things the other way around.

Matched pairs design

A third possible design when carrying out experiments is to use two different groups but to match the participants on a one-to-one basis, in pairs. They would need to be matched on all important characteristics that could make a difference in the study, such as age, sex, socioeconomic status, and intelligence. This can be difficult. The most common use of the **matched pairs design** is comparing behaviour in pairs of twins, in which case matching is quite straightforward.

EVALUATION OF THE DIFFERENT DESIGNS

Independent groups design

➕ Can be used in cases where a repeated measures design cannot be used because the investigation requires separate groups, such as a comparison of men and women, young people and old people, urban and rural dwellers.

➖ There may be important differences between the groups of individuals to start with and these, rather than the independent variable, may be responsible for differences in results.

Repeated measures design

➕ Controls for individual differences between participants (participant variables).

➖ Introduces problems of order effects.

Matched pairs design

➕ Controls somewhat for individual differences between participants.

➖ Matching individual participants into exact pairs is difficult and requires a large number of participants from which to select pairs.

OCR AQA **Designing studies**

Longitudinal

Longitudinal studies follow the *same* participants over a long period of time. Huesmann et al. (2003) (see Chapter 4 on aggression) is a longitudinal study in which people were investigated at intervals over a 15-year period with respect to their television viewing habits and how aggressive they were.

KEY TERMS

Longitudinal studies: the same participants are studied over a number of years, even a lifetime, in order to study changes over time.

Sample: the participants actually used in a study, drawn from some larger population.

EVALUATION

➕ Longitudinal studies allow researchers to see the long-term effects of upbringing and experiences.

➖ Some participants may drop out or be hard to trace during the course of the study, or be difficult to locate, and this can leave a biased **sample**. Those who drop out are not necessarily typical of the rest of the group.

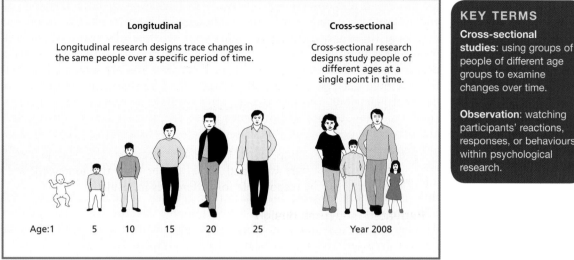

Cross-sectional studies

Cross-sectional studies also look at changes over time, but by comparing people of different ages. Piaget did this frequently when looking at differences in the cognitive ability of children of different ages (see Chapter 9).

EVALUATION

➕ Cross-sectional studies are much quicker and easier than longitudinal studies.

➖ Differences between the groups may not be a result of age but of other factors such as educational background or differences in cultural norms. For example, if comparing 5-year-olds and 12-year-olds on a Piagetian task, some of the differences could be because of changes in educational practice over that time, rather than differences in individuals' cognitive ability. In cases where the age difference between the two groups is very large (say 20 years), any differences may be confounded by the social changes experienced by the two groups. This is known as the cohort effect.

OCR AQA Observations

In a lot of psychological research we simply look at what people (or animals) are doing – we make an **observation**. We then make a record of it and analyse the findings.

Description

It may sound easy simply to watch behaviour and make a note of it (or record it on video) but unless we have a clear idea of precisely what behaviour we are observing, and observe it properly, we will achieve very little. Imagine you and several other people in your psychology class go to observe behaviour in a local supermarket. Once you start your separate observations, you will soon find it impossible to record everything you see, so you need to make a decision as to what particular aspect of behaviour you are interested in. Left to your own devices it is very likely that all of you will choose to observe different behaviour. You may decide, after reading the chapter on non-verbal communication, to look at how much space people leave between themselves and other shoppers and/or if they use their trolleys as a sort of barrier. Is there a difference between men and women in this respect, or between couples and single people? Your friend may have just read the chapter on attachment, and may decide to concentrate only on those people with young children in their trolleys and observe the interaction between carer and child, perhaps following one child–adult couple for 10 minutes then moving on to another. Another friend may look at whether people on their own tend to make quicker decisions about what to buy than do couples. There are lots of types of behaviour to look at.

In order to carry out a good observational study the following things are necessary:

- for all observers involved in the same research operation to have a clear idea of exactly what they are observing;
- to use a system for categorising and recording behaviour (see notes below);
- to use either a recording device (such as a video camera) or more than one observer.

Categories of behaviour in observations

Let us look in a little more detail at the second requirement above, that it is necessary to use a system for categorising behaviour. What the researcher has to do is decide on the categories of behaviour they are interested in. For example, for "aggression" it could be punching, kicking, hitting, verbal abuse and so on. For "attachment" it could be smiling at carer, moving towards carer, being upset when carer moves away, clinging to carer, looking at carer and so on.

ACTIVITY 15.4

Think of categories of behaviour for the following (choose the ones on your own specification):

- Playing
- Showing sex-typed behaviour
- Guarding/defending personal space.

Once the information (data) is collected, it needs to be analysed. Again, this can be a difficult process. For example, if some psychologists were interested in observing aggressive behaviour in a football match, researchers could watch a video of the match and record every aggressive incident. However, there may well be incidents on which the researchers disagree – I'm sure you could think of times when it is difficult to decide if a push or collision between players was actually aggressive. The observers therefore need to be trained in analysing the data. It is then possible to check the extent of agreement between observers. This is known as **inter-observer reliability**. Inter-observer reliability is high if there is a considerable amount of agreement, but low if there is little agreement. Obviously a study that has low inter-observer reliability is a poor one.

ACTIVITY 15.5

Choose two or three other chapters in the book and suggest behaviour that you could observe in a large shopping complex – behaviour that corresponds to the focus of interest in these chapters. Be precise about the exact categories of behaviour that you would look at.

Types of observation

Naturalistic observation

As the name **naturalistic observation** suggests, this involves simply observing behaviour in a natural, everyday situation with observers remaining as inconspicuous as possible so they do not influence the behaviour they are observing.

An example of a naturalistic observation study is Schaffer and Emerson (1964) in Chapter 8 (Attachment).

EVALUATION

➕ This method has high *ecological validity*. This is the extent to which the behaviour being observed reflects behaviour in ordinary real-life situations. These observations therefore tell us a lot about everyday behaviour.

➖ It's not always easy for observers to remain completely inconspicuous and still record the results accurately. This may mean that either behaviour is affected by the observer and therefore is no longer entirely natural, or it is not fully recorded – or both.

Controlled (structured) observation

Controlled (structured) observation is carried out in conditions in which the researcher has some control, such as a laboratory or a specially designed

KEY TERM

Participant observation: an observational research method involving active participation within the study group or organisation by the researcher/observer.

room. For example, sleep researchers study volunteers who are prepared to come into the laboratory and be observed while they sleep. In this case, they would be "wired up" to machines that would make accurate recordings. Not all controlled observations require technical equipment, some simply involve people being observed in an enclosed environment that has been specially chosen because of the type of behaviour the researcher wishes to investigate.

An example of a controlled (structured) observation is Ainsworth's "Strange Situation" study examined in Chapter 8 (Attachment).

EVALUATION

➕ Because the situation is controlled, it is possible to treat all participants in the same way, and thereby make comparisons and generalise outside the group who are being studied. You can also observe people in situations in which you may not find them in everyday life.

➖ This type of observation may lack ecological validity because people are no longer in their natural environment, so their behaviour does not necessarily reflect that found in everyday life.

Participant observation

In **participant observation** the observers take an active part in the group or situation by becoming members of the group they are studying. This allows them to get to know the people concerned and gain a real insight into their behaviour. For example, a researcher might join a group of religious supporters or a football crowd. Sometimes the people being observed know that the observations are being made, but sometimes they are unaware of it.

Try to fit in as a member of the group and remain detached as an observer.

EVALUATION

➕ By becoming part of a group, the observer can gain much greater insight into the behaviour of the participants than if they remain an outsider.

➖ There are ethical problems if people do not know they are being closely observed and records are kept of their attitudes and behaviour. Sometimes this is unavoidable but it is essential that the confidentiality and privacy of individuals are respected by the observer.

➕ Keeping a careful record of the behaviours can cause practical problems. If the observer writes in a notebook all the time, this will affect the behaviour of the people being observed and may even make the observer miss important information. Often, observers keep a diary and try to fill in as much detail as they can as soon after leaving the group as possible.

ACTIVITY 15.6

If you regularly eat in the canteen at school, you could do a participant observation of other students. By becoming one of a group (preferably not doing psychology), you could choose what behaviour to observe and write down as much as you can remember afterwards. There are lots of such opportunities within the school environment.

Now that we have looked at types of observation, we need to be able to distinguish between certain types of observation.

Participant versus non-participant observation

Participant observation (as discussed above) is any observation study in which the observer takes part. **Non-participant observation** is any observation in which the observer remains separate from the people being observed. Naturalistic observations and most structured observations are non-participant observations.

Covert versus overt observations

Covert observations are those in which the observer remains hidden or at least blends in with the scenery, so does not affect the behaviour of those being observed. **Overt observations** are those in which the observers make themselves known to the people being observed (as would be the case for most participant observations).

OCR AQA Case studies

Description

A **case study** is a detailed investigation of a single individual or a small group of individuals. Case studies are useful when a psychologist doesn't want to look at a large representative group of people but at one single individual or small group, usually because they have had unusual experiences, such as severe deprivation. Other examples of where a case study might be of interest are researching the effect of a

---

KEY TERMS

Non-participant observation: any observation in which the observer remains separate from the people being observed.

Covert observations: observations in which the observer remains hidden or at least blends in with the scenery so does not affect the behaviour of those being observed.

Overt observations: observations in which the observers make themselves known to the people being observed (as would be the case for most participant observations).

Case studies: detailed investigation of a single individual or a small group of individuals.

stroke on later personality and behaviour, investigating the effect of a rare genetic disability on later development, or teaching a chimpanzee to use sign language.

EVALUATION

➕ Case studies are useful for investigating the effects of unusual experiences such as deprivation, hospitalisation, or unusual educational experiences. Obviously these conditions could not be artificially arranged but they are of considerable interest to psychologists.

➖ Case studies only relate to one individual or small group and we cannot therefore generalise to others from the result. We have no way of assessing how typical the individual is.

➖ There is a danger that the psychologist who looks at a case study may not be entirely unbiased in their observations. If they believe in a certain theory, for example that lack of attachment leads to delinquency, then they may only look at certain aspects of a person's childhood, in this case how long they were separated from their main carer. However, there may be other circumstances that were also involved.

OCR AQA Surveys

A **survey** is a means of collecting standardised information from a specific population (group of people).

Description
The information gained in a survey is usually obtained by means of a questionnaire, which may be in written form or read to the participant by the person conducting the survey. Generally, a relatively small amount of information is collected from a lot of people. Many of you have probably taken part in a survey, done by a market researcher rather than a psychologist, for the purposes of gaining information that companies can use to maximise their sales.

In a survey, research information is collected from a sample of people who the researcher chooses in such a way that they are a **representative sample** of the larger population.

EVALUATION

➕ Surveys can allow researchers to study large samples of people fairly easily and, provided the samples of people who are used in the survey are representative and are large enough, it is possible to generalise the results to a larger population.

- It may be difficult to obtain a representative sample of the population. Often the questionnaires that are used are only distributed in certain places (such as in a doctor's surgery or in a magazine or by someone in the street) and only certain people will complete them and send them in. These people may be those who feel strongly and/or have the time to spare, and are unlikely to be typical of the population as a whole.

- People may not respond truthfully, either because they cannot remember or because they wish to present themselves in a socially acceptable manner. This may apply when asking people about childhood memories or when doing attitude surveys on prejudice.

OCR AQA Questionnaires

Description

Questionnaires are used in surveys and are particularly useful when trying to investigate people's attitudes. The questionnaire may contain one of two types of questions:

- *Closed questions*: These are ones with fixed alternative responses, such as agree/disagree; yes/no. For example, "Do you have any recollection of your first day at school?" Yes/no.
- *Open questions*: These are ones that give respondents the chance to express themselves more freely. For example, "Describe everything you can remember about your first day at school."

Later in this chapter there is a section on quantitative and qualitative data. Notice that closed questions provide quantitative data (numbers), while open questions provide qualitative data (words/descriptions).

Of course, questionnaires may use a combination of closed and open questions.

An example of the use of questionnaires is Adorno et al.'s study in Chapter 3 (Stereotyping, prejudice and discrimination). They asked people their opinions about, among other things, Jewish people.

ACTIVITY 15.7

Pretend you are a market researcher. You can be working for any kind of company you choose, for example, a group of DVD rental shops. You have been given the task of compiling a questionnaire to find out which are the most popular films, how often people rent DVDs, what determines whether they rent or buy, etc. Compile a questionnaire consisting of some fixed-alternative (closed) questions and some open-ended ones. Distribute to friends, family, or to another class and analyse the results by means of a table and graphs for the closed questions, and a brief description for the open questions.

This questionnaire consists of closed questions; you can only answer "yes" or "no"

Some useful hints when constructing a questionnaire:

• Decide on closed or open questions. Open questions do not allow comparisons between people or statistical analysis. You would not, for example, be able to say that 30% of people believe it is wrong to smack children. However, open questions do give more information.
• Avoid leading questions. A question like "Do you agree that students' grants should be increased?" tends to imply that the person should agree with it.
• Don't ask too many questions.
• Make sure questions are straightforward and can be answered. For example, a question like "How many times have you been to the doctor in the last year?" is very difficult to answer.
• Don't invade people's privacy. Do not ask questions that can cause embarrassment or annoyance.

EVALUATION

Closed questions

⊕ Closed questions are quick to answer and score, and provide information that is useful in making comparisons – e.g. that 54% of people remember their first day at school.

⊖ They provide a very limited amount of information and leave no room for responses such as "it depends on…", which may be valid especially when asking for opinions.

Open questions

⊕ Open questions provide a source of rich and detailed information.

⊖ They take a lot longer to score and, since all responses are different, it is much more difficult to make comparisons between individuals.

OCR AQA **Interviews**

There are many different ways to conduct interviews, ranging from casual chats to formal, standardised, set questions that have to be asked in a particular way. We will consider two different types.

Structured interviews

A **structured interview** involves a list of questions that require the interviewee to choose from a selection of possible answers. In many respects such an interview technique is simply a verbal questionnaire that has closed questions.

KEY TERM

Structured interview: a list of questions requiring the interviewee to choose from a selection of possible answers.

EVALUATION

⊕ It is easy to make comparisons between people because they all answer exactly the same questions. You can gain information such as what percentage of people feel they experience some form of stress in the workplace.

⊖ You can only gain a limited amount of information, none of which is in-depth.

Unstructured interviews

An **unstructured interview** is a lengthier interview aimed at a detailed understanding of a person's mental processes. Often one question is asked at the start in order to focus the main theme of the interview, and the following questions will depend on what answer the interviewee just gave. There are no set questions; the questions depend on the last answer given.

EVALUATION

⊕ Unstructured interviews provide rich insight into the thoughts of individual children or adults, which a standardised format would not allow.

⊖ It is impossible to interview everyone in the same way. One person may talk about something so differently from the way another person does that it becomes almost impossible to compare what two people said.

OCR AQA Correlations

Description

A correlational study involves taking lots of *pairs* of scores and seeing if there is a positive or negative relationship (a **correlation**) between them. Some examples could be to see if there is a relationship between:

- aggression and the amount of violent television watched;
- the amount of stress people experience and illness;
- the IQs of family members.

   If we use the examples above:

- To see if aggression is related to the amount of violent television watched, you would take two measures from each individual person – level of aggression and number of hours of violent TV watched.
- To see if stress is related to illness, again you would take two scores from each person – amount of stress as measured on a stress scale (such as a scale called

> **KEY TERMS**
>
> **Unstructured interview:** an interview beginning with a single question, from which further questions depend on the interviewee's answer.
>
> **Correlation:** a statistical indicator representing the strength of a relationship between two variables. Correlations do not show cause and effect, only that a relationship exists.

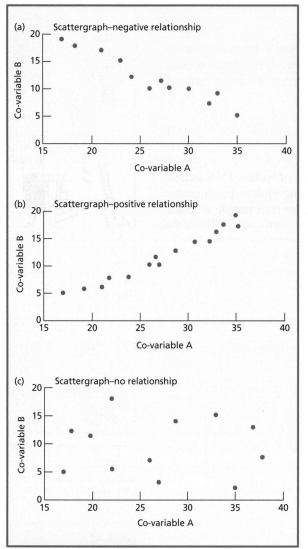

(a) Scattergraph–negative relationship

Co-variable B / Co-variable A

(b) Scattergraph–positive relationship

Co-variable B / Co-variable A

(c) Scattergraph–no relationship

Co-variable B / Co-variable A

the Holmes–Rahe scale which gives a score that reflects how many stressful events a person has encountered in the last 2 years) and the number of days a person has been ill in the past year.

A **positive correlation** means that high values of one variable are associated with high values of the other. For example, there will be a positive correlation between stress and illness if people who score high on the Holmes–Rahe stress scale also take a lot of time off sick. Other examples of variables between which we would expect a positive correlation are between height and weight, and between mathematical ability and scores in physics tests. In each of these cases, as one variable increases, so does the other.

A **negative correlation** means that high values of one variable are associated with low values of the other. We may expect to find a negative correlation between age and speed of running (in adults), between outside temperature and weight of clothes, between work productivity and stress.

If there is *no* correlation between two variables they are said to be **uncorrelated**. There is no relationship, for example, between exam grades and height!

Correlations can be represented in the form of a graph called a scattergraph (or scattergram) with a dot for each participant indicating where he or she falls on the two dimensions. If there is a positive relationship, the pattern of the dots is like graph (b) on the left; if there is a negative one, the pattern corresponds to graph (a) and if there is no relationship, the dots are distributed randomly as in graph (c).

Some correlations are strong, others are weak. For example, students who spend many hours a week reading novels tend to score highly on vocabulary tests; this is a strong positive correlation. Students who spend many hours a week reading novels tend to perform slightly better than average on science tests; this is a weak positive correlation.

KEY TERMS

Positive correlation: a relationship in which as one variable increases, so does the other one.

Negative correlation: a relationship in which as one variable decreases the other one increases.

Uncorrelated: there is no relationship between two variables, e.g. exam grades and height.

ACTIVITY 15.8

Draw a scattergraph to see if there is a correlation between height and shoe size. To do this you need the height and shoe size of a group of people, such as members of your class, then you can plot them and see if the pattern of dots indicates a positive correlation.

EVALUATION

➕ Correlations are very useful for making predictions. If two variables are correlated, you can predict one from the other. If someone is good at maths they may well be good at physics. If someone is highly stressed, they may fall ill.

➖ Correlations only show that a relationship exists between two variables, they do NOT show that one *causes* the other. In Chapter 4, we discussed the fact that even though there is a positive correlation between aggression and amount of violent TV watched, it does not necessarily follow that watching violent programmes causes people to be aggressive. It is possible that people who are already aggressive choose violent programmes to watch. Similarly, even if there is a positive relationship between stress and illness, it does not necessarily mean that stress causes illness. It is possible that being ill causes stress or that poor living conditions cause both stress and illness.

A positive correlation: The taller the player, the higher the score.

OCR AQA Writing an aim and a hypothesis

When researchers carry out a study they start with an aim and then follow this with a more precise statement of what they expect to find.

Aim

The *aim* of a study is usually one sentence that clearly highlights what the researcher is intending to investigate. You have already read many studies in this book that start with the aim. Some examples are:

A negative correlation: The more time spent playing computer games, the less time spent studying.

* To investigate whether young children will imitate an aggressive model.
* To test out the depth-perceptual abilities in two-dimensional pictures in a varied group of people living in the southern regions of Africa.
* To investigate prejudiced attitudes, particularly anti-Semitism (prejudice against Jews).
* To study the attachment behaviour of a group of infants from their early life (this varied from 5 weeks old to 23 weeks) until they were 18 months old.
* To see whether there would be a difference in the recall of words that were structurally, phonemically or semantically processed.

No correlation: Where there is no relationship, variables are uncorrelated.

Hypothesis

A *hypothesis* is a prediction. It is a sentence that states what the researcher predicts the findings could be. The investigator starts with two different hypotheses:

* an alternative hypothesis
* a null hypothesis.

An *alternative hypothesis* states that there will be a difference between two sets of scores, or a correlation between them (depending on the type of study that was done). It is a clear specific statement such as:

- Children who have watched an aggressive model will show a greater number of aggressive acts than children who have watched a non-aggressive model.
- There will be a relationship between reaction time and amount of alcohol drunk.
- There will be more words recalled from questions that ask about meaning compared to questions that ask about structure.

Important point on writing hypotheses

Note that when writing a hypothesis, do this in terms of what is being measured, so that it is very precise. Do not, for example, say that 'children are more likely to be aggressive when watching an aggressive model compared to watching a non-aggressive model' because you have not said how the aggression is measured.

A *null hypothesis* states that there will be no difference or relationship between two set of scores. Examples of null hypotheses are:

- There will be no difference in the amount of aggression shown between children who have watched an aggressive model and children who have watched a non-aggressive model.
- There will be no relationship between attachment type and type of adult relationship.
- There will be no difference in the number of words remembered when they are processed semantically compared with when they are processed acoustically or physically.

You will notice that the alternative and the null hypothesis cannot both be true. The purpose of an investigation is to decide which one is more likely to be true and therefore to choose between them.

OCR AQA Sampling

People undertaking research cannot possibly investigate all the participants in whom they may be interested, so they have to choose a *sample* of them to investigate. The whole population in whom they are interested is called the **target population** and their aim is to choose a *representative sample* from this target population. A representative sample is a smaller group that shares the characteristics of the target population. However, it is by no means easy to select a representative sample, and often practical considerations such as time and who is available mean that inevitably some samples will be biased. The most common sampling methods are as follows.

KEY TERM

Target population: the whole group to which a researcher wishes to generalise the findings.

Random sampling

Random sampling

A **random sample** is a sample in which every member of the target population has an equal chance of being selected. This means that it's necessary to have a list of the whole target population in order to obtain your sample. You can then give each one a number and use a computer program to generate a list of random numbers and you choose the first ones generated until you have sufficient. Alternatively you can use the old fashioned method of putting all the names in a hat and drawing out the number you require.

In reality, random samples are rare in psychology because it is difficult to have a complete list of the target population. Even if you have, there is no guarantee that all of the people you have selected will be available or willing to take part in your study.

Systematic sampling

A **systematic sample** consists of selecting participants at fixed intervals from a list, for example, every 10th or 30th person. If you had a list of all the students in a school by class registers, you could choose every 10th person from the total list. This ensures that you have a certain number from each age group, for example, and thus a reasonable chance of producing a representative sample.

Opportunity sampling

An **opportunity sample** is one that uses anyone who is available and willing to take part. If you

> ### KEY TERMS
>
> **Random sample**: consists of participants selected on some random basis (e.g. numbers out of a hat). Every member of the population has an equal chance of being selected.
>
> **Systematic sample**: consists of participants chosen by a modified version of random sampling in which the participants are selected in a quasi-random way (e.g. every 100th name from a population list).
>
> **Opportunity sample**: consists of participants selected because they are available, not because they are representative of a population.

Opportunity sampling

were to ask your family and friends to be the participants in your coursework, or you asked a teacher if you could conduct a study in their lesson using the available students as participants, then this would be an opportunity sample. It is an easy and practical method to use (and one that many students use when doing coursework) but it is likely to be biased. The sample really depends on who is available at the time, probably from one place, and is unlikely to be truly representative.

OCR AQA Ethics

Doing research in psychology poses a number of ethical problems. For example, there are occasions when, if you told participants what aspect of their behaviour you were interested in, they would behave so differently from normal that there would be no point in conducting the research. An example of this would be Asch's study on conformity (see Chapter 2). So we may have to accept that some deception is required (as long as it's not too harmful), but where do we draw the line? In order to try to make research as ethical as possible, psychologists have to follow a set of **ethical guidelines** when they conduct research. In Britain these guidelines are produced by the British Psychological Society (BPS) and there are equivalent guidelines in other countries. We will have a look at a small number of the most important guidelines:

- *Deception*: Participants should not be deceived unless it is absolutely necessary. Even then, the deception should not in any way be likely to cause the participants to feel uncomfortable or angry, or to raise objections once they are told the real purpose of the study.
- *Consent*: Wherever possible the informed consent of the participant should be obtained. However, as already discussed, it is not always possible to give all the details of the study to participants before they begin.
- *Confidentiality*: Unless it is agreed with participants beforehand, their individual results and any personal information obtained in a study should be completely confidential.
- *Debriefing*: Participants should, where possible, be debriefed. This involves informing the participant of the true nature and purpose of the study at the end, and is especially important if the real purpose of the study has been hidden from them. Of course, in some research such as naturalistic observations or some field studies, participants aren't available to be debriefed.
- *Withdrawal from the investigation*: It should be made clear to participants that they are free to withdraw from the investigation at any time, regardless of whether they have been paid.
- *Protection of participants*: Participants should not be placed under any great stress, nor should they be harmed, either physically or mentally.
- *The use of children*: Obviously development psychologists need to use children in their investigations but they need to be especially careful when they do. Young children cannot give consent, they may be easily upset, and

they may not be able to say that they do not want to do what the psychologist asks them to. When using children in their research psychologists must ensure that they:

- gain the consent of the parent or guardian;
- do not cause the children any upset or embarrassment;
- stop the study if the child shows any reluctance to carry on.

There are no easy answers to ethical issues. It is often a matter of weighing up the "costs" (in terms of factors such as deception) against the benefits gained. For example, in Hofling et al.'s study of the nurses (see Chapter 2), the nurses were deceived and did not consent to being part of a psychological investigation, but it could be argued that the information gained was vitally important.

ACTIVITY 15.9

Consider ethical issues that arose in the following studies. Consider both the negative aspects (e.g. participants were deceived) and the positives (e.g. they were fully debriefed):

- Milgram (1963) (electric shocks) Chapter 2
- Hofling et al. (1966) (nurses) Chapter 2
- Middlemist et al. (1976) (invasion of personal space in toilets) Chapter 5
- Fisher and Byrne (1975) (invasion of personal space in library) Chapter 5
- Ainsworth (Strange Situation) Chapter 8
- Bandura (1961) (Bobo doll) Chapter 4

OCR AQA **Analysing research**

Once studies have been collected, psychologists need to analyse their results, that is, their data. They need to decide the best way of presenting the data in terms of tables and graphs. We will start by looking at the two main types of data that will be gathered.

Types of data

- *Quantitative data*: This term refers to data that take the form of numbers. For example, rating how aggressive a character is in a film or measuring how quickly someone can solve a logical puzzle would generate *numbers*.
- *Qualitative data*: This term refers to data that take the form of words (or any data that are not in the form of numbers). For example, a response to a question like "why do you study GCSE psychology?" would generate *words* as the answers.

EXAM HINT

An easy way to remember the difference between quantitative and qualitative data is that quaNtitative data involve Numbers.

Quantitative data are very useful if we want to make comparisons between groups (e.g. the mean amount remembered by two groups working under different conditions). Qualitative data are useful if we want in-depth detailed information, such as in a case study or concerning people's attitudes.

Descriptive data

To describe data you have collected to a person wanting to know more about your study, you can use analyses like the mode, the median and the mean, or draw tables and graphs of the results.

Measures of central tendency

Mode

The mode is the most common response in a data set. For example, you ask 20 people what their favourite type of chocolate is and you get the following responses:

- Milk – 12
- Dark – 4
- White – 1
- Nutty – 3

The mode is milk chocolate. You would report your findings by stating:

"The modal favourite chocolate in this sample of 20 people was milk with 12 responses."

Median

The median is the middle number in a data set after you have placed the results in rank order. Below is a step-by-step guide to show how to calculate the median:

1. Rank all of your data from the smallest number to the largest number.
2. Eliminate one score from the lowest end of the ranked data and one score from the highest end of the ranked data (called a pair of scores).
3. Continue to eliminate pairs of scores until either one or two numbers are left. If you have an *odd number* of scores in your data set then you should be left with just one number – this is the median. If you have an *even number* of scores in your data set then you should be left with two numbers. In this case, you must complete the following step.
4. Add up the two remaining numbers and divide the total by 2. This is the median.

Example: The following data have been generated by asking a sample of boys and girls how much they like *High School Musical* on a scale of 0–10 (0 = rubbish; 5 = OK; 10 = love it!).

0   2   2   3   4   5   8   8   10   10 10

Using the step-by-step guide above, the median is 5. You would report your findings by stating:

"The median rating for High School Musical in this sample of 11 people was 5. This means that, on average, this sample of people thought the film was ok."

Most research compares *at least* two groups of participants. This is when you can use a median to conclude what your study has found. Therefore, if the *High School Musical* question was asked to a sample of girls and boys you could calculate the median for both groups. Say for example the medians were girls = 8; boys = 2. You would report the findings by stating:

"The medians clearly show that girls like High School Musical more than boys do. The median rating for girls was 8 (indicating they like it a lot) compared to boys which was 2 (do not like it much)."

Mean

To calculate the mean you must complete the following steps:

1. Add up all of the scores you have collected in your study.
2. Divide this total by the *number of scores* that we have just added up.

Example: The following data have been generated by getting participants to solve the same puzzle in the game "Professor Layton and the Curious Village". The speed with which they solved it was measured in seconds.

| 25 | 40 | 40 | 65 | 90 |

So, firstly we add up all of the numbers: 25 + 40 + 40 + 65 + 90 = 260. Next, we divide the total score by the number of scores, which is 5: 260/5 = 52 seconds. You would report the findings by stating:

"The mean time taken to solve a puzzle in the 'Professor Layton and the Curious Village' game is 52 seconds."

As with the medians, you can calculate means for your two groups of participants so you can compare them. For example, the mean times for the above task were split by gender. Girls had an average of 55 seconds while boys had an average of 42 seconds. You would report the findings by stating:

"The mean times clearly show that boys are faster at solving a puzzle from the 'Professor Layton and the Curious Village' game (42 s) than girls (55 s)."

Dealing with anomalous results

There are occasions when you may get one or two very unusual results that may distort your data when they are summarised. For example, if you measured the time taken for the girls to do the Curious Village game (see example above) and the results were 49, 50, 53, 55, 55, 56, 58, 60, 127, then the last score is *anomalous* and we need to be careful how we analyse the data. The median will not be affected by this score and will give a fair representation of the results; the same applies to the mode. However, the mean will be considerably distorted by it and will not be a fair representation of the results. Therefore when you have one anomalous result, it is better not to use the mean as a measure of central tendency but to use the median (and the mode if appropriate).

EXAM HINT

Be prepared to be able to work out a median or mode from a list of numbers. With regard to the median, you may need to show your working. Simply list the numbers in order from lowest to highest and circle the middle one, or draw an arrow between the two middle ones if there is an even number of scores.

Measures of dispersion

It is also useful to know the spread of the scores. The easiest way to do this is to use the *range*. The range is the difference between the highest and lowest scores. So, in the set of scores 4, 5, 5, 7, 7, 8, 9, 12, the range is 8 (12 – 4).

The range is quick and easy to calculate but is distorted by an anomalous score.

Tables, charts and graphs

- *Tables*: Tables should be used to *summarise* data so that whoever is reading it can make sense of the numbers. Therefore, you may wish to present a table that shows the median scores of two groups of participants alongside the range. From this it is easier to draw conclusions about your data.
- *Bar charts*: Bar charts should be used to *summarise* data that are already in separate groups (e.g. males/females). Therefore, when groups are separated out, you use a bar chart to display the information.
- *Line graphs*: Line graphs are used when you are plotting data that are *continuous* along the bottom axis and you want to show a trend. Therefore, you may use a line graph to show changes in the number of criminal acts over time. Another example is shown on the line graph below.

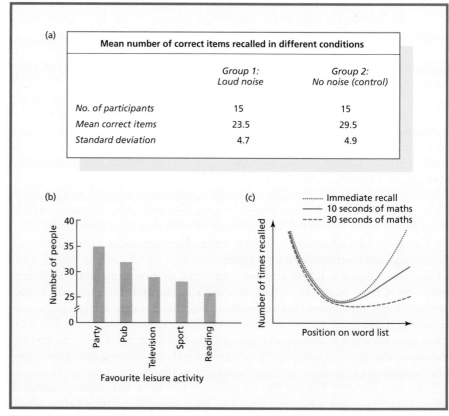

Examples of (a) a table, (b) a bar chart, and (c) a line graph

Evaluating findings

Validity

To evaluate the findings of a study you can write about validity. Validity means accuracy, so you must evaluate just how accurate the findings are. One type of validity is *ecological validity*. This term refers to the extent to which the findings reflect the real-life or real-world behaviour of the participants. You can evaluate a study in two different ways when writing about ecological validity:

1. *The setting of the study*: You can evaluate the ecological validity of a study by looking at the setting it took place in. If the study was in a laboratory, then you could argue it has *low levels* as the setting is controlled and artificial and is not the same as the real world. However, with a naturalistic observation then you could argue it has *high levels* of ecological validity as the participants are being watched in their natural environment.
2. *The task given to participants*: You can evaluate the ecological validity of a study by looking at the task given to the participants. Ask yourself how similar the task is to a task that they would do in real life. So, for example, asking participants to read a list of words, distracting them for a period of time and then asking them to recall the words could have *low levels* of ecological validity as the task is artificial.

Reliability

To evaluate the findings of a study you can write about reliability. Reliability means consistency, so you must evaluate how easy it is to replicate (repeat) the study to see if you *could* get similar results. With respect to an observation study, it is important to know how reliable the observers were (called *inter-rater* or *inter-observer reliability*).

If the study is in a laboratory, then you could argue it is reliable. This is because the high level of controls makes it *easier* to replicate the study. But what about inter-rater reliability?

With inter-observer reliability you must assess how consistent the observers are being. This can be done in a basic way as highlighted in the example that follows.

There are two observers watching some chimpanzees in a zoo. They are tallying up how many times the chimpanzees perform certain behaviours. There are a range of behaviours that are being observed and the researcher wants to see if the observers are being reliable while recording *play* behaviour. After 10 minutes of observation the following results are noted. Observer A recorded 12 instances of play behaviour. Observer B recorded 10.

A very basic way in which we can assess their reliability is to divide the smaller number by the larger number and multiply by 100 to get a percentage reliability score. Therefore for this example it would be:

(10/12) × 100 = 83.3% – the observers were being 83% reliable, which is quite a high score.

AQA Exam-style questions for AQA

Unit 1 question

1. A psychologist conducted a study into the effect of noise on memory. This is what she did:
   - She asked 20 of her students to take part in the study.
   - She split them into two groups by asking them to take a folded piece of paper marked either A or B from a hat. All the As were in one group, all the Bs in another.
   - Group A were asked to watch while 20 words were flashed one at a time onto a screen, then asked to write down how many words they could remember. While they were doing this there was loud music playing in the background.
   - The same procedure was used for group B, except that there was no music playing at all.
   - The psychologist counted how many words each group remembered.

   (a) Identify the independent variable in this experiment. (1 mark)

   (b) Identify the dependent variable in this experiment. (1 mark)

   (c) Identify the experimental design (the participant design) in this experiment. (1 mark)

   (d) Identify the sampling technique used in this experiment. (1 mark)

   (e) Outline **one** disadvantage of the sampling technique mentioned in (d). (2 marks)

   The results of the experiment are shown in the table below.

Table to show the number of words remembered			
Participant	**Group A** **Loud music**	**Participant**	**Group B** **Silence**
1	9	11	12
2	9	12	13
3	11	13	13
4	12	14	12
5	8	12	10
6	18	16	11
7	9	17	9
8	10	18	13
9	11	19	12
10	10	20	10
Total	**103**		**115**

(f) Identify **one** anomalous result in Condition A and state what effect this has on the mean score of the participants. (2 marks)

(g) What is the mode of the scores in Condition A? (1 mark)

(h) Calculate the mean of the scores in Condition B (1 mark)

(i) What is the range of scores in Condition B? (1 mark)

(j) Outline **one** ethical issue the psychologist should have considered before conducting her experiment. (2 marks)

(k) Outline **one** way the psychologist could have dealt with the ethical issue you have identified in your answer to (j). (2 marks)

(l) This study was an experiment. Explain **one** advantage of using this method in psychological research. (2 marks)

(m) Explain **one** disadvantage of using the experimental method in psychological research. (3 marks)

OCR Exam-style questions for OCR

1. (a) In a study, a psychologist used a self-selected sample. Explain what is meant by a self-selected sample. (2 marks)

(b) Name **one** other sampling technique that psychologists can use. (1 mark)

(c) Give **one** disadvantage of the sampling method you have named in (b). (2 marks)

2. (a) Explain what is meant by a laboratory experiment. (2 marks)

(b) Outline **one** advantage of a laboratory experiment. (2 marks)

3. Explain what is meant by gender bias in research. (2 marks)

4. You have been asked to carry out an *observation* to investigate whether 5-year-old boys play differently from 5-year-old girls. The theory is that they play with different types of toys, play different types of games, and interact differently in play.

(a) State a *hypothesis* for this investigation. (2 marks)

(b) Outline where you would draw the sample from for this investigation, and why. (2 marks)

(c) Describe **one** ethical issue you would have to deal with when observing 5-year-olds. (2 marks)

(d) Describe one control you would use in this observation. (3 marks)

(e) Briefly outline how you would carry out the observation to investigate whether 5-year-old boys play differently from 5-year-old girls. (3 marks)

(f) Describe **one** weakness of using an *observation* in this investigation. (3 marks) [OCR, 2008, Specimen Paper 3]

Research methods are central to the study of psychology, so they appear on both AQA and OCR specifications. Although there is a lot of overlap, we will list these separately so you can see exactly what you need to know.

What you need to know AQA

The specification lists the following things that you will need to be able to do for the examination:

Methods of investigation

- The use of scientific methods and techniques that aim for objectivity
- Procedures for each method of investigation:
  - survey methods
  - questionnaires (including closed and open questions)
  - interviews (including structured and unstructured)
  - observation (including categories of behaviour, and inter-observer reliability)
  - case study
- Advantages and disadvantages of each method of investigation (including ecological validity)

Ethical considerations

- Ethical issues in psychological research as outlined in the British Psychological Society guidelines
- Ways of dealing with each of these issues

Methods of control, data analysis and data presentation

- Target populations, samples and sampling methods:
  - random
  - opportunity
  - systematic
  - stratified
- Correlation, including an understanding of association between two variables, and of correlation relationship (without computation of formulae). Advantages and limitations of using correlations
- Calculations, including mean, mode, median, range and percentages
- Anomalous results and their possible effects
- Graphical representations, including bar charts and scatter graphs

What you need to know OCR

The specification lists the following things that you will need to be able to do for the examination:

Planning research

- **Hypotheses**
  - Frame a null hypothesis
  - Frame an alternative hypothesis
  - Distinguish between a null hypothesis and an alternative hypothesis
- **Variables**
  - Distinguish between independent and dependent variables
  - Outline what is meant by an extraneous variable
  - Explain how extraneous variables can be controlled, including standardisation
- **Experimental design**
  - Distinguish between repeated measures and independent groups design
  - Describe the strengths and weaknesses of a repeated measures design
  - Describe the strengths and weaknesses of an independent groups design
- **Sampling techniques**
  - Distinguish between a target population and a sample
  - Distinguish between random sampling and opportunity sampling
  - Describe the relative strengths and weaknesses of random and opportunity sampling, with reference to representative samples and biased samples
- **Ethical considerations**
  - Discuss the issues of informed consent and the right to withdraw
  - Discuss the issue of confidentiality
  - Discuss the issues of protection of participants, including deception, and health and well-being

Doing research

- **Experiments**
  - Describe the use of laboratory experiments
  - Describe the use of field experiments
  - Describe the strengths and weaknesses of laboratory and field experiments
- **Questionnaires**
  - Describe the use of questionnaires as a method of self-report

- Distinguish between open and closed questions
- Describe the strengths and weaknesses of questionnaires

- **Interviews**
  - Describe the use of interviews as a method of self-report
  - Distinguish between structured and unstructured interviews
  - Describe the strengths and weaknesses of interviews

- **Observations**
  - Describe the use of observations
  - Identify the differences between covert and overt observations, and between participant and non-participant observations
  - Describe the strengths and weaknesses of the different types of observations

- **Types of studies**
  - Describe the use of case studies
  - Describe the use of correlation studies
  - Compare the use of longitudinal studies and cross-sectional studies

Analysing research

- **Types of data**
  - Explain what is meant by quantitative data
  - Explain what is meant by qualitative data
  - Describe data collected from investigations

- **Descriptive data**
  - Use and interpret modes
  - Use and interpret medians
  - Use and interpret means

- **Tables, charts and graphs**
  - Use and interpret tables of data
  - Use and interpret bar charts
  - Use and interpret line graphs

- **Evaluating findings**
  - Explain the concept of validity, including ecological validity
  - Explain the concept of reliability, including inter-rater reliability
  - Outline the problems of demand characteristics, observer effect and social desirability

- ◼ **Sources of bias**
  - ◼ Explain the concept of gender bias
  - ◼ Explain the concept of cultural bias
  - ◼ Explain the concept of experimenter bias

Candidates should have experience of using the following methods: experiment, questionnaire, interview and observation. They will be asked to plan an investigation (based on one of the above methods) in the examination.

Planning an investigation

- ◼ **Investigation skills**
  - ◼ Carry out an experiment
  - ◼ Carry out a questionnaire
  - ◼ Carry out an interview
  - ◼ Carry out an observation
- ◼ **Design skills**
  - ◼ State the hypothesis for an investigation
  - ◼ Describe and justify the sample used in an investigation
  - ◼ Describe ethical issues involved in an investigation
  - ◼ Describe and justify how the variables are measured in an investigation
  - ◼ Describe and justify the control of extraneous variables in an investigation
  - ◼ Describe the procedure used in an investigation
  - ◼ Explain the strengths of the method used in an investigation
  - ◼ Explain the weaknesses of the method used in an investigation
  - ◼ Describe how data are analysed in an investigation

Index

Note: References in **bold** are to key terms; those in *italic* are to chapter and section summaries.

Illustration credits

Chapter 1

Page 7 (bottom left): © Bill Varie/Corbis. Page 7 (bottom right): © Cocorophotos/Corbis.

Chapter 2

Page 17: Milgram advert from *Obedience to Authority*. Copyright © 1974 Pinter & Martin: New York. Reproduced with permission. Page 18 (top): From the film *Obedience* © 1968 by Stanley Milgram. Copyright © renewed 1991 by Alexandra Milgram and distributed by Penn State Media Sales. Permission granted by Alexandra Milgram. Page 19: Milgram script from *Obedience to Authority*. Copyright © 1974 Pinter & Martin: New York. Reproduced with permission. Page 23: From the film *Obedience* © 1968 by Stanley Milgram. Copyright © renewed 1991 by Alexandra Milgram and distributed by Penn State Media Sales. Page 38: Reproduced with permission of P.G. Zimbardo Inc. Page 43 (top): From I.M. Piliavin, J. Rodin & J.A. Piliavin (1969). Good samaritanism: an underground phenomenon? *Journal of Personality and Social Psychology*, *13*, 289–9. © 1969 The American Psychological Association. Reproduced with permission.

Chapter 3

Page 58 and page 70: Courtesy of Penn State University Department of Psychology. Page 66: © Corbis. Page 75: © Erin Patrice O'Brien/Corbis.

Chapter 4

Page 84: From Damasio H, Grabowski TJ, Frank RJ, Galaburda AM, Damasio AR, The Return of Phineas Gage: Clues About the Brain from the Skull of a Famous Patient, *Science*, *264*, 1102–1105 (20th May 1994). Copyright © AAAS. Reproduced with permission. Page 87: © Image Source/Corbis. Page 89: Reproduced by kind permission of Professor Albert Bandura. Page 94: © Royalty-Free/Corbis.

Chapter 5

Page 105: Copyright © Paul Ekman. Reproduced with permission.

Chapter 6

Page 140 (left): © Senthil Kumar/Corbis. Page 140 (right): © Gary Salter/zefa/Corbis.

Chapter 7
Page 153: From Lombroso, C. (1876) L'Uomo Delinquente. Milan: Horpli.

Chapter 8
Page 165: © Elyse Lewin/Brand X/Corbis. Page 170 (left): © Design Pics/Corbis. Page 170 (right): © Tom Grill/Corbis. Page 171: Copyright © Science Photo Library. Page 174: © Image Source/Corbis. Page 176: Reproduced with kind permission of Harlow Primate Laboratory, University of Wisconsin. Page 178: © Bernard Bisson/Corbis/Sygma.

Chapter 9
Page 191 (top): © Farrell Grehan/Corbis. Page 191 (bottom): © Brooke Fasani/Corbis. Page 192: Doug Goodman/Science Photo Library. Page 193: © Laura Dwight/Corbis. Page 195: © Laura Dwight/Corbis.

Chapter 10
Page 226 and 227: From Terry, W.S. (2005) Serial Position Effects in Recall of Television Commericals. *The Journal of General Psychology*, 132(2), p.151–163. Reprinted with permission of the Helen Dwight Reid Educational Foundation. Published by Heldref Publications, 1319 Eighteenth St., NW, Washington, DC 20036-1802. Copyright © 2005.

Chapter 11
Page 239 (top): © Mandy Collison. Page 241 (bottom): © Momatiuk - Eastcott/Corbis. Page 242 (bottom): © Frans Lemmens/zefa/Corbis. Page 244: From W. Hudson (1960). Pictorial depth perception in sub-cultural groups in Africa. *Journal of Social Psychology*, 52, 183–208. Reprinted with permission of the Helen Dwight Reid Educational Foundation. Published by Heldref Publications, 1319 Eighteenth St., NW, Washington, DC 20036-1802. Copyright © 1960. Page 248: From R.L. Fantz (1961). The origin of form perception. *Scientific American*, 204, 66–72.

Chapter 13
Page 285: Orion pictures/photofest © Orion pictures.

Chapter 15
Page 308: Hank Morgan/Science Photo Library. Page 320: © Paul Hardy/Corbis.

Going on to study AS-Level Psychology?

If you are following the AQA–A specification, this is the ideal book for you:

AS LEVEL PSYCHOLOGY
FOURTH EDITION
by Michael W. Eysenck

"This excellent new edition of a successful and popular textbook, substantially rewritten, is full of new details, new studies and ideas, all directly relevant to the new specification. Many topics have been updated with current research and new examples and the style is accessible and friendly. There are also very useful online resources to engage students, plus some for teacher use. This is a valuable contribution to the teaching and learning of AS Psychology."

Evie Bentley, Advanced Skills Practitioner for Psychology, West Sussex Adult and Community Learning; Chairperson 1999–2002, The Association for the Teaching of Psychology

This thoroughly updated, full-colour, fourth edition of *AS Level Psychology* has a new focus on the nature and scope of psychology as a science with an emphasis on how science works, and guidance on how to engage students in practical, scientific research activities.

The book includes coverage of six key areas in psychology: Human memory, early social development, research methods, stress, social influence, and abnormality. Chapters focus on the application of knowledge and understanding of the text to help students develop skills of analysis, evaluation, and critical thinking. The book is packed with advice on exam technique and hints and tips on how to pick up marks, giving students the best chance possible of the highest grades. However, unlike other A-Level textbooks ,which focus solely on passing the exam, *AS Level Psychology, fourth edition* is also designed to foster an interest in the study of psychology as a subject with an additional general chapter to introduce the theories and explanations that make psychology a fascinating discipline.

AS Level Psychology, fourth edition is supported by our extensive resource package, *AS Level Psychology Online*. This is available free of charge to qualifying adopters of our A-Level textbooks. Student resources include the AS Level Psychology Workbook, multiple-choice quizzes, animations and interactive exercises, relevant podcasts with key figures in psychology and more. We also provide teacher resources, which include a week-by-week teaching plan, sample essays, chapter-by-chapter lecture presentations, and classroom exercises and activities.

Ψ Psychology Press
Taylor & Francis Group

ISBN 978-1-84169-711-6
£14.99 pbk
Published by Psychology Press

Please visit http://www.a-levelpsychology.co.uk/aqaa for further information.

Going on to study AS-Level Psychology?

If you are following the OCR specification, this is the ideal book for you:

OCR PSYCHOLOGY
AS Core Studies and Research Methods
by Philip Banyard and Cara Flanagan

"This new edition is an excellent resource for the delivery of the new OCR specification. Its lively and colourful presentation makes it highly accessible to students and its broad background and extension material mean it is ideal for teachers seeking to plan engaging delivery of its core studies in a modern context. An all-round winner!"

Anna Ross, Psychology Course Team Leader, Long Road Sixth Form College

This book is endorsed by OCR for use with the OCR AS Psychology specification. Presented in magazine-style spreads to aid the learning process, it gives the who, the what, the where, and even the why of each of the core studies. It also looks at some of the work that followed the studies.

Specifically, it covers:

- Core studies: An abstract of each study plus ample details of the aims, method, results, and conclusions. Guidance is given on how each study can be evaluated, and a wealth of extra materials is provided for each study—practical activities, discussion ideas, multiple-choice and exam-style questions, diagrammatic summaries, further reading, and video links.

- Background to each core study: Information about related research before and after the study; and biographical details of the researcher(s).

- Key issues: Sixteen issues are discussed to cover the themes of the course and prepare students for the long-answer questions.

- A "Psychological Investigations" chapter helps students to understand research methods in psychology—useful support for the Psychological Investigations exam and also for understanding the core studies themselves.

- Exam preparation: Short and long answer exam-style questions answered by students with examiner's comments.

The textbook is accompanied by online student and instructor resources, including answers to all questions posed in the book, a helpful glossary, and a multiple-choice question test bank.

Ψ Psychology Press
Taylor & Francis Group

ISBN 978-1-84169-728-4
£17.50 pbk
Published by Psychology Press

Please visit http://www.a-levelpsychology.co.uk/ocr for further information.